PERSONAL CYBERSECURITY

HOW TO AVOID AND RECOVER FROM CYBERCRIME

Marvin Waschke

WITHDRAWN

Apress®

Personal Cybersecurity: How to Avoid and Recover from Cybercrime

Marvin Waschke
Bellingham, Washington, USA

ISBN-13 (pbk): 978-1-4842-2429-8　　　　　　ISBN-13 (electronic): 978-1-4842-2430-4
DOI 10.1007/978-1-4842-2430-4

Library of Congress Control Number: 2017930630

Managing Director: Welmoed Spahr
Editorial Director: Todd Green
Acquisitions Editor: Robert Hutchinson
Development Editor: Laura Berendson
Coordinating Editor: Rita Fernando
Copy Editor: Mary Behr
Compositor: SPi Global
Indexer: SPi Global
Artist: SPi Global
Cover Image Designed by Creativeart - Freepik.com

Distributed to the book trade worldwide by Springer Science+Business Media New York, 233 Spring Street, 6th Floor, New York, NY 10013. Phone 1-800-SPRINGER, fax (201) 348-4505, e-mail orders-ny@springer-sbm.com, or visit www.springeronline.com. Apress Media, LLC is a California LLC and the sole member (owner) is Springer Science + Business Media Finance Inc (SSBM Finance Inc). SSBM Finance Inc is a **Delaware** corporation.

For information on translations, please e-mail rights@apress.com, or visit http://www.apress.com/rights-permissions.

Apress titles may be purchased in bulk for academic, corporate, or promotional use. eBook versions and licenses are also available for most titles. For more information, reference our Print and eBook Bulk Sales web page at http://www.apress.com/bulk-sales.

Any source code or other supplementary material referenced by the author in this book is available to readers on GitHub via the book's product page, located at www.apress.com/9781484224298. For more detailed information, please visit http://www.apress.com/source-code.

Printed on acid-free paper

PERSONAL CYBERSECURITY

HOW TO AVOID AND RECOVER FROM CYBERCRIME

Marvin Waschke

WITHDRAWN

Apress®

Personal Cybersecurity: How to Avoid and Recover from Cybercrime

Marvin Waschke
Bellingham, Washington, USA

ISBN-13 (pbk): 978-1-4842-2429-8   ISBN-13 (electronic): 978-1-4842-2430-4
DOI 10.1007/978-1-4842-2430-4

Library of Congress Control Number: 2017930630

Managing Director: Welmoed Spahr
Editorial Director: Todd Green
Acquisitions Editor: Robert Hutchinson
Development Editor: Laura Berendson
Coordinating Editor: Rita Fernando
Copy Editor: Mary Behr
Compositor: SPi Global
Indexer: SPi Global
Artist: SPi Global
Cover Image Designed by Creativeart - Freepik.com

Distributed to the book trade worldwide by Springer Science+Business Media New York, 233 Spring Street, 6th Floor, New York, NY 10013. Phone 1-800-SPRINGER, fax (201) 348-4505, e-mail orders-ny@springer-sbm.com, or visit www.springeronline.com. Apress Media, LLC is a California LLC and the sole member (owner) is Springer Science + Business Media Finance Inc (SSBM Finance Inc). SSBM Finance Inc is a **Delaware** corporation.

For information on translations, please e-mail rights@apress.com, or visit http://www.apress.com/rights-permissions.

Apress titles may be purchased in bulk for academic, corporate, or promotional use. eBook versions and licenses are also available for most titles. For more information, reference our Print and eBook Bulk Sales web page at http://www.apress.com/bulk-sales.

Any source code or other supplementary material referenced by the author in this book is available to readers on GitHub via the book's product page, located at www.apress.com/9781484224298. For more detailed information, please visit http://www.apress.com/source-code.

Printed on acid-free paper

Apress Business: The Unbiased Source of Business Information

Apress business books provide essential information and practical advice, each written for practitioners by recognized experts. Busy managers and professionals in all areas of the business world—and at all levels of technical sophistication—look to our books for the actionable ideas and tools they need to solve problems, update and enhance their professional skills, make their work lives easier, and capitalize on opportunity.

Whatever the topic on the business spectrum—entrepreneurship, finance, sales, marketing, management, regulation, information technology, among others—Apress has been praised for providing the objective information and unbiased advice you need to excel in your daily work life. Our authors have no axes to grind; they understand they have one job only—to deliver up-to-date, accurate information simply, concisely, and with deep insight that addresses the real needs of our readers.

It is increasingly hard to find information—whether in the news media, on the Internet, and now all too often in books—that is even-handed and has your best interests at heart. We therefore hope that you enjoy this book, which has been carefully crafted to meet our standards of quality and unbiased coverage.

We are always interested in your feedback or ideas for new titles. Perhaps you'd even like to write a book yourself. Whatever the case, reach out to us at editorial@apress.com and an editor will respond swiftly. Incidentally, at the back of this book, you will find a list of useful related titles. Please visit us at www.apress.com to sign up for newsletters and discounts on future purchases.

—*The Apress Business Team*

Apress Business: The Unbiased Source of Business Information

Apress business books provide essential information and practical advice, each written for practitioners by recognized experts. Busy managers and professionals in all areas of the business world—and at all levels of technical sophistication—look to our books for the actionable ideas and tools they need to solve problems, update and enhance their professional skills, make their work lives easier, and capitalize on opportunity.

Whatever the topic on the business spectrum—entrepreneurship, finance, sales, marketing, management, regulation, information technology, among others—Apress has been praised for providing the objective information and unbiased advice you need to excel in your daily work life. Our authors have no axes to grind; they understand they have one job only—to deliver up-to-date, accurate information simply, concisely, and with deep insight that addresses the real needs of our readers.

It is increasingly hard to find information—whether in the news media, on the Internet, and now all too often in books—that is even-handed and has your best interests at heart. We therefore hope that you enjoy this book, which has been carefully crafted to meet our standards of quality and unbiased coverage.

We are always interested in your feedback or ideas for new titles. Perhaps you'd even like to write a book yourself. Whatever the case, reach out to us at editorial@apress.com and an editor will respond swiftly. Incidentally, at the back of this book, you will find a list of useful related titles. Please visit us at www.apress.com to sign up for newsletters and discounts on future purchases.

—*The Apress Business Team*

For Rebecca

Contents

About the Author

 **Marvin Waschke** was a senior principal software architect at CA Technologies. His career has spanned the mainframe to the cloud. He has coded, designed, and managed the development of many systems, ranging through accounting, cell tower management, enterprise service desks, configuration management, and network management. Each of the many projects on which he worked involved security in some form that had to be designed, implemented, and then supported. He brings a veteran software engineer's understanding to computer security mechanisms and how hackers do their work.

Waschke represented CA Technologies on the DMTF Cloud Management Working Group, DMTF Open Virtualization Format Working Group, DMTF Common Information Model REST Interface Working Group, OASIS Topology and Orchestration Specification for Cloud Applications (TOSCA) Technical Committee, DMTF Cloud Auditing Data Federation Working Group (observer), DMTF Configuration Database Federation Working Group, W3C Service Modeling Language Working Group, and OASIS OData Technical Committee (observer). On his retirement from CA, he was honored as a DMTF Fellow for his distinguished past and continuing significant contributions to the DMTF and he continues his work with the DMTF on cloud standards. He was the editor-in-chief of the *CA Technology Exchange* (an online technical journal). He is the author of *Cloud Standards: Agreements That Hold Together Clouds* and *How Clouds Hold IT Together: Integrating Architecture with Cloud Deployment*.

Acknowledgments

I owe a tremendous debt to all my former colleagues at CA Technologies, Inc. I learned from my colleagues and customers every day I worked at CA. I had daily opportunities to confer with security specialists, antimalware builders, and encryption experts. I talked with customers who had been hacked, asking how it happened and how it affected their business and them personally, how they could have avoided it, and what they would do to prevent it in the future.

Since I retired from CA and began to concentrate on writing about computing, I have pursued another passion: public libraries. I serve on the board of the Whatcom County Library System in Washington State. The library and its patrons inspired me to focus on personal cybersecurity. Special recognition goes to the Executive Director, Christine Perkins, and IT Services Manager, Geoff Fitzpatrick.

My good friend Efraim Moskovitz was my constant sounding board while writing this book. He pushed me on and reined me in as needed. Efraim and I worked together on the CA Council for Technical Excellence for several years and Efraim contributed several articles to the *CA Technology Exchange*, which I edited. Efraim was technical reviewer for both of my previous books with Apress.

My online acquaintance Shawn Coyne made some suggestions on organization in the early stages of this project that were quite helpful.

I also am grateful to the folks at Apress: Robert Hutchinson, whose wit and insight shaped many aspects of the book; Matthew Moody, who helped with perspective and nudged in useful directions; and Rita Fernando, the project manager who gently and tolerantly urged me forward.

Finally, I must gratefully acknowledge my wife, Rebecca, my daughter, Athena, and my grandsons, Matthew and Christoper. They put up with my erratic and reclusive ways while I was working on this book. I cannot thank them enough for this. Christopher, who at 14 is already on his way to becoming a software engineer, gets special credit for answering his grandfather's questions on the Apple user interfaces.

Introduction

I wrote this book to solve two very specific problems for my fellow IT professionals. We all get too many questions from individual computer users who are worried about the security of their personal computers, tablets, and phones. In the industry, the acronym RTFM is hurled at beginners for asking naïve questions. But that is not an appropriate answer to a user concerned about computer security. These folks ask good and important questions that deserve serious answers.

A few years ago, after repeating the same answers many times, I started to look for the right book to recommend. There are many good books on computer security but most of them drift into security for system administrators; this confuses ordinary users and leaves them uncertain. And no one needs to be reminded that the details of computing change rapidly, but the basic principles stay the same. Users need knowledge that will give them a foundation to build on as the details of security issues change.

Many books on personal computer security tend to be highly prescriptive with lots of screenshots and values to fill into specific fields. This is nice, but this aspect of computing changes rapidly and many of these books become confusing within months of publication because interfaces change. Users need simple explanations of what they are doing and why they are doing it, not outdated, detailed instructions. The rate of change has escalated as products adopt automated update practices. Products evolve much more rapidly than a few years past. To stay safe during rapid change, computer users must have a firm grasp of what they are protecting themselves against, how the protections work, and why they need to protect themselves.

The book is divided into three sections. The first section explains how computing has developed, how cybercrime has become a serious problem, and the extent of its severity. The second section examines what government and industry have done to respond. The third section relies heavily on the previous two sections and focuses on what you can do to protect yourself and what to do when you become a victim. Throughout, I have tried to maintain focus on what is wrong, why it is wrong, and how the response works so that a user can apply the advice to any computer they work with.

If I have succeeded in my goal, the users who read this book will be informed, not quite so nervous, and prepared to avoid or actively resist the security issues that plague them. This book will not eliminate user questions to IT professionals, nor will it eliminate the need for operating system and product security documentation. In a world where substantial updates are automatically applied every month, a book like this would not be useful for long if it was only a snapshot of cybersecurity at one moment in time.

Readers may be tempted to skip to the last two chapters. If you are under attack and feel the need to take immediate action, do skip ahead. But then go back and read the preceding chapters. You will find that the recommendations in the final chapters will make more sense, are easier to accept, and can be applied more effectively after you have the background the earlier chapters provide.

What's Biting Us

Who and What Does Cybercrime Hurt?

When I hear the news about the latest computer security breach, I am so dismayed that I want to turn off my smartphone, tablet, and laptop and quietly lock them in the bottom drawer of my desk. But I don't. I have designed and written computer software for decades, and I will not accept that the work that I and many others have done over the years is being subverted by disgruntled misfits, criminals, and thugs. I take a deep breath and think through what has happened and why it took place.

Turning off personal computers does not help much. Lapses in security in other people's computing systems can hurt you as much as a weakness in your own system. Many of the systems over which we have no control are critical to our safety, financial well-being, and even our health.

The dangers seem to have multiplied overnight. The devices that were once useful and entertaining seem to have spontaneously metamorphosed into menaces. Computing began in what seemed like a garden of Eden, far from crime and malice. Early computers were hidden in laboratories and their users were engineers and scientists. Computing as an instrument of crime was not in anyone's mind. But this has changed. Instead of being protected behind locked doors, computers large and small are exposed in ways that could not have been imagined by their inventors. Nearly every computer is attached to networks that can be accessed from anywhere on the planet by almost anyone. Wireless networking further opens computers to both free and malicious access. In this open environment, the computing industry only noticed the

© Marvin Waschke 2017
M. Waschke, *Personal Cybersecurity*, DOI 10.1007/978-1-4842-2430-4_1

opportunities for cybercrime in the last two decades of the millennium. Even then, most computer-related crime was embezzlement and inventory twiddling that could have been done as easily with paper books as by computing.

Computer and software manufacturers were not earnest about security until cybercrime grew into big business at the beginning of the millennium. Previously, engineers tended to think of security as an annoying hindrance to development that could be added in the last stages of a project. If a project got behind, security might be left for the next release. This attitude still sometimes exists, although engineering practices now acknowledge that security must be considered at every stage of product development, including decisions not to build projects that cannot be adequately secured.

Services, such as online banking, which we can scarcely imagine living without, loom as threats in news reports almost every week, and yet we become more and more attached to our plastic. Androids and iPhones burrow deeper and deeper into our lives with texting, email, Facebook, Uber, and hordes of other apps that make busy lives easier. But each of these devices and apps present new vulnerabilities to criminal attack. The vulnerabilities grow with each new device and app.

In their self-interest, computer users must understand the threats, correctly evaluate their potential, and take steps to avoid, block, or disarm attacks. Computer networks are a tough neighborhood. Doing business on the mean cyber streets is a difficult assignment in an environment that changes every day.

This challenge is not that different from challenges we face in other areas. After all, life is a dangerous venture. Heart disease or cancer can strike anyone, but we can improve our odds with exercise and a healthy diet. Driving a car is dangerous, but we can drive carefully in cars equipped with seatbelts, air bags, and anti-lock brakes. There are no guarantees that we will avoid a heart attack or an automobile crash, but our chances significantly improve when we are reasonably cautious. Most people can live a long and satisfying life while following good safety practices. The same applies to the cyberworld.

The cyberworld has no guarantees and there are many tradeoffs, but most people can use and enjoy their computers, tablets, and smartphones without becoming a victim of cybercrime. It's like choosing to avoid sugary soda altogether but occasionally indulge in your favorite dessert. You must intelligently reduce the chances that a calamity will occur. Choosing a car or truck with anti-lock brakes will not guarantee that you will never skid on an icy road, but they will help control the skid and give you a better chance of steering out of a crash into the guardrail. Good cybersecurity practices will not guarantee that you will never be hacked, but they can turn away all but the most persistent hackers and limit the damage when an assailant smashes through your defenses.

Individuals can take heart from the statistics. Despite increases in computer use, cybercrime complaints to the FBI's Internet Crime Compliance Center have drifted downward from 303,809 complaints in 2010 to 269,422 in 2014, a more than ten percent decrease. The significance of this decrease is greater than it may appear because the pool of computing devices has grown, with an increase in the number of smartphones and tablets to the existing pool of laptops and desktops.

Keep in mind that cybercrime is likely underreported. Not every victim of massive credit card theft reports the crime to the FBI. Cyberwarfare and terrorism seldom have individual persons as victims, and their impact is not reflected in FBI statistics. These are some of the most heinous and far reaching crimes, and yet they may not be reflected in the statistics.

Nevertheless, the crimes that are reported to the FBI are significant and they do show a decline, which seems the opposite of what we see on the news. The frequency of news stories on cybercrimes is different from the true frequency of cybercrimes. Cybercrime may simply have become more newsworthy. Later, as I probe into the industry's efforts to deter or prevent computer crime, you may gain some insight into why the FBI numbers have gone down.

The Internet Crime Compliance Center reports that the largest financial losses were from conventional confidence fraud over the Internet and the most frequent complaint was non-payment and non-delivery on Internet transactions. For these crimes, the Internet was a convenient vehicle, but they could have been committed over the telephone or through the paper mails. These reports suggest that good old-fashioned dishonesty and fraud continues to be profitable in the 21st century, but they are not examples that are germane to the rise of crime enmeshed with computer and network technology.

Cybercrime is not quite as threatening to individuals as it appears, but don't underestimate it. For individuals, the biggest threats do not come from hackers breaking into their laptops and tablets. The greatest threats are through break-ins and other mayhem done to computer systems that most people have little or no contact with. When those types of crimes are counted, cybercrimes occur more frequently than anyone would like. Some experts estimate that individual's email account is more likely to be broken into than their house.[1]

Cybercrime

Cybercrime takes many different forms. The most spectacular crime is massive theft of critical personal information. Companies that hold this information can do much to prevent these thefts, but we individuals have little power because we have no control of the vulnerable systems that process and store our information.

[1]CBS. " These Cybercrime Statistics Will Make You Think Twice About Your Password: Where's the CSI Cyber team when you need them?" March 3, 2015.
www.cbs.com/shows/csi-cyber/news/1003888/these-cybercrime-statistics-will-make-you-think-twice-about-your-password-where-s-the-csi-cyber-team-when-you-need-them-/. Accessed December 2015.

SOME USEFUL CYBERSECURITY JARGON

- Attack surface: All points vulnerable to attack on a computer, network, or system. The attack surface usually does not include the human element, which is often the greatest vulnerability.

- Attack vector: A route or method allowing an invader to enter or compromise a computer, network, or system.

- Exploit: An invasion of a computer system. Also the method and the system defects used for an invasion.

- Hacker: Traditionally, someone who writes or studies computer code for their own satisfaction rather than a job or school. Some hackers code for illegal purposes. Hacker now often means "system invader."

- Malware: Malware is any software designed to perform harmful activities. Viruses and worms are both malware.

- Social engineering: Using human weaknesses as an attack vector.

- Virus: A virus is a fragment of code that attaches itself to another file. When the file is accessed, the virus will infect other files. It may spread to other devices by emailing itself or some other method.

- Worm: Worms are programs that travel from computer to computer, usually doing damage along the way. Worms can replicate and move between devices autonomously.

The number of pieces of data and enterprises hacked into are surprising. RSA is one of the largest providers of security certificates used to guarantee that Internet sites are who they say they are. A major security company is, one would hope, an unlikely candidate for a hacker intrusion, but in 2011 RSA was embarrassed to be hacked to the tune of tens of millions of employee records.[2]

People think of hackers as Lisbeth Salander from Stieg Larsson's *Millennium Trilogy* or Garcia on the television series *Criminal Minds*; geniuses who can work miracles from any computer attached to the Internet. In minutes, they hack into any computer anywhere and extract the precise information they need. That is not exactly the way real hacking works.

---

[2]See Taylor Armerding, CIO, February 16, 2012. www.cio.com/article/2399262/data-breach/the-15-worst-data-security-breaches-of-the-21st-century.html. Accessed December 2015.

In the 1960s and 1970s, anyone working on a computer and not performing an assignment from a business, school, or government was called a *hacker*. Programmers and administrators who worked after hours on their own computing projects and students who hunched over terminals working on unassigned tasks were all an anomaly. These enthusiasts occasionally drifted past official rules either unintentionally or from curiosity, but seldom with malicious intent. But as computing advanced, some of these unofficial experts began to take advantage of opportunities for mischief and gain that they discovered in their preoccupation.

The hackers of today have a range of profiles. Some merely push boundaries for pleasure. Enthusiasts who spend hours searching for undocumented ways to change the behavior of their personal computers are at this end of the spectrum. Some of them are *white hats*: hackers who are paid by businesses and law enforcement to find security flaws by acting like *black hats* trying to break in. In the middle of the range are hackers who claim to perform victimless crimes that affect only institutions, not people. Other hackers claim to be activists who only hack for benevolent or political purposes. At the far end, organized criminals use hacking skills to wreck and steal. The most dangerous of these gangsters have adopted the brutal tactics of organized crime. Government or military operatives who create and use cyberweapons often are the authors of the most destructive exploits.

The Target Corporation Heist

How do hackers steal? Examining a well-known exploit helps explain what they do. A few days before Thanksgiving in 2013, hackers began an exploit that eventually stole information from 40 million credit and debit cards from a mass retailer, Target Corporation. To put this another way, more than one person in ten in the entire United States had a card number stolen. The stolen card numbers and other information were spirited off to "dark" trading sites, sort of criminal eBays, and sold for a few dollars apiece to other criminals called *carders*, who manufacture new cards bearing the stolen data. They use the fake cards to purchase expensive items on the unsuspecting cardholder's accounts. The purchased items are often sold on the real eBay.

Like most hacking exploits, the Target heist began with social engineering. See Figure 1-1. *Social engineering* is jargon for tricking a person into revealing information that a hacker can use to gain entrance to a system. The tricks can be elaborate, often involving meticulously prepared fake emails, or simple, like asking someone for their password for a seemingly innocent purpose. Disgruntled former employees are often willing to be social engineered into helping with, or leading, an invasion.

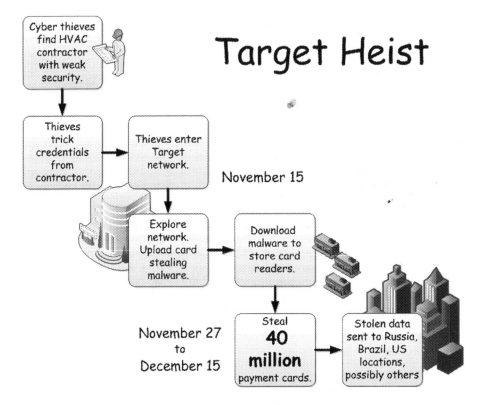

Figure 1-1. The Target heist involved a series of carefully planned steps

Social engineering is less spectacular than *cracking*, a favorite tactic of hackers in the popular media. Crackers obtain user passwords by guessing or de-encrypting password information. Cracking a password is frequently possible, but hackers often decide cracking is too much work. Social engineering is much easier, so some form of social engineering is the first step in most hacking invasions.

For the Target exploit, hackers used social engineering to penetrate a weak point in Target's defensive perimeter. Heating and air-conditioning equipment is now frequently connected to corporate computer networks. Corporate facilities staff use the network to adjust heating and air-conditioning, which is automated for comfort and energy efficiency. Heating and air conditioning contractors log into the system to monitor for issues and make remote adjustments. These contractors are frequently less experienced in managing cybersecurity. The Target hackers began by searching for contractors with connections to Target. They found a heating and air conditioning (HVAC) contractor with unsophisticated security and the kind of connection to the Target network they needed.

The hackers sent emails to the contractor's employees to trick them into revealing a username and password. The social engineering challenge was to send a carefully contrived email that would trick a contractor employee into revealing their password. The effort succeeded and the hackers logged into the Target network. That login was the intrusion that began the exploit. They broke into the system using their knowledge of human nature and gullibility rather than technical knowledge or skill.

The contractor was apparently blind to the situation. They issued a press release stating that their connection was only used for billing, contract submission, and project management. In other words, the contractor was apparently unaware that they were an unwitting attack vector for the plunder that followed.

The hackers gained access on November 15, which was 12 days prior to the sales flurry of Black Friday on November 27. Using their access, the hackers got ready for Black Friday by loading their malicious software into the Target system. The software was then pushed down to most of Target's automated cash registers all over the country. The hacker's software was designed to grab credit card data as customers purchased their goods and slid their cards through card readers attached to the cash registers. The hackers had several days to ready their credit and debit card information collection system. The hackers, like good software engineers, used the time to test their systems before the full-scale launch.

By television hacker standards, the Target hackers were painfully slow and pedestrian, but unlike fiction, they stole real data and hurt real people. They stole so much data that transporting it out of the Target system was a logistical challenge. It is not clear exactly where all the data was sent. They covered their tracks by sending data over difficult-to-trace clandestine networks; the credit card information was eventually sent to computers in the United States, Brazil, and other obscure locations. The stolen data recipient's systems may have been hacked and the owner was not aware that their computer was used for an illegal purpose.

Eventually, the credit card numbers appeared on criminal sites that traffic in goods like stolen credit card numbers. These sites are not difficult to access and they are a ready market for purloined data. Credit card numbers go for a few dollars apiece. As the data gets older, the price goes down as more card numbers are cancelled or flagged with a fraud alert.

Some estimate that Target lost nearly half a billion dollars from this hack, which did not have to take place. There were several points where the breach could have been prevented. The air conditioning contractor could have trained their employees to be more aware of efforts to swipe passwords. Target could have divided up their network so that contractors only had access to data they needed, not critical payment systems. Target could have monitored activity on their network and noticed that an air conditioning contractor was accessing data that had nothing to do with air conditioning. Target could have guarded their point-of-sale systems from installation of unauthorized software. Superior hindsight does not mean culpability for allowing these gaps, but stopping up any one of them could have prevented disaster. Although the issues of a large distributed corporation like Target are different from personal cybersecurity issues, Target's woes offer clues to what can happen on our personal devices. I will discuss them in more detail later.

Tablets and Phones

Smartphones and tablets are replacing the desktop and laptop computers that have been the targets of cybercrime in the past. This does not mean cybercrime will go away. The larger computers still have some uses and some people will always prefer large keyboards and displays, so it is unlikely that big desktops and laptops will completely disappear. More importantly, when size and appearance are ignored, desktops, laptops, tablets, and smartphones are all similar and they have similar vulnerabilities. They all have random access memory, persistent storage, and network connections. Consequently, all are vulnerable to the same kinds of exploits. This book discusses many exploits and techniques that have been directed at desktops and laptops. These same exploits could be directed at smartphones or tablets, and likely will be. The hackers must change some code to work with different operating systems, but the basic pattern will be the same.

If exploits on these devices seem seldom now, it is only because hackers concentrate on the devices that will yield the most return for the least effort. As smartphones and tablets become more prevalent, hackers will direct more exploits in their direction. Devices that appear to be impregnable will begin to be hacked more often.

Cellular phones and phone systems have their own set of issues, but these are mainly privacy issues. For example, hardware, mainly used by law enforcement, can spoof a cellphone into believing the device is a cell tower. The device acts as a middleman who monitors the victim's phone calls and messages and then passes them along to a legitimate tower. Other privacy issues involve accessing the records kept in the cellular system. Much of the wrangling that is going on over cellular phone privacy is about who should have access to what from these records. Since the records are kept on a computer system, they are subject to hacking also. When dealing with computer systems, the question is never whether breaking in is possible. It always is. The critical question is whether breaking in is difficult and time-consuming enough to discourage the most desperate from trying.

Wireless

Wireless networks open up new opportunities for hacking. Open wireless sites such as those in coffee shops, public libraries, hotels, and airports are convenient, but they are also treacherous. Even the sites that have passwords, like many hotels, are dangerous because there is little control over who has the password. Everyone who is using the hotel wireless network has access to all the traffic on the network. A password that is handed out to people whom you have no reason to trust does not protect you on a wireless network.

You may think that secured networks with passwords are there to prevent bandwidth theft. They do discourage bandwidth theft, but the most important reason for securing a wireless network is to keep untrusted persons out. Anyone on a wireless network can listen in on anyone else on the network. In public places, a potential victim has no idea who is nearby with access to the wireless network.

With access to the network, a hacker can watch all the traffic to and from a victim's computer, which could be a laptop, smartphone, or tablet. While hackers are watching, they can skim any data they care to. A victim connecting with any site that might reveal valuable credentials or other valuable data invites a watching hacker to steal it. Encrypted transmission and virtual private networking make hacking more challenging, but a hacker who is willing to invest resources into obtaining the data can succeed most of the time.

Unsecured home systems are equally vulnerable. Some hackers drive through neighborhoods with their laptops, searching for unsecured wireless networks. When they find an unsecured, or poorly secured network, they can monitor the data on the wireless network, or use the network as a base for attacks. The attacks will appear to come from the compromised home wireless network.

Not all security standards are equal. The earliest wireless security standards were developed in the late 1990s and have been shown to be completely insecure. A hacker using readily available tools needs only minutes to break in. Unfortunately, the old standards (WEP and WPS) are still used occasionally. The currently preferred wireless security standard (WPA2) is safer. A long random password is difficult to crack, but a persistent hacker with abundant computing resources may still be able to break it.

Wireless networks can be treacherous in other ways. Most devices, especially smartphones, are set up to attach to a wireless network whenever one is available. The phone user may think they are using the cellular network and therefore they can log into their bank in relative safety. In fact, the smartphone may have latched onto a hacker-infested open network.

Wireless networks are a convenient pleasure, but they must be used with caution.

Crimes Against Devices

Can a network-controlled electric kettle be hacked? Sure. An electric kettle controlled by a smartphone may be an attractive idea. Use your smartphone to turn on the kettle from your bed and have boiling water when you arrive in the kitchen. Nice. But that kettle could be an open door into your wireless network. You can follow the article mentioned in footnote below to get the details on how to hack into one model of kettle.[3] The steps are not difficult. The hack relies on sloppy programming and weak passwords. The group who produced the kettle were probably veteran kitchen appliance designers but new to networks and software. They would have been excited about an innovative new product and likely did not give a thought to a security review.

The fitness tracker you wear on your wrist is also hackable. One brand of tracker has been subjected to an attack in which a security researcher connected to the tracker through Bluetooth, changed data, and deposited code. The code was automatically uploaded the next time the tracker connected with its display on a laptop or smartphone.

Bluetooth has about a 30-foot range. You could be sitting on a bus and the nondescript guy sitting a couple seats away fiddling with his Android could be loading your wrist tracker with malware that will be loaded into your phone the next time you sync up. Before you know it, your friends are getting offensive messages that you did not send, but are from your phone.[4]

Personal cybersecurity extends beyond the traditional desktop and laptop personal computers to tablets, smartphones, and everything else that is connected to our home networks. Items in our homes, such as security cameras, electronic locks, and heating-air-conditioning systems, that are connected to the Internet are especially vulnerable. It's bad enough that our bank accounts can be looted and our identities stolen, but we also have to worry about our children being spied upon in their beds, invaders electronically turning off alarms and unlocking our front doors, and our houses burnt down by malicious meddling with the controls on our furnaces. Checking on our children

---

[3]Phil Ducklin. "Internet of Things- do you really need a kettle that can boil your security dry?" Naked Security. October 10, 2015. https://nakedsecurity.sophos.com/2015/10/20/internet-of-things-do-you-really-need-a-kettle-that-can-boil-your-security-dry/. Accessed December 2015.

[4]Alexandra Burlacu. "Experts Warn It Just Takes 10 Seconds To Hack Fitbit Fitness Trackers: Here's Fitbit's Response." *Tech Times*. October 24, 2015. www.techtimes.com/articles/98427/20151024/experts-warn-it-just-takes-10-seconds-to-hack-fitbit-fitness-trackers-heres-fitbits-response.htm. Accessed December 2015. Fitbit denied that the hack can do damage. Let's hope that they are working on a fix. They would not be the first to stick their head in the sand and hope the problem goes away.

and controlling our house remotely is a remarkable modern convenience, but it can also be a threat. This is the Internet of Things. Like the heating and air conditioning contractors that became the route of attack in the Target heist, the designers of devices that are newly online can be unfamiliar with security practices and leave the devices they design poorly protected.

Large corporations and government agencies are attractive to cybercriminals because the loot available for plunder is usually much greater than the loot on personal devices. A personal device may hold a few credit cards, credentials for a few personal bank accounts, and not much else. Corporate systems may hold millions of credit cards and access to billions of dollars. To the individual, this comparison is no solace when their laptop, tablet, or smartphone is breached.

What Are Hackers Looking For?

By far the most common reason for invading a computing device is money, although a few hackers breach systems to make a political point or as a personal assault on the device owner. Obtaining access to personal email often goes with this sort of assault. Others invade with an intelligence or military objective. Still others are just snooping. Nevertheless, most hacking is for money.

Money can be made from a compromised computer in various ways. Personal data suitable for stealing an identity can be sold readily on the black market. Payment card information can also easily be sold, but a personal device is not likely to yield many cards compared to a business. Beyond stealing data, ransom is a possibility. An intruder can disable a critical resource, such as encrypting a file system, and then demand payment for releasing the resource.

Hackers may also try to "own" a victim's device. An "owned" device is under control of the hacker. Usually, the hacker obtains administrative control of the device and has deposited code or scripts that prevent the true owner, or anyone else, from taking back control. An owned device can be very useful. It can become a slave computer that is part of a mass spam mailing machine. It might be used as a relay in an effort to obscure the source of an attack. Perhaps the worst part of having an owned computer is that the rightful owners may not be aware of the mischief their computers are performing.

Perhaps the most sinister use of owned devices is spying. Some malware can be installed that will capture the screen images, take control of the device's camera, and install key loggers that record every stroke from the keyboard, as well as spirit away all the files on the system. Techniques like this are used by law enforcement and other government agencies for investigation and spying. Criminals use malware like this for less savory purposes such as stealing financial credentials or extortion. Cyberbullies and stalkers also use this kind of malware.

How Do Hackers Get In?

We have all heard about master hackers who have nearly supernatural powers for guessing or cracking passwords, but that is not the most common way personal devices are invaded. There are much easier ways.

Social Engineering

Social engineering, as mentioned previously, is security jargon for using psychology and sociology to trick victims into revealing critical information such as passwords. In a business, disgruntled employees might give away passwords to harm their employer. A hacker might call an individual on the telephone, posing as someone from an Internet provider, credit card company, or some other person with a legitimate interest in computing devices or accounts. The masquerade is to trick victims into revealing their usernames, passwords, and other critical information.

Phishing

Phishing is favorite method that uses deceptive emails. The invader sends a seemingly legitimate email to a user. The email requests an account and password for a seemingly legitimate reason. In the simplest form of phishing, the clueless victim replies with the requested account and password.

Since few people fall for that ploy anymore, subtler variations have appeared. One variant asks the victim to click on a link to a fake web site. The fake might be a clever reproduction of a legitimate site such as the victim's bank. The victim logs in to the fake bank, and the phisher snaps up the victim's bank credentials.

In another version of the fake website, the phishing expedition turns into a drive-by in which malware is deposited on the victim's device. Drive-bys are explained in the next section.

Yet another phishing ploy uses an attachment that contains malware that is executed when the user tries to open it. An even more malicious variety embeds a script in a photograph or graphic that runs when the photo is opened. In some malware deposit versions, no password needs to be harvested. The malware establishes a backdoor into the device and the invader has access.

Drive-bys

Another method is the drive-by attack. The user is lured to a malicious website that, when it opens in a browser, executes scripts that deposit malware. Usually the malware opens access to the hackers who later work their mischief.

Drive-bys usually occur on dodgy sites designed to attract the unwary. They often promise compromising photographs of entertainment stars, over-the-top tax advice, or too-good-to-be-true weight loss schemes.

Man-In-The-Middle

A man-in-the-middle attack inserts a third party between two communicating systems. For example, a victim might attempt to use an online interface to pay off a mortgage with a large wire transfer. The hacker hijacks the network connection between the victim and his bank, and inserts himself in the middle. When the victim sends the transfer request, the hacker intercepts the request, inserts his account as the recipient of the transfer, and sends the modified version to the bank. When the bank sends the confirmation to the victim, the hacker intercepts the confirmation and puts the original recipient back in. Neither the bank nor the victim is aware of the attack. The money is transferred to the hacker and the victim assumes the transfer went through until the mortgage company asks about the expected payment. See Figure 1-2 for a graphic depiction of a man-in-the-middle attack.

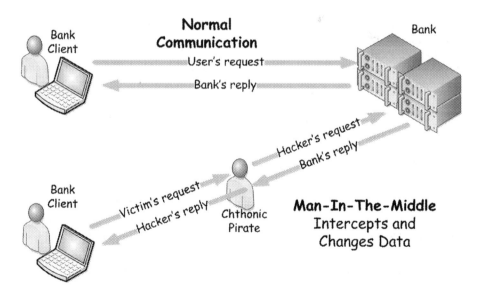

Figure 1-2. The man-in-middle interrupts normal communication between parties

A variant method inserts a fake version of a website a victim intends to connect with. The hacker then scoops up the information that victim enters, sends whatever they want to the target, and returns to the victim whatever the hacker wants the victim to receive.

In another man-in-the-middle exploit, an attacker sets up his laptop as a hot spot in a public place and names the hot spot something plausible like "Free Wi-Fi." When users connect, the attacker skims the incoming data for valuables like bank credentials and passes on the connection to a legitimate Wi-Fi service.

How often man-in-the-middle attacks occur is contested. Some experts think they occur frequently; others think they are rare. This is an indication of the difficulty of detecting man-in-the-middle attacks. If the connection is a normal unsecured connection, a man-in-the-middle is nearly impossible to detect. Using a secured connection, the browser may raise an invalid certificate error. (I'll discuss certificates later, but reliable certificates are a foundation of Internet security.) The error *may* indicate a man-in-the-middle attack, but there are other trivial reasons for certificate errors and a well-executed man-in-the-middle attack can avoid certificate errors.

Man-in-the-middle attacks can be used in different ways. Besides changing the intent of interactions, they can be used to glean information about the client or to deposit malware on the victim's computing device.

Trojans

Remember your history? A Trojan horse is something dangerous that looks innocuous. A Trojan file looks like a file that should be there, but was placed on a computer by an attacker. Hackers and anti-virus tool developers play cat-and-mouse. The anti-virus tool writes code to find the Trojan and the hacker writes code to hide it. Trojans often are carefully designed to have the same name and size as legitimate files, but when they are executed, they can do almost anything, especially if they are executed with the administrative privileges necessary to make critical changes to a device.

Trojans are often used to install back doors. To do this, a Trojan typically has to modify the device's settings and operating rules, and install code to permit the back door to work. Often, after the back door is installed, the Trojan will send a message to the attacker to let them know that the door is ready. The attacker then has secret and private remote access to the victim's computer.

Back doors are not the only thing that Trojans can do. A Trojan might go to the user's email address list and transmit it to the attacker, who will use it to target phishing attacks on the victim's friends and acquaintances. Or the Trojan might be purely destructive and garble the victim's files, delete them all, or encrypt them and request ransom for decryption.

Remote Access Tools

Remote access tools (RATs) are the key that unlocks computing devices to attackers. Each computer platform (Windows, Linux, Android, iOS) has its own remote access tools. Many are built for legitimate purposes like remote maintenance, but hackers use them for mischief.

The granddaddy of remote access tools is Telnet, a protocol and software for interacting with remote systems that was developed in the late 1960s, an era when security was not an issue. Telnet is implemented on almost all platforms, but it is highly insecure. Today, security experts discourage using Telnet, yet it is still widely available, simple to use, and popular for command line services that only deal in public data. Hackers look for sites where Telnet is enabled and use it to gain remote control. It is an easy tool for novice hackers to use. Fortunately, on Windows and most versions of Linux, the user has to intentionally configure the device to accept Telnet. Telnet-enabled victims are rare and Telnet hacks rarely succeed. When they do, the invader can take over the victim's device, stealing data or setting it up as a slave to perform whatever nasty acts the invader chooses.

Telnet is not the only way to get remote access. Secure Shell (SSH) was designed to be a successor to Telnet. Secure Shell requires that an entity logging in must identify itself using secure credentials and passwords. The data that passes through Secure Shell is encrypted. Someone wishing to tap into the data must decrypt it first. This makes Secure Shell more private than Telnet, but only as private as Secure Shell encryption is strong. Users of Secure Shell are much safer. However, hackers have developed ways around Secure Shell and do use it to enter systems, perhaps using credentials snapped up in a phishing expedition. If invaders succeed using Secure Shell, their access is equivalent to Telnet. Invaders can take over the computer and steal data. Hacking in through Secure Shell has an added benefit to the invader: his communication to the victim device is probably not visible to law enforcement, which is very convenient.

Windows Remote Desktop Connection is another route into a Windows machine. Using Remote Desktop, a support technician can enter a machine and examine firsthand the settings of the computer and witness issues as they occur. Hands-on engagement through Remote Desktop can resolve issues quickly. The alternative, verbal descriptions of issues, is often inadequate. Remote access is powerful, but dangerous. If the support technician happens to be an attacker in disguise, he has the keys to the kingdom. There are few limits to the damage that can be done.

There are also back door remote login tools that were written as invasion tools. Neatly packaged versions of many of these tools can be downloaded from sites on the Internet. Most of them are designed to access versions of Microsoft Windows. Microsoft has steadily hardened its security and these tools have become more difficult to write.

Hacking novices don't need any knowledge of Windows security to download remote access tool packages available on the Internet. These packages install a remote access code on the targeted computer and a client on the hacker's computer. Some of these installations are polished and easy as any commercial installation. A hacker without programming skills and little knowledge of security can install these tools and, in minutes, start stealing data or subverting the target computer to the hacker's purposes.

These hacking packages rely on security flaws in their target. When flaws are discovered, the operating system and software vendors hurry to fix the flaws before invaders can make use of them and deliver patches to their users. By the time a hack is packaged up for download, patches are likely to be available that will thwart exploits. But availability of patches does not mean the patches have been applied. Users of prepackaged hacks search for unpatched devices, and they often do not have to search far.

Zero-Day Attacks

A zero-day attack is an attack on a previously unknown security flaw. When honest researchers or developers find a flaw, they notify the owner of the flawed software so they can develop a patch. That starts a count of days until the flaw is patched and the patch is publicly available. If a flaw is never reported, the count is zero and it is a zero-day flaw, simply a zero-day. When a hacker discovers a previously unknown flaw and launches an attack, the attack is a zero-day attack.

Zero-days have a market. The discoverer of a zero-day flaw, depending on how effective it might be, can sell the flaw on a black market exchange for thousands of dollars. Large criminal organizations are said to have stockpiles of zero-day flaws to use when the need arises. Government cyberwarfare organizations all over the world also are said to have stockpiles of zero-days, and have teams searching for zero-days to add to their stockpile. Some may be willing to pay for zero-day flaws found outside their organization. Much of this effort is directed toward the ubiquitous Windows operating system, but efforts are also aimed at Linux, mainframe systems, smartphone and tablet operating systems, industrial control systems, and any other systems that might yield control or monetary advantages.

Zero-days may provide routes into systems, but after a zero-day is used, it can be detected. Then it is no longer a zero-day and its value plummets. Instead of zero-days, social engineering is often the hacker's first choice because it is easy and reliable. Phishing, drive-bys, and man-in-the-middle activity are also less expensive that zero-days, but sophisticated sites often avoid these more conventional attacks.

Password Cracking

A password cracker discovers their victim's password without the participation of the victim. Cracking is more difficult and time consuming than social engineering. Usually, it is reserved for accounts that are likely to yield a large return for the effort and are resistant to social engineering. The extra effort is often applied to breaking into a corporate or institutional system rather than an individual. Celebrities like movie stars and high school principals are also likely victims of cracking, Still, anyone can be the victim of a cracker.

Password crackers typically first try to guess passwords. People are not as unique as they may think when choosing passwords. A handful of passwords are used all the time; "password", "drowssap", "123456", and so on are all good first guesses for crackers. If the cracker has a little knowledge of his victim, other good guesses are birthdays, anniversaries, relative's names, and pet names. These are easy to glean off Facebook and other social media. An experienced hacker is adept at using these resources to make good guesses. If guessing fails, the next step is often a brute force attack that tests many possibilities. Running through every possibility takes too many resources to be practical. One strategy is called a dictionary attack, which limits candidate passwords to words from a dictionary and runs through every word in a dictionary, perhaps including variants like replacing "a" with "@." With sufficient computer speed and storage, brute force attacks that were impossible a few years ago are now run every day. Some sophisticated algorithms can make brute force attacks more efficient. However, even the most powerful brute force attacks cannot reliably conquer long random passwords.

For highly resistant passwords, other attacks assault the password encryption algorithms themselves. Researchers regularly discover flaws in even the most secure encryption schemes. Highly trained hackers, often military personnel, are no doubt able to break any password they care to, although the resources required may be huge and the cracking methods may be so secret that they are reserved for extreme situations and are not likely to be used on an individual account.

I will talk more about managing passwords later.

Denial of Service and Botnet Invasions

Denial of service (DoS) and botnets are related attacks that occur frequently. They are responsible for both economic disruption and annoyance. Denial of service attacks are often performed by botnets.

Denial of Service

Denial of service is a common way of attacking business and government websites. A denial of service attack is usually a flood of input messages that exceeds the processing capacity of the attack's target, and the rush of bogus messages blocks the site's legitimate customers. In other words, the customer is denied service. The customer usually sees the denial as performance so sluggish as to be unusable, or a site that is completely unresponsive. Businesses lose sales or other transactions and their reputation for service.

A more advanced form of denial of service is called *distributed denial of service* (DDoS). A distributed attack is from more than one source at the same time. Distributed attacks are more effective than single attacks because the volume of messages is greater and they are more difficult for the victim to fend off. Botnets are an effective way of launching distributed denial of service attacks. More on botnets later.

The types of messages sent during an attack vary. One form is a barrage of emails. Other attacks use high-level protocols such as hypertext transfer protocol (HTTP). Others use lower-level protocols that bypass much of the processing of the higher levels. Some attacks are designed to damage servers and make them unusable in addition to overwhelming their capacity. Some of these attacks increase processor speeds, which can cause the processor to overheat and fail, possibly permanently.

Although denial of service attacks are not considered as sophisticated as some other types of attacks, they are becoming more frequent. Between 2013 and 2014, the frequency of distributed denial of service attacks has roughly doubled. A sample of 70 attacks measured by the volume of data thrown at the victim has also increased sharply.[5] The number of denial of service attacks continues to increase, although some experts predict that the intensity of each attack may go down because larger numbers of smaller attacks are harder for authorities to track down.

---

[5]See Arbor Networks. "Arbor Networks 10th Annual Worldwide Infrastructure Security Report Finds 50X Increase in DDoS Attack Size in Past Decade." `www.arbornetworks.com/news-and-events/press-releases/recent-press-releases/5351-arbor-networks-10th-annual-worldwide-infrastructure-security-report-finds-50x-increase-in-ddos-attack-size-in-past-decade`. Accessed December 2015.

As the tools used by the attackers evolve to avoid detection and make attacking easier, the details of attacks change, but the concept of denial of service remains the same.[6] As attack techniques evolve, strategies for evading attacks also evolve.

Botnets

Personal computing device users are more involved in denial of service attacks than they may think. Distributed attacks are often executed by systems called *botnets*, which run on the personal computing devices of unsuspecting victims.

Botnet is an elision of "robot" and "network." A network of robots, or bots, is a botnet. Bots are devices, usually personal computers, that have been commandeered to do the bidding of a *bot master*. Bots are recruited using techniques such as phishing and drive-bys. See Figure 1-3.

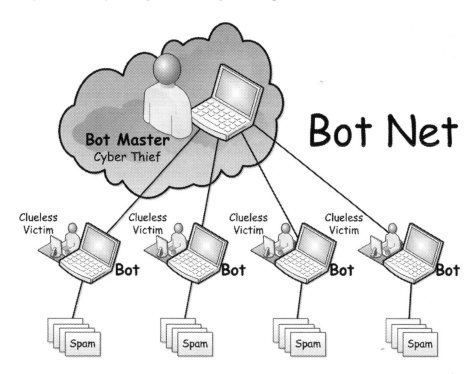

Figure 1-3. Victim computers become bots under the control of the bot master

---

[6]See Akamai Technologies, Inc. "State of the Internet Security Report Q3 2015." www.stateoftheinternet.com/downloads/pdfs/2015-cloud-security-report-q3.pdf. Accessed December 2015.

Bots receive orders from the master. Depending on the sophistication of the botnet, a bot may take only simple orders, or they may be able to execute complex programs.

The user often is unaware that their device has become a slave to the bot master. Bots are not always active, and when they are, the slave device may be slow and occasionally hang, but these symptoms can be explained by any number of conditions. Most bots can be detected and removed by anti-malware software, although the bot software changes frequently to evade detection.

Botnets can be huge. Some nets have had millions of users, although lately there is a trend to limit sizes to tens of thousands. The rationale is guessed to be that bot masters have decided many smaller nets are harder to detect and shut down than a single mega-net. Individual bots are relatively easy to detect and remove compared to taking down an entire botnet. The nets can be managed in intricate hierarchies, as peer-to-peer networks, or other patterns. Even the botnet servers may be installed on compromised devices to thwart pursuit of the bot master. Authorities may take down a botnet and see it reappear a few months or weeks later.[7]

Tracing a net back to its origin can be very difficult. When an Internet message arrives, the author and location of origin may be buried in the body of the message, but they are not a required part of the wrapper where the information necessary to send the message appears. The only thing required on the wrapper is an address for the recipient and an address for a return message.

An analogy with paper mail may help fix Internet communications in your mind. The post office requires some information on the envelope, but the contents of the envelope can be anything the sender wants, similar to the requirement that an Internet message wrapper must have an address and a return address, but the body can be anything. The required envelope information is an address that the post office will use to deliver the letter. The envelope can have a return address, but the letter will still be delivered if the return address is blank, incorrect, or deceptive. The Internet is similar. Messages must have a deliverable address. If the address is wrong, the message can't be delivered. End of story. An origin address is also required. In this the Internet is tighter than the post office, which ignores absent return addresses; but the Internet is lax about the contents of the origin address. Like a return address, it can be deceptive. The lack of a requirement for a verified return address on paper letters has been the crux of many mystery novels about anonymous threats and blackmail, which is not far from what can happen on the Internet.

---

[7]For an overview of the size and resilience of botnets, see Karl Thomas, "Nine Bad Botnets and The Damage They Did," February 25, 2015. www.welivesecurity.com/2015/02/25/nine-bad-botnets-damage/. Accessed December 2015.

To further complicate Internet messages, Internet addresses are not like a street address. They are more like street directions for getting to the address. They can be simple and direct, or they may be complicated and intentionally difficult to follow. Even when the directions are simple and direct, pinning down the exact device that sent a message is often difficult or impossible because a group of devices may have the same address. For example, a home Wi-Fi network with several devices is usually seen from the outside as all having the same address. The home Wi-Fi router, which is plugged into an Internet feed, sorts out the addresses. These routers keep tables that they use to match incoming messages to the correct device, but these tables usually don't stay around for long, so finding the exact match later may be impossible. People who want to be anonymous make sure the directions are excruciatingly difficult to follow and their tracks are wiped out instantaneously. Most networks work more or less this way. Botnets and hackers in general rely on the vagaries of Internet addressing to evade discovery.

Botnets are used for several kinds of mischief. I've mentioned launching distributed denial of service attacks. Much of the Internet's spam is distributed by botnets. Each bot sends out spam, combining into an avalanche of email. At some times, botnets have been estimated to generate from 10% to 20% of global email traffic. Besides launching distributed denial of service attacks, botnets can be used to provide the computing resources for cracking passwords or mining cyber currency like Bitcoin. The owners of botnets sometimes offer botnet services for sale on the same exchanges where credit card information is sold. Criminals with few computing or network can use these services to launch their own attacks.

Cyberwarfare

Cyberwarfare is a threat that individuals can do little to prevent but puts all in danger. Cyberwarfare means surreptitiously entering the computer networks of another nation in order to do harm, spy, or steal information. Like many Internet threats, the possibility of waging cyberwarfare comes from the wide accessibly of the Internet. Cyberwarfare is fought with the same tools as a hacker attack.

Cyberwarfare can harm us in many ways. An attack on the power grid could leave part or all of the country without electricity. Industry and commerce would stop. An attack on the financial system would stop our debit and credit cards from working and reduce the stock and commodity markets to shambles, which could hinder the economy for years to come. Nuclear plants, oil pipelines and refineries, railroads, and air traffic are all vulnerable to cyberattack and disastrous industrial accidents; fires and crashes are sure to result. The effect could exceed the destructive power of an attack with nuclear weapons.

Cyberwarfare is also found in tactical military fights. For example, a cyber assault can blind defense radar systems to approaching air attacks. Cyberattacks can scramble battlefield communications networks. The potential uses are many, and most of them are probably secret.

Less open countries like China and North Korea are better prepared for cyber defense because their networks are more easily shut off from the outside world than more open countries like the United States. The first defense against a prolonged cyberattack is to shut off networks from the Internet. Open countries like the United States do not have mechanisms in place for isolating the entire country from the Internet quickly and easily.[8]

Also, in less developed countries, computer networks have a smaller role in industry and commerce. Control networks are little used in their utilities. In other words, less developed countries do not have extensive systems to defend.

A cyberwar places the highly developed nations in a lopsided position. An advanced country like the United States has great resources for launching cyberattacks, probably exceeding those of any other country, but they also have the greatest vulnerability because the make most use of computer systems in their economy. In addition, their networks are largely privately owned. These private owners may not feel that cyber defense is their responsibility, but their networks are a logical point for defensive measures.

To be effective, a cyberattack relies both on computing access to critical systems and on knowledge of the workings of the content of the system. For example, an attack on a power grid requires knowing how to run the equipment that the computer system controls. Without that knowledge, the attacker won't understand the effects of his attack, and instead cascading blackouts that blanket the country, the whole attack may fizzle into a minor event. This applies to all infrastructure cyberattacks. Attacking a financial system, air traffic control radar, or petroleum pipeline pumps and valves all require knowledge of the system to be attacked if the attack is to be a success. Infrastructure knowledge may be as hard to obtain as the computing skills necessary to hack into adversary systems. Consequently, a complex infrastructure such as a power grid or pipeline may not be as vulnerable to cyberattack as it might appear.

Traditional military strategy has difficulty with cyberwarfare. A cyberenemy may not be detectable until long after the damage is done. It may be difficult to ever identify the enemy. During the Cold War, strategies were based on

---

[8]Countries that are able to shut off the outside world have their own vulnerabilities. They may be isolated against their will by a hostile attack on their gateways. A country, active in international business, such as China, shut off from online business contact with their international partners by a hostile cyberforce could be economically devastated.

detecting and neutralizing enemy missiles and bombers before they could do damage. A cyberattack may begin long before any effects are seen. For instance, the attackers may stealthily place scripts or snippets of code in place months before the visible attack begins or a worm may be launched that slowly winds its way through the network, searching for vulnerable points. The attack itself may be undetectable: a series of flaming oil train crashes may seem to be unrelated until months later when an internal system review reveals hacked code in the railroad control system. All of this must present challenges to military strategists for whom a nuclear attack was unmistakable.

Misuses of Cyber Systems

Cybercrime is not limited to attacks on computing systems. The Internet and the applications that run on it, such as Facebook and email utilities, can be abused and cause as much or more harm than the most vicious hacker. According to the 2014 Internet Crime Report from the FBI, confidence fraud and business email compromise accounted for 140 million dollars in victim losses.[9] These crimes do not involve hacking. They use email and other forms of Internet communications in a legal fashion for illegal schemes.

Cyberbullies

Humans bully each other all the time. The desire to push other people around and make them feel bad is a perennial characteristic of human nature. Bullying among children and teenagers appears in the news often. The Center for Disease Control estimates that in 2013, one in seven high and middle school students were bullied in school. They also estimate more students were bullied electronically: one in five.[10]

The effects of cyberbullying, especially among children and teenagers, is troubling. Teenage suicides have been attributed to cyberbullying. Suicide is the most extreme form of loss of self-esteem, but many lesser forms, such as declining grades, depression, acting out, and drug use. At the most extreme, mass killings, such as Columbine, are blamed in part on cyberbullying. Unlike physical bullying, cyberbullying often occurs in the victim's home, which turns what should be a sanctuary into a crime scene.

---

[9]See Federal Bureau of Investigation, Internet Crime Complaint Center, 2014 Internet Crime Report. www.ic3.gov/media/annualreport/2014_IC3Report.pdf. Accessed December 2015. p. 47.
[10]Center for Disease Control. Bullying Fact Sheet. www.cdc.gov/violenceprevention/pdf/bullying_factsheet.pdf. Accessed December 2015.

Electronic or cyberbullying is a form of cybercrime that is quite different from data theft. Bullies do not invade systems by taking advantage of security weaknesses. Much of the time, bullies do the same things that ordinary computer users do: they send emails, they send messages, they post photographs on Instagram and Facebook. In doing these things, the bullies don't break computer system rules or encroach into forbidden areas. Instead, they maliciously break social rules by using these innocent tools to cause pain and anguish to their victims.

FORMS OF CYBERBULLYING

- Cyberbullying: Using computer, mobile phone, and network facilities to support deliberately hostile activities intended to harm an individual or group.

- Impersonation: Creating fake accounts or taking over accounts to present a demeaning false persona.

- Shunning: Maliciously excluding an individual from an online group that they ordinarily would be free to participate in.

- Threats and harassment: Using computer, mobile phone, or network facilities to threaten or discomfort an individual or group.

- Trolling: Trolls make disruptive, bad-tempered, or demeaning comments in public forums and post vitriolic product reviews.

Cyberbullying is easy; individuals weakly inclined toward injuring others can be drawn into acts that they would probably not perform if the effort and risk was greater. Physical bullying relies on the bully's power, which may be from physical strength, economic advantage, social position, or other traits. Cyberbullying requires only malice.

Social media makes communication easier and more efficient than physical interaction. Opening a Facebook page and posting a photograph of your latest family gathering is easier than physically visiting each friend to present a photograph. Unfortunately, the same efficiency applies to bullying. Bullies can take embarrassing photos of their victims and broadcast them to hundreds of friends in seconds. Without much effort, the identity of the bully can be obscured from the victim and their cohort. The prevalence of cyberbullying is not surprising. Malicious uses subvert the good intentions of the developers of social media, which is an unfortunate irony.

Authorities also have more difficulty dealing with cyberbullying than physical bullying. In the old version of the schoolyard brawl, the hulking bully threatens his scrawny victim, the principal rushes out, separates the combatants, and sends the bully to detention. Cyberbullying is much different. The aggression is hidden on the network. If the victim does not tell, the authorities are likely not to find out. If the victim tells, the authorities have to investigate before they can act. Authorities may be eager to pursue the bully, but this investigation is not nearly as easy as the old-school walk across the school yard.

What can be done to avoid cyberbullying? Cyberbullying is behavioral, not technical. Technical solutions may help identify bullying patterns in the use of computers and networks and help find the bully, but technical solutions are unlikely to prevent bullying. Most social media, such as Facebook, offer to remove objectionable material and restrict or ban users who don't conform to published community standards. However, cyberbullies can conform to social standards and still hurt their victims.

Changing a social pattern is not like tightening security on a financial site or patching a flaw in a browser. Successful anti-bullying campaigns in schools or communities usually involve raising awareness of the problem and convincing victims to seek help instead of suffering in silence. The same applies to cyberbullying. If all cyberbullying victims realized that help is available, and managers and administrators can move to neutralize the bully, far less cyberbullying would occur. Some bullies will be clever enough to circumvent any barriers to abusive activity. Without the cooperation of the victim in spotting abuse, little can be done. This can be accomplished only when potential victims know what bullying is and how to find help. This applies especially to children and young people.

Social Media Abuses

Social media is one of the wonders of the Internet. Services like Facebook bring families and friends together and provide a communication channel for community organizations and governments. Unfortunately, the qualities that make social media effective and desirable to ordinary users also attract cybervillains.

Social media, such as Facebook, Google+, Pinterest, Instagram, Twitter, and others assume that people are sincere and well-intentioned. That is as true for most social media users, as it is in life. But there are exceptions and when the sample is large, the number of exceptions is also large. Facebook has around a billion users[11] and Twitter has over 300 million users.[12] If one in a thousand users are bad eggs, Facebook has a million and Twitter has 300,000 bad ones.

The bad eggs who want to maneuver in the background and avoid being identified like electronic social media. Anonymity is easy in electronic communications. A user can take on different personas to suit their purposes.

---

[11]See http://newsroom.fb.com/company-info/. Accessed December 2015.
[12]See https://about.twitter.com/company. Accessed December 2015.

Impersonation, using another person's identity or shapeshifting, is not difficult. There are legitimate, or at least innocuous, reasons to be a shapeshifter on Facebook or Twitter, but shapeshifting also can cover up crime or vicious behavior. An impersonator can damage or destroy the reputation of the person impersonated. A shapeshifter can commit mayhem and disappear into another persona.

Geography means little on the Internet. Delivering a message from a block away can take longer than a message from the other side of the planet. Although some nations attempt to limit traffic in and out of their country, the Internet has no borders. An ordinary user has no easy way of finding the geographical origin of a message, and there are ways of hindering even forensic experts from finding the origin of a message. Geographic obscurity is a boon to miscreants. A scurrilous post on a Facebook timeline that appears to be from a hometown local could be from anywhere: Eastern Europe, South America, West Africa, anywhere. Unless someone tries to ferret out the origin of the message, no one will ever know where it came from. And even a smart cyberferret cannot guarantee that the origin will be found.

The anonymity and ignorance of location are in the design of the Internet. When the Internet was developed, an important goal was to connect existing networks into the Internet with minimal changes to their configuration. This was to promote rapid and wide expansion of the Internet. Requiring a verified identity and location of the sender would have complicated the interface between networks. Consequently, geography and authenticated identity are not part of the Internet's design.

Social media attracts users because social ties are built and reinforced on the media. Distant relatives can be brought into family events. Acquaintances can converse and become real friends. With the casual exchange of images and communication, trust is easy to establish.

The combination of anonymity, ease of impersonation, and easily obtained trust with little oversight and few rules is an ideal environment for gulling the unwary. Predators of every stripe love a communication channel like Facebook, which gives them access to over a billion trusting users. They can hide behind a fake persona and not reveal their location. A grizzled and tattooed convicted felon can plausibly impersonate a 6-year-old girl. If he is good at mimicking the mannerisms of a little girl, his deception can go undetected and he is free to use the guise of an innocent to indulge in mischief and mayhem. This kind of deception, which is possible on all forms of social media based on the Internet, including chat rooms, provides opportunities for many varieties of troubling activities.

At the least destructive end of the spectrum, are trolls who deceive, insult, and disrupt discussions. Some trolls are genuine cyberbullies; others are only distracting and annoying grumps. At best, they ignore the rules of social discourse and are distracting and annoying. At worst, they bully their victims with insults.

Other mild forms of social media abuse are phony reviews of various kinds. Businesses get bad reviews from competitors and biased good reviews are submitted by proprietors and their friends. Retail sites like Amazon have to deal with both bogus good and bad reviews. Some shady businesses offer reviews in bulk for a fee. These scams rely on the anonymity and openness of the Internet.

There are many lucrative and elaborate scams. An often-reported and lucrative Internet crime in 2014 was automobile fraud. The fraud commonly begins on a website or a solicitation from an acquaintance on social media or via email. The fraudster offers to sell an auto at an attractive price, probably an unreasonably low price. The fraudster explains that he is in the armed forces, about to be sent overseas, and needs quick money, or some similar story tailored to evoke incautious empathy. The victim transfers the money, perhaps by wire transfer or Western Union. The vehicle never materializes and the fraudster disappears in to cyberspace. Per the FBI, this was a common Internet fraud in 2014. Almost 1,800 victims lost a total of 56 million dollars.[13] And that is reported victims, which could be lower than the actual number of victims.

Sinister organizations like the Islamic State of Iraq and Syria (ISIS) or other hate groups use social media to promote and recruit because social media is an effective vehicle for any kind of subversive activity. The dilemma is that subversion and legitimate dissent are not easily differentiated. This dilemma is a challenge to a democratic and free society like the United States. Dangerous, subversive groups are hard to distinguish from legitimate dissenters. Both subversion and suppression of dissent threaten democracy. Consequently, protecting legitimate social media users and preventing misuse of social media at the same time is difficult.

Social media is subject to the same techniques as other Internet services. A link on Facebook can be as dangerous as a link anywhere else. A click on a social media site that leads to a page that requests confidential information like passwords or credit card numbers is likely to be harmful. Pages can also deposit drive-by malware that opens your device to the hacker or performs other mischief. Caution is advised. Later, I will talk about how to avoid and deal with this type of threat.

---

[13]See Federal Bureau of Investigation, Internet Crime Complaint Center, 2014 Internet Crime Report. www.ic3.gov/media/annualreport/2014_IC3Report.pdf. Accessed December 2015. p. 41.

Where Are We?

Has this chapter scared you? I hope so. Cybersecurity is very serious. Cybercrime can harm individuals profoundly. Life savings can be lost. A stolen identity may plague a victim for decades. Spam may be only an annoyance, but when it is a phishing expedition or an attempt to deposit malware on your computer, it can do serious damage.

Public wireless networks are convenient, but they also harbor grave dangers.

Social media has enhanced our lives, and has made us vulnerable to bullies and scammers.

Cyberwarfare is another worry. I happen to believe that cyberwarfare is a more dangerous threat than the terrorism that has captured public attention. Highly industrialized countries are more vulnerable than under-developed countries. The under-developed countries may lack expertise, but expertise can be developed or bought. Unorganized hackers with few resources do damage every day. What can a well-organized and funded military group do?

What can we do to protect ourselves?

Why Is Computer Security So Weak?

Come On, Guys! Can't You Do Better?

The history of computers for the last 80 years has been a fall from innocence. The story begins in a protected place where computer crime as we know it today was non-existent. As the computing community delved deeper into the computer's potential, the computing garden was gradually infiltrated by cybercrime. The Internet let in all comers, including those remarkably lacking in innocence, to an unprepared community, and the scene was set for cyber-mayhem. This chapter describes the road to mayhem.

© Marvin Waschke 2017

M. Waschke, *Personal Cybersecurity*, DOI 10.1007/978-1-4842-2430-4_2

The security problems of today are traceable to the origins of computing. The form of security used for early computers is almost irrelevant to contemporary cybersecurity. In the best of possible worlds, protection for users would be built into the foundation of computer design. But that could not happen because early computer designers had no concept of protecting the user from intrusion and damage, and certainly no idea that computers might be connected together into an enormous worldwide web. The fundamental decisions in the early stages of computer design do not correspond to the needs of the present. Hardware and software engineers are still dealing with the traces of these early decisions.

Babbage and Lovelace

Charles Babbage is usually cited as the inventor of the programmable computer and Ada Lovelace as the first computer programmer. They lived and worked in the early and mid-19th century. Although Babbage and Lovelace were clearly brilliant and far ahead of their time, their accomplishments were only tenuous influences at best on the scientists and engineers in the first half of the 20th century, who began the line of development that leads to the computers of today.

Babbage first designed what he called the Difference Engine. The device required a skilled and innovative machine shop for its construction, pushing the limits of Victorian technology. The Difference Engine was a calculator that could calculate logarithmic and trigonometric tables, which were important for navigation, but it was not programmable. A later design called the Analytic Engine was programmable. Ada Lovelace wrote programs for the Analytic Engine. None of Babbage's designs were completely constructed during his lifetime, although a modern replica of a version of the Difference Engine was built and successfully tested in 1991 at the Science Museum in London.[1]

The Babbage devices were analog, not digital. Electronic digital computers represent numbers and symbols as discrete values, usually voltages in electronic circuits. The values depend on voltages falling within ranges. In modern computer memory, a value must be either 1 or 0; an intermediate value is impossible. The zeroes and ones combine to express everything else.

An analog computer depends on physical measurements rather than discrete values and must be manufactured with great precision to produce correct results. Babbage designed more complex and powerful computers than those that proceeded his, but he stayed within the analog tradition. Moving from analog to digital was one of the accomplishments that began modern computing.

---

[1]See the Computer History Museum, "The Babbage Engine," www.computerhistory.org/babbage/modernsequel/. Accessed January, 2016. The output mechanisms were not completed until 2002.

Babbage's triumphant innovation was programmability. He designed his Difference Engine to calculate by *finite differences*, a mathematical method that applies to many problems, but is much narrower than the range of problems that can be addressed by a programmable computer. The Analytic Engine was programmable; it could be given instructions to solve many different problems. In fact, computer scientists have proven that the Analytic Engine could solve any problem that a modern digital computer can solve, although impractically slowly.[2]

Ada Lovelace not only devised programs for the Analytical Engine, she conceived an important concept of modern programing: numeric codes can represent symbols. For example, the code "97" represents the letter "a" in most computers. A series of numeric codes like this can represent a page of text. This simple insight moves computing from numerical calculation to manipulating language and general reasoning.

Since Babbage's designs were not built in his lifetime, security was never an issue, but it is easy to imagine that a simple lock on the mechanism, a guard, or a lock on the door would have adequately protected the machinery. In addition, it is hard to imagine anyone wishing to interfere with a machine cranking away at calculating a table of logarithms. If anyone had, the ordinary means for dealing with theft or trespass would probably have been adequate.

Unfortunately, the great discoveries of Babbage and Lovelace were forgotten and had to be reinvented in the 20th century. World War II marked the beginning of modern computing.

The Programmable Computer

The development of contemporary computing began in earnest during the buildup to World War II. Early computers were primarily military. They were developed for two tasks: aiming big naval guns and breaking codes. Both were intense numerical tasks that had to be performed under the fierce pressure of war.

Before computers, these tasks were performed by squads of clerks with simple calculators such as mechanical adding machines. Methods were developed for combining the results of each human calculator into a single calculation and checking the results, but the process was still slow and errors were common. An incorrect ballistic calculation could hurl expensive ordnance off-target, resulting in lost battles, sunken friendly ships, and injury or death. Cracked codes could determine the outcome of battles, turn the course of war, and save lives. Prompt and accurate calculations were vital to national survival.

---

[2] The Analytic Engine is "Turing complete." This is not the place to discuss Turing computers, but "Turing complete" is a mathematical definition of a general computer.

The first calculation machines were analog and like Babbage's Difference Engine. These machines were faster and more accurate but they could perform only one type of computation. If a cipher changed, the machine was useless until it was rebuilt. A device that could perform different types of calculation without torturous rebuilding would be more efficient and useful. Babbage's Analytical Engine might have filled the bill, but it was long forgotten and probably too slow.

Digital electronic computers were faster and easier to build than analog, and development in the 1940s was almost entirely digital. Computing took a huge step forward when calculating instructions joined data in computer input. The first computer to combined program instructions with data input was the Electronic Discrete Variable Automatic Computer (EDVAC.)[3] John von Neumann (1903-1957) wrote and released the first report on the design of the EDVAC. He is considered the inventor of the program-stored-as-data architecture, for which Babbage and Lovelace had postulated the basic ideas but never actually implemented, and were forgotten until after their ideas had been reinvented. Modern computers are based on the von Neumann architecture.

The von Neumann architecture gives computing one of its most important characteristics: its malleability. Computers are limited by their resources, such as storage and memory, but they can be made to execute an unlimited array of algorithms with different goals. The range of capabilities is wonderfully large and these capabilities can be changed at will while the computer is in operation. Without this malleability, computers would not have the many uses they have today.

But malleability makes computers subject to subversion in ways that other kinds of systems do not face. A computer program can be changed while it is in operation. The changes can have a huge impact but can be hard to detect. For example, an enemy programmer who gained access to a computer like the EDVAC system for aiming a ballistic missile could, with sufficient skill, be able to subtly reprogram the system to miss or hit the wrong target without changing the physical device. If the computer had to be physically rebuilt to make the change, it would be much harder to mount such an attack surreptitiously.

This new kind of threat meant new kinds of security measures, but the new threats were not apparent. Threats that involved physical contact with the computer could be stopped by existing practices. Posting guards and screening the scientists and engineers involved in critical projects was routine military research practice long before computers. Some engineers at the time may have thought about the new vulnerabilities in von Neumann's architecture, but they were quickly shoved to the back of the desk by more pressing concerns.

---

[3]Encyclopedia.com, "Early Computers," www.encyclopedia.com/doc/1G2-3401200044. html. Accessed January 2016.

The notions of intrusion on the physical machine and intrusion into the running software naturally were conflated. Today, we often hear of computers invaded by hackers from the other side of the planet, but before networks became prevalent, interrupting the software without getting near the hardware was impossible. The only way to subvert a computer was to slip through a security gate. What invaders might do after they got past the gate was a secondary question. The mindset and skills needed to program were so rare in the early days, the director of a project might be more inclined to hire an invader rather than send them to jail.

On the other hand, separation of hardware and software transformed computers into the flexible tool that now dominates so much of our society and economy.

The Mainframe

Unlike most technology companies, the origins of International Business Machines (IBM) go back to the late 19th century when the company manufactured tabulating machines, time clocks, and other business equipment. IBM held patents on the Hollerith key punch, which became prevalent as the input and output medium for mainframe computers. Until World War II, IBM continued to develop and manufacture tabulators and mechanical calculators for accounting systems. Shortly before the war it developed a non-programmable electronic computer and became involved in defense development, converting some of its manufacturing capacity to manufacturing ordnance, but it retained its focus on computing, participating in some large government efforts to develop computers. IBM leveraged access to government research into dominance in computer manufacture. With its history in both business and research, IBM could then dominate both research and business applications of computers. The phrase for the time was "Big Blue and the seven dwarves." Big Blue was a nickname for IBM and the seven dwarves were Digital Equipment, Control Data, General Electric, RCA, Univac, Burroughs, and Honeywell.[4]

As computer hardware became more compact, smaller computers became viable. These were built as cheaper alternatives to mainframes and required less space and fewer staff to run. They were known as *minicomputers* and were frequently set up as multi-user systems in which computer processing time was distributed among the users, each having the illusion of complete control of their own computer. These multi-user systems have security challenges.

---

[4]Shayne Nelson, "The 60s - IBM & the Seven Dwarves," June 1, 2004, http://it.toolbox.com/blogs/tricks-of-the-trade/the-60s-ibm-the-seven-dwarves-955. Accessed January 2016.

User data must be separated and protected from other users. Unauthorized users must also be prevented from interfering with other users. These concerns were addressed by UNIX, an operating system developed by AT&T. The UNIX source code was offered to educational institutions. A flurry of innovation followed and many variations of UNIX appeared. Eventually UNIX evolved into today's Linux. IBM introduced timesharing also, but used a different method that evolved away from timesharing to become a key technology of cloud computing.[5]

The Personal Computer (PC)

The earliest personal computers preceded the IBM PC, but the IBM PC was the first to enter the workplace as a tool rather than a toy. The IBM PC was introduced in August of 1981. Measured against the personal computers of today, the 1981 IBM PC was puny. The processing capacity of a desktop now is several orders of magnitude greater than that of the first PC. Yet, the first PC was equipped to perform serious work. IBM offered word processing, spreadsheets, and accounting software for the PC, whose monitor and keyboard was destined to appear on every desktop in every business.

When PCs were introduced to the workplace, they were appliances: super powered typewriters that made corrections without retyping the document; automated spreadsheets for data analysis and tabular records; and streamlined accounting systems for businesses. These appliances were isolated islands, accessible only to their owners. The personal in "personal computer" was literal; it was not a node in a communication web.

Early PCs were usually not networked with other PCs or any other type of computer system, although they might be set up to emulate a terminal attached to a mainframe or minicomputer. A terminal is nothing more than a remote keyboard and display. When a PC emulates a terminal, the emulation software is designed only to receive screen data from the mainframe or mini and translate it to a PC screen image. The emulation software also passes PC keyboard input to the mainframe or mini. When a PC is emulating, the PC is only a conduit. No data on the PC changes and the host, mainframe or mini, can't distinguish between a PC and a dedicated terminal. A person needing both a PC and a terminal could claw back some real estate on the top of their desk by replacing the terminal with an emulator on their PC and the company need only buy one expensive device instead of two.

Hard drives did not appear in PCs until the second model of the IBM PC appeared. The earliest PCs used audio cassettes for storage. Later, users relied on small floppy disks for saving information and backing up. The floppies usually

---

[5]The technology is virtualization of which I will talk about later.

ended up in a box, possibly locked, on the user's desk. Both their processing and the data were isolated and inaccessible to everyone but the PC owner. An isolated PC on every desk was the vision of many in the PC world. This vision was nearly realized in the late 1980s and early 1990s.

Isolated and relatively cheap PCs could be and were purchased by business departments rather than IT and were considered closer to office machines than real computers that deserved the attention of the trained technologists from the IT department. Although mainframe security differs from PC security, IT staffs are aware of data protection, unlike most office workers. Generally, left on their own, most workers are unaware and basic security practices, such as regular backups, are neglected or never established.

PC practices could be rather chaotic, varying greatly from department to department. Since each department often purchased their software and hardware independently, compatibility was hit and miss. Although these practices were inefficient, the PC increased departmental efficiency enough to justify continued departmental purchases of PCs and software. PC security, other than preventing thieves from carrying off expensive pieces of equipment, was not a recognized need. Theft of memory cards was common enough that locks were often placed on computer cases. Only the occasional loss of unbacked-up data from a disk crash reminded managers that PCs require a different kind of attention than an electric typewriter or copier.

Occasionally, you hear of offices that brought in computer services regularly to dust the interior of their PCs, but neglected to back up their data. Dusting the interior of PCs is occasionally needed, but in a typical clean office environment, dusting may not be required until after a PC is obsolete. Backing up is a continual necessity. Such misplaced priorities are an indication of system management without a clear understanding of threats.

The predominant PC operating system, Microsoft Disk Operating System (MS-DOS), was a single-user system. Its code would not support more than a single user. Microsoft licensed a second operating system, . Like Linux today, Xenix was derived from UNIX, the venerable mini-computer operating system. UNIX was a multi-user operating system that built substantial security, like limiting user authorization, into the core of the system. Xenix inherited multi-user support and some of the security built into UNIX.

The isolated PC vision could get along well without investments in the cumbersome and performance-sapping mechanisms of a multi-user systems and networking. For a while, Microsoft thought Xenix would become the Microsoft high-end operating system when PCs became powerful enough to support Xenix well. That view changed. Microsoft distanced itself from the Xenix operating system in the mid to late 1980s and began to concentrate on its own high-end operating system, NT.

NT did not begin as an operating system that concentrated upon security and did not inherit the security concerns of Xenix. It was still anchored in the milieu in which each PC was an island with minimal contact with other computers. Security as we think of it today was still not a driving concern. NT did provide greater stability and freed Microsoft from limitations that came from operating with the early processor chips that were used in early PCs. Current Microsoft operating systems are still based on the NT design, although they have evolved substantially.

Microsoft and the other hardware and software vendors could have chosen to develop more secure multi-user systems, but there was little apparent need. PCs were not powerful enough to drive multi-user systems well. At that time, most people's vision for the PC was an isolated personal device on every desk and in every home. Although the technology for networking computers was available, it was not implemented at first. The cost of installing wiring and the lack of apparent benefit may have affected this.

The Local Area Network

The introduction of the Local Area Network (LAN) was a milestone on the path to the end of innocence for personal computing. A LAN is a network that connects computers over a small area, often a building or a floor in a building. A network connection transforms a desktop PC into a communication device. The new power that a LAN connection conferred was not understood when LANs were introduced. Few realized that the versatile machine on everyone's desk could no longer be managed and maintained like a high-end typewriter.

At first glance, a LAN connection appears to be a minor enhancement to the PC's capabilities. LANs were often positioned as a cost reduction measure. Connected PCs could share resources like disk storage. Instead of investing in large storage disks for each PC, a single *file server* could be equipped with a disk large enough to store everyone's files. Centrally stored data could be stored and served back to the PC of anyone who needed the files. PC hardware was much more expensive then and this was a tempting possibility. Some PCs were deployed that had little or no local storage and operated entirely off the central file server.

Documents written at one desk were instantly available for revision at a dozen other desks on the LAN. Eventually, this mode of working would become very common. It connects with the concept of the *paperless office*, an office in which all documents are stored and maintained in electronic form. These documents are passed from person to person electronically rather than as paper. The path to a paperless office was longer than expected.[6] Shared disks were an early step forward that inspired enthusiasm, but it took cloud implementations and tablets to substantially reduce the amount of paper used in offices.

A LAN without an external connection can only connect the computers on the LAN. Documents could not be delivered to remote offices without a connection to another type of network, called a Wide Area Network (WAN). Before the Internet, wide area communication was usually reserved for large enterprises. Computer communications with customers or suppliers was usually not available. Teletype communications, based on the telephone system, was generally used for business-to-business document transfer. Faxing, also based on the telephone system, was gaining ground during this period.

Email was available, but on an isolated LAN or group of LANs connected on a WAN, the reach of email was limited. A cobbled together UNIX system based on dialup modems could transfer email from one isolated LAN to another, but it was difficult to learn and set up, relying on the UNIX command line. Delivery was quirky and depending on dialup connections that were easily snarled. It was not fast and reliable like the Internet-based system everyone uses today.[7]

Even with its limitations, email and early network forums began to thrive and foreshadow the current popularity of social media. Today's arguments over the ethics of spending time on Facebook at work resemble the passionate debates that once raged over the legitimacy and ethics of using company email to set up a lunch date with a colleague.

---

[6]BusinessWeek, "The Office of the Future", June 1975, www.bloomberg.com/bw/stories/1975-06-30/the-office-of-the-futurebusinessweek-business-news-stock-market-and-financial-advice. Accessed February, 2016. This article is a pre-PC discussion of the paperless office. It documents the mixture of views prevalent at the time. This article seems to assume that a paperless office would consist of terminals connected to a central mainframe. In the future, a LAN of connected PCs would be thought of as a better architecture.

[7]Danny Weiss, "Eudora's Name and Historical Background", www.eudorafaqs.com/eudora-historical-background.shtml. Accessed February 2016, offers some interesting insight into the early days of email.

LAN Security

The appearance of LANs inspired new thinking on computer security. A LAN fits a secure-the-perimeter model, which is an extension of the concept of locking doors and surrounding buildings with fences. Ethernet is almost the only LAN protocol used today. The Ethernet standard specifies the way bits and bytes are transmitted in patterns that are identified, received, and sent on the conductors that connect individual PCs on a LAN. The Ethernet design was conceived in the mid-1970s at the Xerox labs in Palo Alto. The Institute of Electrical and Electronics Engineers (IEEE) published an Ethernet standard in 1983.[8]

Usually, computers and other devices connected to an Ethernet LAN determine a security perimeter that prohibits or limits access to the LAN. The LAN perimeter may be nested inside a wide area network (WAN) perimeter that might be within an even wider corporate perimeter. See Figure 2-1.

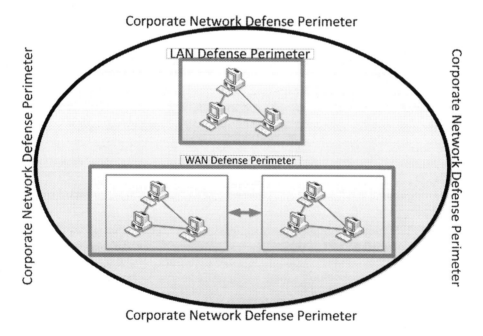

Figure 2-1. Defense perimeters nest

---

[8]IEEE, "The 40th Anniversary of Ethernet", 2013, http://standards.ieee.org/events/ethernet/index.html. Accessed February 2016, offers a brief history of the Ethernet standard.

The attack surface of an isolated LAN is limited to physical access to the computers connected to the LAN plus the cables and network gear that tie the network together. In most cases, an isolated LAN can be protected by restricting access to rooms and buildings. A physically secured LAN is still vulnerable to invasion by rogue employees or attackers who penetrate physical security. Cabling and wiring closets were added the list of items to be physically secured, but, for the most part, a LAN can be secured in the same way isolated PCs can be secured.

Many enterprises are not limited to a single building or compact campus. If a geographically spread organization wanted to network all their PCs together, they had to step up to a WAN to connect widely separated sites. WAN services, at that time, were usually supplied by third parties using the telecommunications voice transmission infrastructure. Often the telecoms themselves offered WAN services. This opened inter-LAN communication to tampering from within the telephone system. With each step, from isolated PC, to PCs connected to a LAN, to LANs connected by WANs, PCs became more useful and began to play a more important role moving data from employee to employee and department to department, and consolidating data for management. However, with each step, the PC on the desk became more exposed to outside influences.

Although the vulnerabilities of a LAN are greater than those of a disconnected PC, developers were not spurred to rethink the security of the hardware and software designs of the PC. The developers remained largely oblivious to the threats that were coming.

The Methodology Disconnect

Mainframe software was almost always mission critical; few businesses could afford to use expensive mainframe resources on anything but mission critical projects. The downside of these critical projects was the frequency of missed deadlines and dysfunctional results. These failures cost millions of dollars and ended careers. Cost-overruns and failed systems often seemed more common than successes. The managers in suits responded with a rigid methodology intended to ensure success. A project had to begin with a meticulous analysis of the problem to be solved and progress to an exacting design that developers were expected translate to code without deviation from the design.

The methodology had some serious flaws. Often in software development, new, better, and more efficient approaches are only visible after coding is in progress. The methodology was a barrier to taking advantage of this type of discovery. In addition, the methodology provided every player with opportunities to blame someone in a previous stage for failure, or toss issues over the wall for the next stage to resolve.

This was the state of software engineering for a distributed environment when I first entered PC development. The atmosphere was heady. Development had broken away from the mainframe.

Programming offers unlimited opportunities for creativity and can be more art than science. Many developers who were attracted to the creative side of coding did not thrive in the regimented mainframe development environment. For these developers to be part of a small team, each with their own computer under their control, on which they could experiment and push to the limits and beyond, was like a trip to Las Vegas with an unlimited bankroll.

New products popped up everywhere and the startup culture began. In the exuberance of the time, security was more a hindrance to development rather than a basic requirement. Although most developers knew that networking was about to become a mainstay of computing, they still preferred to tack security to the end of development process and leave the hassle of signing in and proper authorization to the testers. After all, it was not like a timesharing system; no one could get to a PC sitting on an office worker's desk or in someone's living room.

The Internet

The Internet was the next stage in the transformation of the personal computer from a stand-alone appliance like a typewriter or a stapler into a communications portal. Home computers were transformed in the same way, connecting home and office to a growing world of information, institutions, and activities. See Figure 2-2.

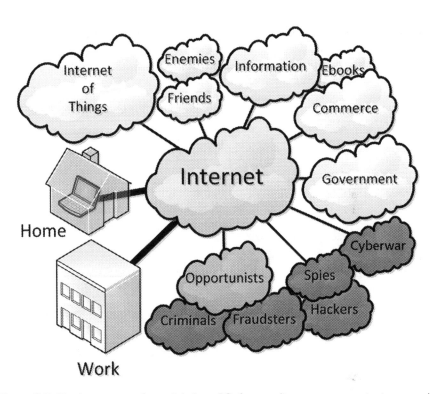

Figure 2-2. The Internet transformed desktop PCs from appliances to communications portals

Network

The Internet is a network that connects other networks. When a business' network connects to the Internet, all the computers that connect to the business' network join the Internet.

The computers connected in a network are called *nodes*. Nodes shows up often in computer science terminology. The Latin meaning of node is knot, a meaning that the word retains. In networking jargon, a node is a junction, a knot, where communication lines meet. Most of the time, a network node is a computer, although other network gear, such as switches and routers, are also nodes. When connected to the Internet, nodes are knitted together into a single interconnected fabric. Some nodes are connected to each other directly, others are connected in a series of hops from node to node, but, when everything is working right, all nodes connected to the Internet are connected and can communicate. At present, there are over three billion nodes connected into the Internet. The exact number changes continuously as nodes connect and disconnect.[9]

---

[9]Internet Live Stats, "Internet Users," www.internetlivestats.com/internet-users/. Accessed February 2016. This site delivers a continuous readout of Internet users based on statistical modeling and selected data sources.

The Internet led software designers and developers to think about computer applications differently. Instead of standalone programs like word processors and spreadsheets, they could design systems that provided complex central services to remote users. Timesharing mainframes and minicomputers had hosted applications that offered services to users on terminals, but the Internet offered a network, which is more flexible. In a network, nodes connect to any number of other nodes. A terminal in a typical time-sharing architecture communicates with a single host. In this architecture, terminals usually were not sophisticated and relied on the host for all computing. Communication between terminals must be routed through the central host. This kind of architecture is hard to expand. At some point, the number of terminals exceeds the load the host can support and the system has reached its limit. Sometimes the capacity of the central host can be increased, but that reaches a limit also. See Figure 2-3.

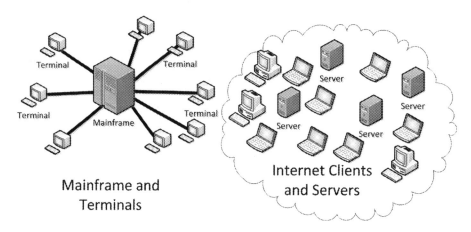

Figure 2-3. A mainframe spoke-and-hub pattern differs from the Internet pattern

Within a network like the Internet, a system can expand by adding new servers, nodes that act like a mainframe host to provide information and processing to other client nodes, in place of a single host mainframe. With the proper software, servers can be duplicated as needed to support rising numbers of clients. On the Internet, users do not connect directly to a single large computer. Instead, users connect to the Internet, and through the Internet, they can connect to other nodes on the Internet. This connectivity implies that servers can be located anywhere within the reach of the Internet.

As the Internet blossomed, developers still tended to assume that no one was malicious. In the early 1990s, I was part of a startup that was developing a distributed application. Our office was in Seattle and our first customer was a bank located in one of the World Trade Towers in Manhattan. One morning, one of the developers noticed that some odd data was appearing mysteriously in his instance of the application. After a minute, he realized where it was coming from. Our first customer was unknowingly broadcasting data to our office. Fortunately, only test data was sent, but it could have been critical private data. If our customer had gone into production with that version of the product, our little company would have ended abruptly. The defect was quickly corrected, but it was only caught by chance. The development team missed a vital part of configuring the system for communication and did not think to monitor activity on the Internet. Until that moment, we did no testing that would have detected the mess.

Of course, our team began to give Internet connections more attention, but it would be a decade before Internet security issues routinely got the attention among developers that they do now. Mistakes like this were easy to make and they were made often, although perhaps not as egregious as ours.

Communication Portal

The decentralized connectivity of the Internet is the basis for today's computers becoming communication portals that connect everyone and everything. Utilities like email are possible in centralized terminal-host environments, and attaching every household to a central time-sharing system is possible and was certainly contemplated by some pre-Internet visionaries, but it never caught on. Instead, the decentralized Internet has become the ubiquitous communications solution.

Much of the expansion of home computing starting in the mid-1990s can be traced to the growth of the home computer as a communications portal. A computer communications portal has more use in the home than a stand-alone computer. Before the Internet, most people used their home computer for office work or computer games. Not everyone has enough office work at home to justify an expensive computer, nor is everyone taken with computer games enough to invest in a computer to play them. The communications, data access, and opportunities for interaction offered by the Internet alter this equation considerably.[10]

The expansion of communication opportunities has had many good effects. Publishing on the Internet has become easy and cheap. Global publication is no longer limited to organizations like book publishers, news agencies, newspapers, magazines, and television networks. Email is cheaper and faster than paper mail and has less environmental impact. Electronic online commerce has thrived on the ease of communication on the Internet.

---

[10]Of course, it did not hurt that the price of computers began to plummet at the same time.

The Internet has reduced the obstacles to information flow over national boundaries. The browser has become a window on the world. New opportunities have appeared for both national and international commerce. Social media has changed the way families and friends are tie together. The transformation did not happen overnight, but it occurred faster than expected and is still going on.

The computer as a communications portal appeals to many more people than office functions and games. Everyone can use email and almost everyone is receptive to the benefits of social media. When the uses of computers were limited to functionality that required technical training, computer owners were a limited subgroup of the population with some level of technical insight. The group of those interested in social media and email has expanded to include both the most technically sophisticated and the most naïve. The technically naïve members of this group are unlikely to understand much of what goes on behind the scenes on their computer and its network. This leaves them more vulnerable to cybercrime.

Origins

The Internet did not spring from a void. It began with research in the 1960s into methods of computer communication and evolved from there to the Internet we know today. Often, the Internet is said to have begun with the development of the Advanced Research Projects Agency Network (ARPANET)[11], but without the network technology developed earlier, ARPANET would have been impossible.

ARPANET and the Internet

In the 1950s, mainframes in their glasshouse data centers were nearly impregnable, but a different wind had begun to blow. In the late 1950s, Joseph Lickliter (1915-1990), head of the ARPA, began thinking about connecting research mainframes as part of the research ARPA performed for the defense department. Lickliter wanted connect computers to provide access to researchers who were not geographically close to a research data center. He called his projected network the "Intergalactic Computer Network" in a memo to the agency.[12]

---

[11]ARPANET is sometimes called the Defense Advanced Research Projects Agency Network (DARPANET). ARPA was renamed DARPA in 1972.
[12]http://history-computer.com/Internet/Birth/Licklider.html. Accessed January 2016.

Lickliter brought together researchers from the entire country. This group eventually developed the ARPANET. The network was designed to connect research computers, not, as is sometimes reported, as a command and control system that could withstand nuclear attack. Lickliter went on to other projects before the network was realized, but he is often called the originator.

The first incarnation of the ARPANET was formed on the west coast between Stanford, University of California Los Angeles, University of California Santa Barbara, and the University of Utah. These were university research centers, not top secret military centers, nor were they commercial data centers, processing inventories and accounts.

The concept of tying together isolated computers and knowledge was compelling. The objective was to include as many research centers as possible, not raise barriers to joining. At the height of the Cold War, fear of espionage was rampant, but apparently, no one thought about ARPANET as a means for spying on the research center network and little was done to secure it, beyond the usual precautions of keeping the equipment behind lock and key. The early ARPANET did not include commercial datacenters. Therefore, there may have been some concern about data theft, but money and finances were not on anyone's mind.

During the 1980s and the early 1990s, two networking approaches contended. The ARPANET represented one approach. The other was IBM's Systems Network Architecture (SNA). The two differed widely, reflecting their different origins.

Businesses needed to connect their computers for numerous reasons. Branches need to connect to headquarters, vendors to customers, and so on. To serve these needs, IBM developed a proprietary network architecture unrelated to the ARPANET. The architecture was designed for the IBM mainframes and minicomputers used by its business customers. It was implemented with communications equipment that IBM designed and built specifically for SNA. Non-IBM hardware could connect with SNA to IBM's equipment, but SNA was not used to connect non-IBM equipment to other non-IBM equipment. In other words, SNA was only useful in environments where IBM equipment was dominant.

Almost all networks today are based on what is called a *layered architecture*. Instead of looking at network transmission as a single process that puts data on and takes data off a transmission medium, a layered architecture looks at the process as a combination of standardized parts that are called *layers*.

When put together for communication, the layers are called a *network stack*. For example, the bottom layer, called the *physical layer*, is concerned with signals on the transmission medium. This layer knows how to translate a message into the physical manifestations the transmission media must have. If the medium is copper wire, the layer is a software and hardware module designed and built to put modulated electrical signals on copper wire at the proper voltage and frequency. If copper wire is replaced by optical fiber, the copper wire module is replaced by an optical fiber module that reads and writes light pulses. When a layer in the stack is replaced, the other layers do not have to change because each layer is designed to interact with the other layers in a standard way.

Layers work like an electric plugs and sockets. It doesn't matter whether you plug a lamp or an electric can opener into a wall socket. Both will work fine. Also, the electricity could come from a hydro-electric dam, a windmill, or a gas generator out back. The lamp will still light and you can still open the can of beans because the socket and the electricity is the same. You replace a layer in a network stack in the same way. If what goes in or comes out meets its specification, what happens in between does not matter. You can think of each network layer as having a plug and socket. An upper layer plugs into the socket on the next lower layer. If each pair of plugs and sockets meet the same specification, the stack works.

A layered network architecture is a tremendous advantage, as is the standard design of electricity sources and electrical appliances. When the need arises, you can switch sources. If you lose power during a storm, you can fire up your private gas generator and the lamp still lights. This also applies to networking. If copper is too slow, you can replace it with optical fiber and replace the copper bottom layer module with a fiber module. This saves much time and expense because the entire network stack does not need to be rewritten. When connecting to another network, only the top layers where the connection occurs need be compatible. Typically, networks are divided into seven layers. The bottom layer is the only layer that deals with hardware. The rest are all software.

In addition to being an early adopter of a layered network architecture, ARPANET used *packet switching* for message transmission. Packet switching divides a message into chunks called *packets*. Each of these packets is addressed to the destination network node. Each packet finds its own way through the network from one switching node to the next. A *switching node* is a special computer that can direct a packet to the next step toward the target address. Since there is usually more than one way to travel from source to destination, the network is resilient; if one path is blocked, the packet is switched to another path and the packet eventually gets through. When all the packets arrive at the destination, they are reassembled and passed to the receiving program.

A group researching a military communications network that could survive a catastrophe, such as a nuclear attack, discussed the concept of a packet switching network. The ARPANET was not developed by this group, but the ARPANET team put packet switching to work in their network and gained the resiliency that military communications required.

There are other advantages to packet switching beyond resilience. It is very easy to connect to an ARPANET-style network. Part of this is due to the layered architecture. For example, if a network based on a different transmission technology wants to join the Internet, they develop a replacement layer that will communicate with the corresponding layer in the ARPANET network stack and they are ready to go without re-engineering their entire implementation. When a new node joins the Internet, other nodes do not need to know anything about the newcomer except that its top layer is compatible. The newcomer only needs to be assigned an address. The switching nodes use the structure of the address to begin to direct packets to the newcomer.

The layered architecture facilitates ease in entry by not mixing lower level concerns and application code. Application changes do not require changes deep in the stack that would prevent connections with nodes without the lower level changes. This explains the rich array of applications that communicate over the Internet with nodes that are unaware of the internals of the application.

ARPANET also developed basic protocols and addressing schemes that are still in use today. These protocols are flexible and relatively easy to implement. A layered architecture and packet switching contribute to the flexibility and ease. The basic Internet protocol, Transmission Control Protocol over Internet Protocol (TCP/IP) conducts messages from an application running on one node to another application running on a node, but it is the job of the node, not the network, to determine which application will receive the message.

The flexibility and ease of connection profoundly affected IBM's SNA. By the mid-1990s, SNA was in decline, rapidly being replaced by the Internet architecture. SNA was hard to configure, required expensive specialized equipment, and was hard to connect to non-SNA systems. By the mid-1990s, SNA systems were often connected over Internet-type networks using *tunneling*: hiding SNA data in Internet messages, then stripping away the Internet wrapper for the SNA hardware at the receiving end. This added an extra layer of processing to SNA communication.

The SNA connection from computer to computer is relatively inflexible. There was no notion of sending or receiving a message to or from another computer that any application able to handle the message could respond to the message. This is one of the features that makes Internet-style communication flexible and powerful, but it also eases intrusion into application interaction, which is the basis of many cybercrimes. It is not surprising that financial institutions were late to replace SNA with the ARPANET-style networking of the Internet.[13]

---

[13]For a detailed technical description of SNA in a heterogeneous environment, see R. J. Cypser, *Communications for Cooperating Systems: Osi, Sna, and Tcp/Ip*, Addison-Wesley, 1991.

An ARPANET-style layered network architecture separates the authentication of the source and target of a message from the transmission of the message. Generally, this is advantageous because combining transmission and authentication could degrade the performance of transmission as identities and credentials are exchanged. Proving who you are requires complex semantics and negotiations. Quickly and efficiently moving raw bits and bytes from computer to computer does not depend on the semantics of the data transferred. Including semantics based authentication slows down and complicates the movement of data.

The ARPANET architecture choice was practical and sound engineering, but it was at the expense of the superior security of SNA.[14] In SNA, unlike ARPANET, transmission and authentication were combined in the same layer. This meant that adding a new node to a network involved not only connection but authentication, proving who and what the new node was. This made adding new nodes a significant configuration effort, but it also meant that the kind of whack-a-mole contests that the authorities have today with hacker sites would be heavily tilted in the authorities' favor.

Taken all together, a layered architecture, packet switching, and a remarkable set of protocols add up to a flexible and powerful system. These characteristics were chosen to meet the requirements that the ARPANET was based upon. The ARPANET was transformed into today's Internet as more and more networks and individuals connected in.

World Wide Web

The World Wide Web (WWW), usually just "the Web," is the second part of today's computing environment. Technically, the Web and the Internet are not the same. The Web is a large system of connected applications that use the Internet to communicate. The Web was developed to share documents on the Internet. Instead of a special application written to share each document in a specific way, the Web generalizes document format and transmission. From the end user's standpoint, the visible part of the Web is the browser, like Internet Explorer, Edge, Firefox, Chrome, and Safari.

A browser displays text received in a format called Hypertext Markup Language (HTML). Computers that send these documents to other nodes have software that communicates using a simple scheme that creates, requests, updates, and deletes documents. The browser requests a document and the server returns with a document marked up with HTML. The browser uses

---

[14]Not everyone agrees on the security of SNA. See Anura Gurugé, Software Diversified Services, "SNA Mainframe Security," June 2009, www.sdsusa.com/netqdocs/SNA. Security.090721.pdf. Accessed February 2016.

the HTML to decide how to display the document. The richness of browser displays is all described and displayed following HTML instructions. Although this scheme is simple, it has proved to be exceptionally effective.

And it goes far beyond simple display of documents. The first web servers did little more than display a directory of documents and return a marked up copy to display in an HTML interpreter. Browsers put the request, update, and display into a single appliance. Browsers also implement the hyperlinks that make reading on the Internet both fascinating and distracting. A hyperlink is the address of another document embedded in the displayed document. When the user clicks on a link, the browser replaces the document being read with the document in the hyperlink. Everyone who surfs the Net knows the seductive, perhaps addictive, power of the hyperlink.

As time passed, servers were enhanced to execute code in response to activity on browsers. All web store fronts use this capability. When the user pushes an order button, a document is sent to the server that causes the server to update an order in the site's database and starts a process that eventually places a package on your front porch.

The documents and markup languages passing between the client and server have become more elaborate and powerful as the web evolved, but the document-passing protocol, Hypertext Transfer Protocol (HTTP), has remained fundamentally unchanged. In fact, the use of the protocol has increased, and often has nothing to do with hypertext.

Most applications coded in the 21st century rely on HTTP for communication between nodes on the network. Servers have expanded to perform more tasks. Many uses of the protocol do not involve browsers. Instead, documents are composed by programs and sent to their target without ever being seen by human eyes. The messages are intended for machine reading, not human reading. They are written in formal languages with alphabet soup names such as XML and JSON. Most developers are able to read these messages, but no one regularly looks at messages unless something is wrong. Typically, the messages are delivered so fast and in such volumes that reading all the traffic is not feasible. The average user would find them incomprehensible.

The Web has evolved to become the most common way of sharing information between computers, both for human consumption and direct machine consumption. Even email, which is often pure text, is usually transferred over the Web.

The ubiquity of data transfer over the Web is responsible for much of the flourishing Internet culture we have today. Compared to other means of Internet communication, using the Web is simple, both for developers and users. Without the Web, the applications we use all the time would require expensive and tricky custom code; they would very likely have differing user interfaces that would frustrate users. For example, a developer can get the current temperature for many locations from the National Weather Service with a few lines of boilerplate code because the weather service has provided a simple web service. Without the Web, the attractive and powerful applications that communicate and serve us would not be here.

Opportunities for development are also opportunities for crime. Developers are challenged with a learning curve when they work on non-standard applications. They are much more effective when they work with standard components and techniques. The Web provides a level of uniformity of components and techniques that make development more rapid and reliable.

However, these qualities also make criminal hacking more rapid and reliable. An application that is easier to build is also easier to hack. A hacker does not have to study the communications code of a web-based application because browsers and communications servers are all similar. The hacker can spot an application to hack into and immediately have a fundamental understanding of how the application works and its vulnerable points.

The Perfect Storm

As marvelous as personal computing devices, the Internet, and the World Wide Web are, they are part of a perfect storm that has propelled the flood of cybercrime that threatens us. The storm began to hit in the late 1990s.

The very success of the PC has engendered threats. PCs are everywhere. They sit on every desk in business. They are on kitchen tables, in bedrooms, and next to televisions in private homes. In the mid-1980s, less than 10% of US households had a PC. [15] That rose by a factor of six to over 80% percent in 2013. [16]

Contrast this with the 1970s when the Internet was designed and began to be deployed among research centers. The Internet was for communication among colleagues, highly trained scientists, and engineers. In 2013, the training of most Internet users did not go beyond glancing at a manual that they did not take time to understand before throwing it into the recycling bin. In 1980, computer users were naïve in a different way; they expected other users to be researchers and engineers like themselves, but they were also sophisticated in their knowledge of their software and computer equipment, unlike the typical user of today. The 1980 user was also more likely to know personally the other users on the network with whom they dealt.

---

[15]See "Top Ten Countries with Highest number of PCs," www.mapsofworld.com/world-top-ten/world-top-ten-personal-computers-users-map.html.

[16]Thom File and Camille Ryan, "Computer and Internet Use in the United States: 2013", U.S. Census Bureau, November 2014. www.census.gov/content/dam/Census/library/publications/2014/acs/acs-28.pdf. Accessed February, 2016.

Users today are often dealing with applications they barely comprehend and interacting with people they have never seen and know nothing about. This is a recipe for victimization. They are using a highly complex and sophisticated device that they do not understand. Many users are more familiar with the engine of their car than the workings of their computer. Unlike the Internet designers, users today deal with strangers on the Internet. Strangers on the street reveal themselves by their demeanor and dress. Through computers, Internet strangers can be more dangerous than street thugs because they reveal only what they want to be seen and readily prey on the unsuspected.

Computer hardware and software designers have been slow to recognize the plight of their users, both businesses and individuals. Until networked PCs became common, PCs only needed to be protected from physical theft or intrusion. The most PCs needed was a password to prevent someone from the next cubicle from illicit borrowing. Consequently, security was neglected. Even after PCs began to be networked, LANs were still safe. Often, security became the last thing on the development schedule, and, as development goes, even a generous allotment of time and resources for security shrank when the pressure was turned on to add a feature that might sell more product or impress the good folk in the C-suite. In an atmosphere where security was not acknowledged as a critical part of software and hardware, it was not developed. Even when it was thought through and implemented, experience with malicious hackers was still rare, causing designs to miss what would soon become real dangers.

The Soviet Union crashed in the 1990s, just as naïvely secured computers were beginning to be connected to the Internet, which was engineered to have a low bar of entry and designed with an assumption that everyone could be trusted. One of the consequences of the fall of the Soviet Union was that many trained engineers and scientists in Eastern Europe lost their means of livelihood. In some locations, government structures decayed and lawlessness prevailed. The combination of lawlessness and idle engineers who were prepared to learn about computing and connecting to the Internet was fertile ground for the growth of malicious and criminal hackers looking for prey.

The Internet is borderless. Unless a government takes extraordinary measures to isolate their territory, a computer can be anywhere as soon as it connects. If a user takes precautions, their physical location can be extremely hard to detect. A malicious hacker located in an area where the legal system has little interest in preventing hacking is close to untouchable.

The Web and its protocols are brilliant engineering. So much of what we enjoy today, from Facebook to efficiently managed wind-generated power, can be attributed to the power of the Web. The ease with which the Web's infrastructure can be expanded and applications designed, coded, and deployed has the markings of a miracle. However, there is a vicious downside in the ease with which hackers can understand and penetrate this ubiquitous technology.

The perfect storm has generated a loosely organized criminal class that exchanges illegally obtained or just plain illegal goods in surprising volumes, using the very facilities of the Internet that they maraud. And these criminal bazaars increase the profit from crime and the profits encourage more to join in the carnage.

A solution is under construction. The computing industry has dropped its outmoded notion that security is a secondary priority. More is being invested in preventing cybercrime every year. Crime does not go away quickly; perhaps it never disappears, but with effort, there are ways to decrease it. One of the ways is to be aware and take reasonable precautions. The next chapter will discuss some of the technological developments that help.

How Does Computer Security Work?

It's Harder Than It Looks

Cybersecurity is a complex and highly technical subject that uses many tools. It starts with the security provisions built into the chips that power the computer. Software must comply with rules established in hardware and use those rules to enforce more complex security policies. Much of security also depends on the way the software is used. This chapter explains some of the basic tools and principles that are used in secure computing.

Security in Hardware

Computer hardware enforces most security. One or more central processors are at the heart of every computer. The processor manipulates digits, calculating the results of moving and combining digital values. Although the digital values are sequences of zeroes and ones, they are interpreted as numbers or characters and the ways in which they combine can be arithmetic or logical.

© Marvin Waschke 2017

M. Waschke, *Personal Cybersecurity*, DOI 10.1007/978-1-4842-2430-4_3

The processor does this by following rules built into the processor chip and following the instructions in the programs that run on the computer. The program instructions are digital values themselves. Instructions are carried out at blazing speed, measured in billions of instructions per second. A 2.4 GHz processor can execute 2.4 billion instructions per second.

The processor in most personal computers is based on the Intel x86 architecture, the architecture of the processor in first IBM PC. Processor architectures determine the instructions the processor will execute and how it controls and moves values from place to place in the processor and memory. The x86 architecture of the first PCs has been expanded to be faster and do more, but the basics have remained the same and most instructions that would execute on the early x86 processors are in use today.

One of the key features of x86 is *protection rings*. Programs are assigned modes, usually called *supervisor* and *user*. These are similar to account types like *administrator* and *user*. A process in supervisor mode operates in what is called Ring 0 and can execute all instructions. A process in user mode, Ring 3, cannot execute some instructions that are called *privileged instructions*. Rings 1 and 2 are for code that interacts directly with hardware and can execute instructions not available in user mode, but fewer than the instructions available in supervisor mode.

The foremost job of protection rings is to keep the system from crashing. A user mode process must not crash the system and destroy the work of other processes. Some program instructions can do this easily when misused. These are the privileged instructions that can only be executed by processes in supervisor mode. Ring 0 supervisor processes are usually part of the operating system. Neither Windows nor Linux use Ring 1 or 2. Applications, the programs that ordinary users execute, are limited to safe instructions and run in user mode, Ring 3. If a Ring 3 process needs to use a privileged instruction, it must ask the operating system to perform it. Protection rings permit ill-conceived Ring 3 applications to execute instructions that may cause their own process to self-destruct or die, but, if the protection rings are doing what they are supposed to, they cannot execute instructions that invade reserved resources or crash the computer.[1]

---

[1] There are exceptions. The earliest PC x86 processors did not have protection rings. Any MS-DOS program could execute any instruction, which gave DOS programs wonderfully destructive power. When protection rings were added to the x86 architecture, Windows still allowed every program to execute every instruction because some old programs required privileged instructions to work. Since some of these old programs were important to customers, ring protection was not added to Windows when rings appeared. Microsoft engineers added partially effective code to protect the system, but many "blue screen" crashes could not be prevented. These issues were resolved over time. Now Windows uses ring protection and the system is more reliable. Linux never had the backwards compatibility issue because it is based on UNIX, which used ring protection early.

Protection rings also prevent users from interfering with each other. Users cannot affect processes or resources they do not own unless they request privileged instructions. Sometimes an application must execute instructions that could be dangerous to other users. To execute the privileged instructions, the Ring 3 application must ask the Ring 0 operating system to do it. The operating system will examine the authorization of the user and what they are requesting, and then reject unauthorized or dangerous requests. Hackers try to get around these restrictions, and sometimes they do. One way is to feed a program input that will cause a privileged call to crash in such a way that the hacker gets Ring 0 privileges. At that point, the hacker has complete control of the computer for any havoc they care to perpetrate.

The ring mechanism is at the heart of the distinction between administrative and user accounts. As users, taking more privilege than needed is a temptation. An increase in authority over the computer can save time, but it invites dangerous mistakes, and users with unnecessarily high levels of privilege are vulnerable to hackers who want to usurp the power to themselves.

Authentication and authorization are aspects of a system that amplify and rely upon protection rings to provide the finely articulated security we see today. This will be covered in detail in a later section.

Encryption

Encryption converts a readable document to an unreadable one. Decryption converts a previously encrypted document back to the original readable text. Unencrypted text is often called *clear*. Most encryption schemes use a secret key that the receiver of an encrypted document uses to restore the encrypted document to readability. The secret key can take many forms. Sometimes it is a code book that converts words and phrases to other words and phrases. Or it can be a rule like "replace each character with the character four places ahead in the alphabet." In computing, a complex mathematical formula transforms the message to and from the encrypted form. The key is a value that the encryption formula processes with the clear text to generate the encrypted text. The key must be supplied to reverse the formula and return the message to readability.

Encryption is used to protect data in transit between computers. Speedy encryption and decryption is especially important when transferring data. Encryption is also used to protect data at rest, which is usually data that is stored on a disk. Frequently, the encrypted data resides on a remote disk in the cloud.

A good encryption scheme for computers must meet several criteria. First, encrypting and decrypting a message must be fast and efficient; neither encryption or decryption can take too much memory or processor time. Some decrease in computer performance is tolerable for increased security, but no one is happy with sluggish performance. The encryption algorithm must also be hard to crack. Choosing an encryption algorithm is tricky. An algorithm that is slow to decrypt is also slow to crack by the brute force method (trying every possible key until the right one pops out). Thus, it requires a performance and security tradeoff. A rule of thumb is that an encryption scheme is good if the time it takes to break the encryption without the key is longer than the shelf-life of the data it protects, but that is a difficult requirement to meet.

The National Institute of Standards and Technology (NIST) is a part of the United States Department of Commerce, which provides guidance on encryption and other aspects of computer security. It performs intensive testing on encryption schemes and publishes the results. The federal government requires compliance with many NIST recommendations for systems used by the government.[2]

Symmetric vs. Asymmetric

There are three broad types of encryption that are important in computer security: symmetric, asymmetric, and hashes. Hashes are closely related to encryption, but they have somewhat different purposes.

Most people are familiar with the first: symmetric encryption. A single key is used for both encryption and decryption. This is what we ordinarily expect from encryption. See Figure 3-1.

Symmetric Encryption

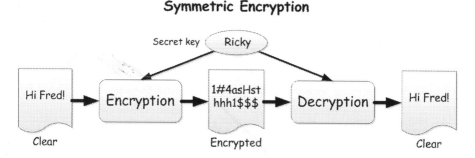

Figure 3-1. Symmetric encryption uses the same key for encrypting and decrypting

---

[2]See "NIST Cybersecurity Portal," www.nist.gov/cybersecurity-portal.cfm. Accessed February 2016.

For example, naval headquarters and a ship at sea share the secret key. Headquarters encrypts a message with the secret key. The ship receives the message, decodes it with the key, and responds with a message encoded with the same secret key. This system works well when there is a clear sender and receiver who can safely share a secret key. Symmetric encryption/decryption is generally faster than the alternative, asymmetric encryption, so it often used safe transmission and storage of data where speed is important. But other purposes for encryption have other requirements.

Asymmetric encryption uses different keys for encryption and decryption. Asymmetric keys are generated in pairs using special algorithms. These paired keys have the property that a message encrypted using one of the keys can only be decrypted using the other key in the pair. The encrypting key will not decrypt the message it encrypted. Only the other key in the pair will decrypt the message. See Figure 3-2.

Asymmetric Encryption

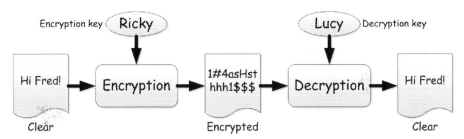

Figure 3-2. Asymmetric encryption uses different keys for encryption and decryption

Requiring separate keys means that sender and receiver do not share a secret key that they both know. Under some circumstances, this is a big advantage.

THE MAGIC OF ASYMMETRIC ENCRYPTION

The algorithms used for asymmetric encryption are complex but the idea behind them is simple. Start with a hard-to-factor number, such as 4757. It is the product of two prime numbers: 67 and 71. We can use these facts to perform an elementary, if trivial, asymmetric encryption.

Ricky wants to send a secret numeric message to Lucy. He can't use symmetric encryption because he has no way to get a shared secret key to Lucy. He goes to an encryption master to set up an asymmetric encryption system. The master gives the key 67 to Ricky. He sends Lucy a postcard bearing the key 71. Ricky may or may not peek at the postcard with Lucy's key; Lucy doesn't know Ricky's key. The encryption master gives Ricky a black box for encrypting numeric messages. Ricky can input a message and his key to the encryption black box. Inside the box an algorithm multiplies the message by the input key and divides by 4757. The result is the encrypted message. The encryption master gives Lucy a similar box for decrypting. If she inputs the encrypted message and her key to the box, out will come the decrypted message. Inside the black box, the encrypted message is multiplied by the key and the result is the decrypted message.

Ricky's romantic secret message is 11. (I told you this would be trivial.) He uses the encryption box to encrypt the message with his key (67). Inside the encryption box the calculation is

11 * 67 / 4757 = 0.15492957746478873239436619718311

Ricky's encrypted message is "0.15492957746478873239436619718311" which he paints on a rock and throws through Lucy's window, an insecure transmission, but the message is safely encrypted.

Lucy decrypts the message using the decryption box and her key (71). The result is

0.15492957746478873239436619718311 * 71 = 11

Note that if Ricky forgot the contents of his message and tried to decrypt it with his key, the result would be

0.15492957746478873239436619718311 * 67 =
        10.380281690140845070422535211268

A failure. All Ricky can do with the tools given him by the encryption master is encrypt messages for Lucy. Similarly, Lucy can only decrypt messages from Ricky with her key. Only her key, and no other, will decrypt a message from Ricky.

This is, of course, a weak algorithm and not very useful example, but it illustrates how different keys can be used for encryption and decryption. Non-trivial asymmetric encryption encrypts complex messages and is not easily cracked. Producing the key pairs is a challenging aspect of asymmetric encryption.

Public and Private Keys

Usually, one asymmetric key is designated *public* and the other key designated *private*. Depending on the goal of the encryption, either the encryption key or the decryption key can be designated public. The public key is broadcast to a large group and is not secret. The private key is secret and is kept secret by an individual or special group.

When the encryption key is public, anyone in the public group can use it to encrypt a message, but only a holder of the private decryption key can decrypt the message. Therefore, the members of the public group can send secret messages that can only be decoded by the private group because the decryption key remains secret.

Suppose a detective agency is doing secret work and needs to be careful with communications with their operatives. The agency could issue a public encryption key to all of their operatives. Then their operatives could send private encrypted messages back to the agency, certain that the messages were secret from everyone, even the other public key holding operatives, because the agency holds the only private key that will decrypt the messages. But there's a problem: the agency can't be sure which operative sent the message.

Electronic Signatures

Electronic signatures solve the message source problem. Signatures use asymmetric encryption, but the keys are reversed. The decryption key is the public key and the encryption key is held private.

In the agency example, the operatives each receive a unique private encryption key. The agency makes each operative's public key. Operatives send a message to the agency that is certain to be from them by encrypting the message with their private encryption key. When the message gets back to the agency, they can verify who sent the message by checking whose public key will decrypt it. Now each operative can send messages that are guaranteed to come from them.

There is still a problem. The message sent by the agent is not private because the decryption key is public. Anyone with the agent's public key can read the message. The encryption assures the reader of the message source but not its secrecy. However, the message can be kept secret by asking the agent to encrypt a short text (their name, for example) with their personal private encryption key, insert the encrypted text into the message, and encrypt the entire message with the agency's public key. The privately encrypted text in the larger publicly encrypted text is the agent's signature.

When the message arrives at the agency, the agency uses its private decryption key to decrypt the message. Then the agency verifies the source of the message by decrypting the message with the agent's public decryption key. This way, the agency receives a secret message from a guaranteed source.

Electronic signatures are useful in many ways. Electronically signed software assures users that the software is not pirated or tampered with by a cybercriminal. They are also used to verify that the websites are not fakes set up to trap the unwary. For this purpose, they usually are combined with hashes or digests.

HTTP and HTTPS

Hypertext Transmission Protocol (HTTP) is the protocol that controls messages traveling in the World Wide Web. HTTP is not a secure protocol. A network snooper can easily intercept and read the information in any message. This is a gaping security hole for critical information. The hole was closed by an addition to the HTTP standard, which is called Secure HTTP or HTTPS.

HTTPS encrypts the message and verifies that the receiver of a message is who it appears to be using electronic signatures. The protocol is rather complex. The sender and receiver negotiate the encryption algorithm to be used and exchange encryption keys securely. See Figure 3-3.

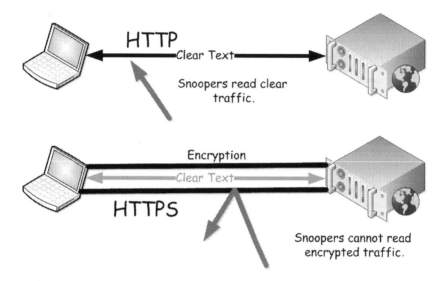

Figure 3-3. HTTPS protects messages with encryption

Hashes and Digests

Hashes are related to encryption, but hashed messages are not intended to be decrypted. In fact, a hash is one-way encryption; a hash that can be decrypted is not useful. A more precise name for the hashes that are used in security are *one-way hashes*. They are also called *digests* or *message digests*.

In general computer programming, a hash is a way of assigning a simple tag for each item in a list. You can hash a list of words by using the first letter of each word as its tag, which is called *the hash*. The hash of "Lupaster" is "L," the hash of "Reggie" is "R," and so on. This is not a very useful hash because it has many collisions. A collision is when two or more values hash to the same thing. For instance, "Apple," "Antique," and "Atom" all hash to "A." Second, it's too easy to reverse this hash because a computer can easily list all the values that hash to "A."

A good cryptographic hash function does the following:

- It is infeasible to reverse.

- It has no collisions.

- Its output values are all the same length.

- The hashed output from two input values that differ only slightly will be drastically different.

Hashes are called *digests* because a hash function can condense a document, even a large document, into a short digest of the original document. Since even a slight change in the original will produce a big change in a good digest, digests can be used to prove that a document has not changed when downloaded or in transmission. The source sends a digest along with the message. The receiver calculates the digest of the document and compares it to the digest sent by the source. If the two match, the receiver knows the document has not been tampered with or corrupted. When digests and electronic signatures are combined, downloaded software is much safer because the receiver is certain that the software received is an exact match to the software sent by the sender who is verified with an electronic signature.

Hashes are also important in verifying passwords, which will be covered in the "Authentication" section.

Authentication

In general, authentication proves that a thing is what it is claimed to be. Authentication in computer security is a special case of general authentication that proves that a person or an entity acting as a person, such as a script, is what they claim to be. Someone enters a user or account name claiming to be the user or account owner and the system challenges the supplicant to prove that the user id is theirs.[3] See Figure 3-4.

Authentication

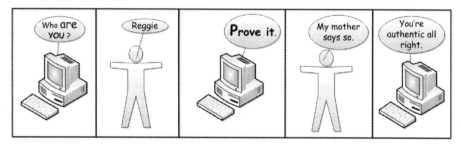

Figure 3-4. Authentication verifies the identity of the user

---

[3]*Supplicant* is security jargon for a person or agent attempting to authenticate.

In early days of computing, a valid user id was adequate to gain entry to the system. Systems are seldom so trusting any longer. The current equivalent of this approach is a blank password, which is a very weak form of authentication.[4]

Most of the time now, systems will not proceed without something that substantiates a user's claim to a user id. There are three types of substantiation:

- Something the user knows, such as a password or an answer to a security question.

- Something the user possesses, such as a wrist band, a cellphone, a mechanical key, or an email address.

- Some artifact inseparable and unique to the user, such as a fingerprint, retina scan, or face scan.

Several substantiating factors can be combined for increased certainty. Multi-factor authentication is often used for increased security.

Often the substantiation is a password, but not always. It depends on what the system will accept. See Figure 3-4 above. The "Password Alternates" section discusses some of them.

Passwords

Everyone knows about passwords, but some implementations of passwords are better than others. In current security practices, most passwords are a pair: a user id and a secret password. If the password goes with the id, the claimant gets into the system. That's simple.

What happens in between gets complicated. For a simple implementation, all that is necessary is a table stored in a file. Each row in the table has a user id and corresponding password, both in clear text. When a user attempts to authenticate, the system scans the table for the user id that the supplicant entered. If there is no matching user id in the table, the supplicant has no account. If the user id is in the table, the system compares the password presented by the supplicant with the password corresponding to the supplicant's user id in the table. If the two passwords match, the supplicant is allowed in. If the user id isn't present, or the password does not match, the supplicant is not authenticated. There are problems with this simple implementation, although it was used when innocence still prevailed. Later, the password file was encrypted to prevent snooping on passwords.

---

[4]The cybersecurity team usually offer the keys to the clown car to enterprise users with blank passwords.

Securing Passwords

Most password schemes now use one-way cryptographic hashes rather than encryption. If a password is encrypted rather than hashed, it can be decrypted with the key. If a hacker obtains the key, they can quickly decrypt all the passwords in the password database. A cryptographic hash has no key and cannot be reversed. Encoded passwords never need to be decoded. The system performs a hash when the supplicant offers the password and compares it to the stored hash. Since encoded passwords never need to be decoded, using an encryption with a key is an unnecessary risk. See Figure 3-5 for the entire process. Note that there is a large vulnerability: hashing the password before it is sent to the authenticator may not be practical. More typically, the clear password is sent. You will see in a moment how that gap can be closed.

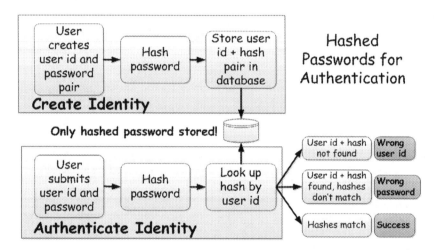

Figure 3-5. Unencoded passwords are never stored in current password practice

How Passwords Are Cracked

Passwords are not invulnerable. They can be compromised in several different ways. Computer users can reduce the chances of password compromise by following good password management practices and being aware of the threats.

Password Theft

Reliable authentication relies on passwords that are kept secret. The system must be hardened against hacker's attacks. The most vulnerable point of attack is the supplicant's practices for keeping passwords secret. If the supplicant can be forced or tricked into revealing a password, authentication is compromised.

As usual, breaching a system with social engineering is easy and quick compared to more technical methods, and very little can be done technically to harden human nature against gullibility and deceit.

Social engineering is not the only way passwords are stolen. Whenever a clear password is placed in an unsecured file, into email or some other insecure messaging system, the password can be stolen by an industrious hacker.

Snooping

Social engineering is not the only way to break a password system. Another point of vulnerability is the connection between the supplicant and the system. If the supplicant is on the same computer as the system, the connection is most likely all in memory and difficult to break into, but a remote login is subject to network snooping. Encrypting the messages interchanged in password validation and creation will prevent network snooping.[5] Secure sockets and secure HTTP are common methods, although some older applications developed their own methods of secure transmission.

Reading unencrypted network traffic is trivial for hackers. Entering a password into a website that does not use encryption is an open invitation for password snoopers. The first version of the HTTP standard documented basic authentication. The method is easy to implement but insecure because it does not protect user id and passwords from snooping in transit. A newer method, digest authentication, uses a cryptographic hash. Since digest authentication is somewhat more difficult to implement, some websites still use basic authentication. Digest authentication is not as secure as using another web security alternative, Secure HTTP (HTTPS). HTTPS encrypts the entire message as well as the password and user id and it also verifies that the message is sent to the intended server. When computers and networks were slower, HTTPS was noticeably slower than HTTP. Websites tended to use HTTPS only when exchanging credentials. This practice has declined as the HTTPS overhead has become less noticeable. Sites like Google and Facebook use HTTPS for all communication on the Web; in fact, HTTPS has become the most common way of hiding passwords from hacker and securing communications on the Web.

---

[5] I have to add that *side channel* assaults are a possibility. They are a sophisticated form of snooping that use external factors like the size and response times of messages to siphon off information about a system. The derived information may be approximate and incomplete, but perhaps enough to stage a breach. See Shou Chen, Rui Wang, XiaoFeng Wang, Kehuan Zhang. "Side-Channel Leaks in Web Applications: a Reality Today, a Challenge Tomorrow," May 2012.
http://research.microsoft.com/pubs/119060/WebAppSideChannel-final.pdf.
Accessed February 2016.

Cryptographic Attacks

Cryptographic attacks assault the encryption or hash algorithm. They come in several forms, but they all require mathematical sophistication. One such attack is called a *collision attack*. Some hash algorithms, which were previously thought to be secure, have proven capable of producing the same hash for two passwords. If a hacker could take advantage of this, they might generate an alternate password for a user id without knowing the real password.

Cryptographic attacks can be more theoretical than real for sites following best practices because they are certainly more difficult than stealing or snooping and could, depending on the circumstances, be slower than brute force cracking. However, there have been sites that continue to use deprecated cryptographic hashes that have been shown to be insecure.

Brute Force

Brute force attacks are more common. A brute force attacker tries different passwords until they find one that works. Some finesse makes the task quicker, but brute force is not subtle. The method assumes that the hash algorithm, user id, and hashed password value are known. Usually the hacker will break into the system by some means and steal the password file or database. Personal computers usually have only a few user id/password pairs to crack and are therefore not as desirable as a corporate server with thousands of ids.

The hacker could simply begin by hashing sequential possibilities like "a", "A", "ab", "Ab", "aB", "AB", "AZ" and so on until a hash pops out that matches the user's hashed password. The method is systematic and brute force in the extreme.

Guessing

Hackers know that users have favorite passwords. For instance, "password" is said to be the most used password. "1234" is another chestnut. Hackers, and security researchers, compile lists of these. You can get a list of the 10,000 most common passwords hashed with a popular algorithm from the Internet.[6] Hackers use lists like this to skim off the easy candidates. The time for scanning a list like this is trivial (seconds for a smartphone) and hackers tend to favor fast, high-performance servers. Some experts estimate that 60% of passwords at most sites will appear on these lists.

---

[6]See www.passwordrandom.com/most-popular-passwords. Accessed February 2016. If you think you have a crack-proof password, check here. You may be surprised.

Dictionary

The next level of attack is a *dictionary attack*. A dictionary attack tries every word in a dictionary, and perhaps some common combinations of words. With faster processors, they will probably throw in a few substitutions: "kat" for "cat", random capital letters, anything obvious. For example, "Eleph@nT" might fall to a dictionary attack. For a dictionary attack, the hacker will probably use sophisticated in-memory storage techniques called *rainbow tables* to reduce the memory required and speed processing. Note that mixing upper-case and lowercase letters, numerals, and symbols is not as good a suggestion as it was when cracking machines were less powerful. The number of possibilities to try in a dictionary attack gets large, but it is nothing compared to the huge number of random choices.

Ultimate Force

If a dictionary attack fails, the next stage is true brute force, which is required to crack passwords that are neither common nor in the hacker's dictionary.

At this point, the hacker needs heavy duty resources. A hacker will probably not make this effort without strong motivation because the time and computing resources are expensive. Nevertheless, such an effort is possible.

An ordinary computer is not adequate at this stage. Hackers build special computers that can execute hash algorithms at very high speeds. Graphics processors happen to be well-suited to this. Calculating the next set of pixels to display for a high-resolution, fast-moving subject requires similar capacities to hashing an arbitrary string of characters. Password cracking computers use many graphics processors to process candidate passwords very rapidly. One example, reported on in 2012, uses 25 graphics processors to execute 63 billion guesses per second. If this specialized computer were to test the 10,000 popular passwords referred to above, it would finish in two millionths of a second. An ordinary dictionary attack would still take less than a second.[7]

Figure 3-6 shows an important characteristic of brute force attacks. Brute force cracking of a random password that is not in a popular choice table or subject to a dictionary attack is subject to simple mathematical rules. The table below crunches the numbers for a simple example. The password character set is a common one: digits, lowercase and uppercase letters, and a few special symbols. Altogether, there are 64 possible characters. For a password

---

[7]Dan Goodin, "25-GPU cluster cracks every standard Windows password in <6 hours," Ars Technica, December 2012. http://arstechnica.com/security/2012/12/25-gpu-cluster-cracks-every-standard-windows-password-in-6-hours/. Accessed February 2016. Note that this reference was three years old when it was accessed. Hardware has advanced in the mean time.

of a single character, there are 64 possibilities. For two character passwords, for each possible first character, there are 64 possible second characters. With each added character, the number of possibilities is multiplied by 64. The number of possibilities rises rapidly. The table shows that a 5-character password has over a trillion possibilities. The number may seem formidable, but a 63 billion guess per second cracking machine can try them all in less than a second.

HOW TO BUILD A CRACKING MACHINE

Today, building a high-speed brute-force cracking machine is not extremely hard. It relies on two technologies. First, big data analysis has developed very effective algorithms for combining the efforts of large numbers of relatively small computers to perform gigantic tasks. The second is the availability of relatively low-cost, high-speed processors that are specifically designed to efficiently perform the mathematical manipulations involved in encryption. These processors are readily available because both encryption and high resolution moving computer graphic images require high-speed, high-throughput numeric processing. In other words, a high-end graphics processor (GPU) is just the thing for cracking passwords. Combining a large number of GPUs into a big data-style parallel processing array for cracking processing is not a job for a first-year computer science student, but by their second or third year, some could handle it. The cost would be in five figures perhaps—but well under the "governments only" price range. It's certainly possible with some help from the "dark side."

Looking down the table, a 7-character password will take a little over a minute, but a 14-character password will take close to ten million years. In short, longer is better. The exceptions are choices from the table of popular choices or the dictionary table. From the table, a 10-character password is quite safe. No hacker would be likely to be willing to wait for 200 days to crack a password. Since cracking machines are bound to get faster, a 12-character password would be a safer choice.[8]

This table brings out an important aspect of password strength. The strength of a password depends on the character set the hacker thinks you are using, not the character set in the password. In Figure 3-6, the length of the password determines the probability that the password will be cracked, not the mixture of characters in the password. If the password does not fall under guessing and dictionary attacks, an all-lowercase 12-character password would still be very time consuming to crack. Stringing together random word combinations into long passwords can be easy-to-remember and strong.

---

[8]I've skipped over another factor for simplicity. Even though there are trillions of possibilities, there is always a chance that the hacker will win the lottery and get a hit early in its process. The probability of a hit within an interval can be calculated, but I don't want to discuss it here. Longer is still better.

Password Length	Possibilities	Seconds	Minutes	Days	Years
1	64	> 1			
2	4096	> 1			
3	262144	> 1			
4	16777216	> 1			
5	1.07E+09	> 1			
6	6.87E+10	1.1			
7	4.40E+12	69.8	1.2		
8	2.81E+14		74.5	0.1	
9	1.80E+16			3.3	
10	1.15E+18			211.8	0.6
11	7.38E+19				37
12	4.72E+21				2,375
13	3.02E+23				152,018
14	1.93E+25				9,729,155

Character Set: 0-9 a-z A-Z !@#$%& (64 possible characters)
Password cracking computer processing 63 billion guesses/sec

Figure 3-6. Password length determines the difficulty of brute force cracking

Death of Passwords

The death of passwords seems to be announced by some important person in the computing industry every few months. For good reason. Strong passwords are a human-computer interaction catastrophe.

Memorizing a 12-character random password, say 2kLc%Arr3$7#, is not easy for most people and accurately typing a random sequence can be frustrating. Not only that, but passwords should be changed frequently in case the password has been stolen through social engineering or snooping.

The result is that most people ignore safer practices. Most passwords in use are on the popular passwords list or subject to dictionary attack, are seldom changed, and are often used for several accounts.

There are alternatives to passwords, but they have their own drawbacks. Possessions, like cellphones, can be lost or stolen. Personal physical artifacts, like fingerprints or face scans, cannot be changed if they are compromised. Fingerprints, for example, have been compromised with casts taken from fingers. One can easily imagine a method that uses a 3-D printer to convert a photograph of a fingerprint to create an ersatz finger to fool a fingerprint reader. If one print is compromised, the user can substitute a different finger, but there is a limit. Secret questions have been proven to be easily guessed by hackers who do a bit of prying into social media and other public records.

Passwords are a problem but they are also familiar, and techniques for programming password systems are well known. There are also methods built around the password system for sharing authentication. A site does not need to have its own authentication. Instead, it can use authentication provided by another site. Facebook, Google, and other sites provide authentication services. This reduces the number of passwords that a user must manage.

The best alternative to passwords on the horizon now is multi-factor authentication, which continues to use passwords but includes other factors such as a message to your phone containing a PIN you must enter to complete the authentication. Combining passwords with physical artifacts like fingerprints is also more secure. A weaker password combined with other factors can be more secure than a strong password alone.

Authorization

After a user is authenticated, they can be assigned rights to the computer and system resources. Rights could be permission to read or write certain files, or permission to execute programs or use services. All activities on a computer system can be controlled by offering or holding back authorization. See Figure 3-7.

Authorization

Figure 3-7. Authorization determines what an authenticated person or agent can do. Contrast authorization to authentication in Figure 3-4

Authorization follows authentication, although it may not be obvious that authorization is taking place. Unlike authentication, which is usually based on challenge and response, authorization takes place in the background and is only visible from its effects. Authentication and authorization are often confused or conflated because they seem to take place at the same time.

An enterprise begins by defining a general security policy. The security policy usually specifies what is valuable to the organization and who should be able to access the valuables. Security policies refer to groups and roles rather than individuals and may include non-computer–related valuables such as buildings and manufacturing equipment.

An authorization policy is more specific, indicating specific resources such as file names and processes. System administrators configure hardware and software to enforce the policy. The first step in authorization is to assign authenticated people or agents to groups such as "system administrators" or "human relations staff." When an authenticated member of the human relations staff attempts to read a personnel record, they will be permitted, but they would not be allowed to reboot a critical server.

In Windows, there are two pre-defined groups, "administrator" and "user." When Windows is installed, the first user is placed in the administrator group. This is practical because ordinary users are not authorized to install applications or make most system configuration changes and there are usually many installations and configurations that have to be made when the operating system is installed.

However, good security practice is to authorize users to do their job and nothing more. This practice prevents users from venturing into areas where they may do damage and it applies to a personal computer as much as it applies to a global corporation. The ordinary user group on Windows is adequate for most uses of a personal computer and most of the time, users should not have administrator authorization. The Windows default may not be the best choice.[9]

Personal computer users are not limited to the two default authorization groups. Custom groups can be created with access to specific files and programs. If you have several users that you want to restrict to certain areas, you could create different groups assigned to different account types and give each user a different account type. Logging in with different types can be a way of foiling hackers when they break in and find they are in a limited group without free reign over the system.

Isolation

Thinking back to the Target heist, one of Target's basic problems was that after the hackers got into their system, they had free reign. They entered as facilities subcontractors and made their way into critical financial records.

---

[9]A word of caution: you must be cautious when changing authorizations. If you end up with no way to log in with administrator privileges, you are in a horrible pickle. Check the documentation, understand it, and proceed carefully.

Secure systems are isolated from the outside world and they are segmented so that an intruder who breaches the outer wall will be limited to a single segment.

Structuring a system like a boat with watertight chambers and a heavy puncture resistant steel hull is one way of limiting the effects of intrusion. If heavy outer hull is punctured and one of the chambers begins to leak, the boat will not sink because the intact chambers will keep the boat floating. Only a portion will be damaged. An enterprise can do the same thing. Each functional area can be sealed off and all interaction with other areas can be controlled and monitored.

In extreme cases, an *air gap* can be established. Two networks with an air gap have no electrical connection between them, neither wired nor wireless. To transfer data from one network to the other, the data has to be placed on a properly sanitized medium like a flash drive[10] and then physically carried to the other network. The storage on a device like a laptop can also be used like a flash drive to move data from one network to another. Perhaps this is not a good practice because a laptop is much harder to sanitize than a flash drive. Other measures include network diodes: hardware and software devices that allow data to move in one direction only.

These practices apply to personal computers as well. A PC owner thinking about segmentation could decide to place confidential documents on a flash drive or an external hard drive and disconnect them when they are not in use. Another example is to have a separate computer that is not connected to the Internet used for confidential work. Some people who are distracted by the Internet do this for other reasons. Thinking about how the system is used and how to segment it to prevent losing everything in an invasion can substantially increase the security of a personal system.

Firewalls

The fundamental purpose of a firewall is to create a perimeter that isolates the interior from attacks from the outside of the firewall.

Perimeters are a fundamental form of isolation and firewalls help enforce perimeters. Think about what a system without a perimeter is like. It would be as if the entire system were built in an open field without a fence or other border around it. Anyone could walk in and look at the system machinery and pull a lever here, turn a valve there, and bring the system to a halt. After a few nasty episodes, the management would probably put a perimeter wall around the system and allow no one in.

---

[10]Flash drives are sometimes used to spread malware. In circumstances like this, the flash drive should be reformatted to guarantee that malware is removed before it is used. There have been cases in which air gaps have been breached by this method.

Unfortunately, a system inside a wall with no openings may still have problems. Customers and suppliers are stuck outside the wall. The system might be fine, but the business might die. Management and the IT department must think again. What they need is a system that permits some transactions in and out, and blocks others. The rules for permitting and blocking transactions could be complex and difficult to implement, but the programmers claim that is their job.

A firewall is an implementation of rules permitting and blocking transactions. It selectively isolates a system from the outside world. The selectivity of an IT firewall differentiates it from a general firewall like the firewall between the engine and the passenger compartment of an automobile. An automobile firewall blocks all fires, but an IT firewall picks and chooses which fires it will stop.

Core mission of a personal computer firewall is to stop all unsolicited incoming transactions. The firewall will reject any message from a node outside the firewall that is not a response to a request from a computer inside the firewall.

This rule is not as restrictive as it might seem. For instance, a widget on a computer desktop shows the outside temperature. You might expect that whenever the temperature changes, some server outside the firewall sends a message with the new temperature. This is not the case. The widget on the desktop requests a new temperature periodically, which would pass through the firewall without an issue. Whenever possible, interactions with outside resources are designed to request information, not receive it unsolicited.

There are exceptions when a process running on a node outside the firewall must send an unsolicited message. These messages will pass through the firewall if the site is on the firewall's whitelist. Messages from a node on the whitelist are always accepted. The other side of the coin is the blacklist. Messages from the blacklist sites are always rejected, even when they are solicited. A blacklisted site could be a known malware source.

Firewalls are a critical element in both personal and enterprise site security. Personal firewalls are usually implemented as software. The Windows firewall is a prominent example, although most of the antivirus vendors also have their own software firewalls.

Enterprises usually rely on firewalls implemented as hardware. The job of a firewall becomes progressively more difficult as the volume of transactions rises. A software firewall can reduce the performance of the PC it protects when the transaction volume is high. When a firewall is protecting hundreds or thousands of users, maintaining satisfactory performance is more than software can provide. Enterprise firewalls are typically hardware appliances that use firmware and dedicated memory to filter incoming and outgoing messages.

Most home computer networks have what could be called a pseudo-firewall that is based on Network Address Translation (NAT). The usual home system has a small router attached to the Internet. All the computers in the house are connected to the router, either by cables or wirelessly. The router distributes incoming messages to the connected computers. Every computer connected to the Internet has a unique address. The computers in a home network have a different kind of address that cannot be seen on the Internet. The router has its own address that is visible on the Internet and it sends and receives messages from other computers on the Internet. The router does a bit of magic. The home computers send all the messages to the router. The router transforms the messages so they look like they came from the router, and sends the messages on to the Internet. For all appearances, the messages came from the router. When replies arrive, the router sends them to the correct home computer. Only the router is visible to the other computers on the Internet and the home computers are invisible.

This invisibility is helpful, but hackers have found many ways to work around NAT. It does not provide an adequate perimeter for a home system.

Virtualization

Virtualization is another tool for isolation. Virtualization is the simulation of a computer in the memory of a host system. A virtual computer, usually called a *virtual machine* (VM), can be created and destroyed at will. There are many uses for virtual machines because they are easier to manage than a physical machine, especially when they are implemented in such a way that they can migrate from physical machine to physical machine.

Virtualization is the key to cloud implementations. A cloud consumer can request a VM without knowledge of the physical device where the VM is running and the cloud provider can migrate the VM to other devices at will. This permits great flexibility for both the consumer and provider.

A VM running on a computer, often called a *guest*, looks like a computer inside a computer. Install a new operating system on the guest and it is a freshly minted machine. Alternatively, you can install a *snapshot* that you have taken of a machine in a state you want to reproduce and have a duplicate of the machine.

Trying a new operating system can be a problem. If you install the operating system directly on a computer, you have to go to the trouble of restoring from a backup if you want to go back to your old system. A VM solves that problem. Create a VM, install the new operating system, and experiment with it on the VM. If you decide you don't like the operating system, shut down the VM; the operating system is gone, and your computer is unchanged.

A VM can be configured to use memory rather than a hard disk for storage. When the VM is shut down, everything that it has written disappears. Every local record of the guest's activity is gone. If it happened to be infected by malware, the infection is wiped out. If you are concerned about privacy, there is no record.

Malware researchers intentionally infect VMs to study virulent software safely. The researchers close all network ports or turn off the virtual network adapter completely. With no disk and no network connection, the infection can't spread and the researchers can poke and prod, examining the characteristics of the specimen and devising a detection and removal strategy.

Personal users can use a VM as a safe haven for critical tasks like bank transactions by launching a clean VM and performing the transaction from the VM. Malware may have infected your computer without you knowing it, but the chance of malware slipping into the new VM is very slight. When the transaction is complete, you can shut down the VM and it disappears.

VMs also can be used to test install applications that might be infested with malware or to visit questionable websites. You can also open email attachments in a VM when you suspect an attachment is legitimate but you are not sure. Perform the risky action on the VM and delete the VM when you are finished.

Attack Surface Reduction

The attack surface of a system is all the points where a system is vulnerable to attack. An armadillo rolled up into a tight ball showing only leathery plates has minimized its attack surface by hiding its soft and vulnerable belly. Computer users can minimize the attack surface of their computers, perhaps not as efficiently as a three-banded armadillo, but they can isolate themselves from some threats.

Any point where data can move in and out of a system is part of the attack surface. These include

- Network and USB ports
- CD or DVD drives
- SD card slots
- External SATA hard drive ports
- Wireless and Bluetooth radios

Older or newer devices may have other vulnerable connection types. Every one of these connections could be exploited to break into and take over or damage a system. The threats that come in through the network are well-known. Any external storage device, whether a flash drive, an SD card, or an external hard drive, can be a carrier for malware. CDs and DVDs also can contain malware. Wireless network connections are especially vulnerable to intrusion through unsecured public wireless services. Bluetooth may not often be thought of, but it also can be a route into a computer.

The first step to reducing the external connection attack surface is to remove, disconnect, unplug, or turn off any of external connection facility that is not used. The second is to be vigilant over what is plugged into ports. USB flash drives loaded with malware and left in parking lots to attract office workers are a popular method of attack.

Wireless networks and Bluetooth connections are useful and convenient, but turning them off when they are not in use reduces the danger that a miscreant will use them as an entry point.

Other attack surfaces that can be reduced are the programs installed on the computer. Most programs have exploitable defects that may never be known, but there is a risk that a criminal may discover them at any time. By removing all unused software, the attack surfaces of the unused software are also removed.

For example, manufacturers often preinstall utilities for maintaining their computers. These can be problematic because many users don't use them. They are frequently only slight improvements over similar and more familiar utilities that are part of the operating system. These utilities can have flaws that can compromise security.[11] Removing them reduces the attack surface.

Services and daemons are programs that run in the background without a user interface. Many of them are started automatically when the computer boots. These too are attack surfaces that are bound to have exploitable flaws. Quite often, there are unused services set to start automatically. Switching them to start manually or disabling them will reduce the attack surface and occasionally improve performance by freeing resources for more useful processes.

There are also processes or tasks that are started for no understandable reason. These processes may have been left behind by an application that started them but neglected to shut them down. These processes simply wait for input or a termination signal. Hackers are always on the prowl for idle processes running with administrative privileges. Sometimes, a hacker can feed data to the program that will cause it to crash and confer its privileges on the hacker, who is then able to wreak any havoc they care to.

The tasks and services lists reveal the beating heart of the computer more accurately that a cardiologist's echocardiogram. Weeding services and processes from the task list is tough. There is no easy way to spot the rogues. You must become familiar with which processes are legitimate and which are not and a feeling for the CPU time and memory activity that each process should have. If you get it wrong and kill a legitimate task or service, you have programs crashing or losing stability. The entire operating system may crash.

---

[11]For an example, see Kif Leswing, "Another Huge Security Hole Has Been Discovered on Lenovo Computers" http://fortune.com/2015/12/08/lenovo-solution-center-hack/. Accessed February 2016.

On the other hand, a user with a good feel for what should be running and how a normal system behaves on detailed level can reduce their attack surface and keep their system stripped of extraneous performance-sapping activity. By watching the task and services list, Googling process names, and judiciously stopping tasks, a user can become an expert on their own computer. Such a user may be able detect and remediate zero-day attacks before other instrumentation raises an issue.

Damage Reduction and Prevention

Computer users can minimize or prevent damage from successful exploits.

Best practice for enterprises is to maintain a comprehensive information security plan. The plan identifies the elements of the system that are critical to the enterprise. For instance, account documents are critical to most businesses and must be given more attention than office supply inventories. The plan documents

- Who is responsible for the information asset;

- Where and how the critical assets are maintained;

- The enterprise policies, laws, and regulations that may apply;

- How they are secured;

- The steps to take when the asset breached. These steps include who is to be informed and how the system is to be restored.

For large enterprises, the information security plan is a thick document that is revised continually to keep up with changing computing personnel and business practices.

Enterprise security experts often say that an information security plan is the most important tool for keeping IT safe. Personal computer users do not need a formal document like a business should have, but taking an informal inventory of information assets and thinking through security and what to do if a hacker succeeds in getting into the system is a powerful tool.

You may want to answer questions like:

- Are financial records stored on my personal computer? How are they protected from unauthorized access?

- How is my email protected? Where is it stored?

- Do I have data that belongs to my employer on my personal computer? Do I have my employer's permission? Have I secured it according to my employer's rules?

- Do I have valuable personal documents or other files stored on my computer? Are they securely backed up?

- Do I have documents that may be of little monetary value, but are of great value to me? Photographs and videos often fall in this category. Are they properly backed up?

Having answered these questions, you may want to consider investing in some USB drives and storing some of this sensitive information offline. You also might consider investing in a backup system. Also, you might consider whether you are getting worthwhile benefits that balance the risks from storing your employer's data on your computer.

Encryption

Encryption can prevent many types of data theft and intrusion. For example, a hacker may break into a personal computer, but if the computer's files are encrypted, the hacker may not find anything to steal. Encryption has become increasingly important in enterprise computing because workplaces are changing and successful exploits have become more frequent. Employees work from home or places like coffee shops. Encryption has become an important tool for protecting information assets that are outside controlled premises or vulnerable to exploits. These benefits apply to personal computers as well as enterprise systems.

Unfortunately, encryption is surrounded by controversy on exactly how secure it is. Successful encryption requires an entire implementation, not just a strong encryption algorithm. For instance, the Microsoft BitLocker file encryption system, which has been a part of Windows since Vista, combines an encryption algorithm with hardware key generation.[12] In theory, BitLocker is very secure because its algorithm is strong. However, some believe that Microsoft built a backdoor into BitLocker for government agencies. They may have, or they may not. There are vehement partisans on both sides. Some say backdoors for proper law enforcement are good, others say backdoors are always bad. The point is that it is never good to assume that encryption, or any other technology, is infallible. For securing data on a personal computer, perhaps the only thing to say is that even flimsy encryption will defeat an inept hacker, and which is an improvement over no encryption.

---

[12]See Niels Ferguson, "AES-CBC + Elephant diffuser: A Disk Encryption Algorithm for Windows Vista," http://css.csail.mit.edu/6.858/2012/readings/bitlocker.pdf. Accessed February 2016. This is a paper by the developer of BitLocker from Microsoft, providing a rather technical discussion of the encryption algorithm and hardware used in BitLocker.

Antivirus

Antivirus, or antimalware, tools find and remove malware. They do not prevent viruses and other malware from infecting computers; they detect and remove the malware after the computer has been infected. Antivirus products began to appear in the 1980s, not long after viruses began to appear. A virus is code that reproduces itself and travels to other computers. Other varieties of malware do not reproduce like viruses. Early antivirus products only detected and removed viruses. As other malwares appeared, the antivirus tools expanded to combat them.

The fundamental mechanism used to detect malware is the signature. The signature can be as simple as a file name and size, but they are often more sophisticated, capable of detecting malware that is disguised and hidden. More sophisticated signatures match patterns in compiled code and scan settings found in registries and other configuration files.

Signatures are both the strength and weakness of antivirus tools because the proper signature has to be devised and installed in the tool before the tool can detect and remove a virus. An antivirus tool is helpless against a virus that has no signature because no antivirus team has seen the virus. Malware developers are always busy devising new viruses, which they test against the major antivirus tools. It is a cat-and-mouse game that guarantees that some viruses will go undetected. Nevertheless, the antivirus tools protect against thousands of viruses.

Signatures are not the only way that antivirus tools work. Some use *heuristics*, rules of thumb that identify suspicious processes by their activity rather than a signature. Other methods examine the layout of binary files to identify patterns that are characteristic of viruses. Instead of scanning the computer periodically, some tools monitor the system continually, watching for anomalies as they occur. This is good, but can affect performance.

Antivirus tools have become more effective as automatic updates over the Internet have shortened the time between discovering a virus in the wild and the tool being prepared to detect and remove it. However, hackers have dealt with antivirus tools for a long time and they have become adept at thwarting them. Therefore, antivirus tools are only one line of defense against cybercrime.

Backing Up

Users may not think of backups, saving copies of the data stored on a computer, as a security tool. However, a good backup is the final protection for a compromised computer. With a current backup, a computer can be taken down to bare metal, where every bit and byte of software is removed and the system is cleaned to nothing but the hardware. After the system is thoroughly cleaned, the system can be built up again to its state at the time of the backup.

Although a backup is the ultimate defense, they are not infallible. Some malware buries itself into the firmware in non-volatile memory and crawls out again after the computer is restored. In that case, even the firmware has to be replaced. Also, the unfortunate fact is that backups are only as reliable as the person administering them. Good backup procedure relies on several backups. One should be off-site in a location where it will not be destroyed if a disaster strikes the computer. Backups should not be accessible to ransomware, as they may be on a hard drive. Finally, backups have to be tested regularly. Malfunctioning equipment, such as hard drives, can write unreadable backups, and have a habit of doing so at the moment they are needed most.

The Tools We Will Never Have

Two things are always true about security in general and personal cybersecurity in particular. Criminals will always be eager to break into our computers to steal and do damage. Second, there will always be flaws in our systems, which give the criminals the opportunity to do their malicious deeds.

Computer engineers can build systems that are more resistant to attack. Security has been improving steadily for more than a decade. In 2000, password hashing algorithms were weaker, recommendations for strong passwords were rare, hacking techniques that are now commonly stopped were waiting to be put to use. Home computer firewalls began to appear and have improved steadily. Antivirus tools have improved and are almost universally installed. Security updates are automated and occur, for the most part, silently in the background. Engineers are now aware of coding habits that are likely to leave flaws that hackers can use to break in or cause damage. Quality assurance testing now actively and intensely goes after security holes. These are all real advances that have made computers much more resistant to hacking and are likely to continue to improve security.

Security is much better, but more criminals are striking and plotting to strike every day. And make no mistake, some of the criminals are as skilled and dedicated as the engineers building the computer systems. For every new technique for thwarting attacks that is developed, inspired hackers are searching for ways to break or go around it. And eventually they do succeed, although success is getting harder and harder for them.

Nevertheless, the perfect toolset that will prevent every breach is not on the horizon and is not likely ever to be there. The computing environment itself, offering more services every year and gaining more users daily, continually adds new challenges. The growth in the power and compactness of the computer is always predicted to be close to the end, but each year, they get smaller, cheaper, and more powerful. The global attack surface grows as these tiny powerhouses are used for more purposes that invite exploitation and their complexity increases.

We cannot expect a perfectly secure environment because the dangers and the potential to exploit our devices increases to match the effectiveness of our tools. Nevertheless, the security of our computers has increased. The challenge is to grow our safety faster than the criminals assault us. Fortunately, we have many tools today that we can learn to use more effectively instead of hoping for perfect tools.

Your Computer Is a Target

What Are the Shady Hombres After?

Don't be fooled into thinking that your personal devices and data are safe because they are not as tempting as business computer systems. Unless your data is uniquely desirable, it is true that your personal smartphones, tablets, laptops, and desktops are not as rich a target as corporate servers that hold payment card information for millions of customers, myriad personnel records, employee health data, and proprietary documents to sell on the black market. Businesses will pay large ransoms when profitable business is slowed or halted by a clever hacker. Hacking into national and international businesses and governments is the big time for hacking. The most skill and effort is directed toward the big targets.

Despite tempting business and institutional targets, hackers still have abundant time and energy for attacking individuals. Although the payload may not be as great, breaking into a personal computer is often less risky and technically easier than breaking into a corporate or government system.

© Marvin Waschke 2017

M. Waschke, *Personal Cybersecurity*, DOI 10.1007/978-1-4842-2430-4_4

Security specialists sometimes rank cybercriminals based on their expertise and their supporting organizations. The most powerful are highly trained and experienced government agents and military personnel with nearly unlimited equipment and support staff. They are prepared to break in anywhere and their potential for mayhem is as unlimited as their resources. At the other end of the scale are *script kiddies*. They have little training or experience, but they know how to download prepackaged hacking software from the Internet and follow the instructions to damage their victims.

No system is safe from a top-flight and well-supported cyberinvader, but a carefully secured personal system can give pause to even the best. A personal computing device on which security is ignored is up for invasion by a script kiddy.

Unsecured personal computing devices are sitting ducks with valuables that cybercriminals want. An unsecured personal system is an easy and tempting target, especially to invaders at the low end of the skills and resource spectrum. In this chapter, I will go into detail about what these invaders want and the damage they can do. Chapter 9 details the steps individuals can take to secure their personal computing devices. Using Chapter 9 your devices will no longer be easy targets waiting for an invasion. If you get scared, you can skip to Chapter 9. However, I suggest that you first read the intervening chapters, or you may make the worst mistake of all: thinking that the steps to secure your computer are not worth the trouble.

Pwning

Pwing is hacker and gamer slang. Legend has it that years ago, a numb-fingered hacker gained access and control of an enemy's computer and intended to crow about it in an Internet chat session. Instead of typing "I own you," his finger missed the "o" and hit the adjacent key, "p," typing "I pwn you." From that day on, taking control of someone else's computer was known as *pwning*. Gamers picked it up and use it to mean "I totally dominate you in this game." Other gamers maintain pwn is a misspelling that appeared in a video game. Which story is true? It is hard to say.

The pronunciation is variable. Some say it is pronounced "pone" as in corn-pone; others pronounce it "pawn" as in chess; yet others insist it has no pronunciation because it is only used in text messages and chat rooms.

The sources are notoriously unreliable. No matter which origin or pronunciation, being pwned is unpleasant.

Birth of a Pwn

It is easy to joke about pwning, but it is also the quintessential hack job and a building block of most sabotage and cybercrime. Desktops, laptops, tablets, and smartphones all can be and are pwned. Some vendors claim their devices are invulnerable. That has repeatedly been proven untrue.[1]

Although it is possible to break into a system directly in several ways, the most frequent attacks are through phishing and drive-bys. A phisher tricks his victim into opening an email attachment, which executes and infects the victim's machine or leads the victim to a phony web site where they are tricked into entering their credentials. The executed code usually establishes an entrance to the system (backdoor) that the hacker can use surreptitiously. The code will also send a message to inform the hacker that a new device has been pwned. A drive-by does the same thing but instead of email, it uses weaknesses in web browsers to fire off code that infects the victim's device. Drive-bys are harder to avoid than phishing expeditions because victims can avoid infection from phishing by not opening attachments or entering credential; to avoid drive-bys, the victim must avoid clicking on links to drive-by sites or avoid executing the code used by drive-by sites.

When a victimized machine is infected, the hacker obtains access to the victim's device through a backdoor, which is also called a remote access tool (RAT). The RAT could be distributed with the operating system, like the Windows Remote Desktop or something special coded up by the hacker. Documented points of entry are usually not called backdoors, but they do similar things. There are many legitimate uses for RATs, such as remote maintenance and troubleshooting, but they are also hacking tools. Hackers usually prefer to use RATs designed for hacking, which are clearly backdoors. There are a number available for downloading. In a pwn, the RAT may be opened up immediately, but it is often easier to open the RAT on the next boot of the victim's computer.

If the victim is lucky, antivirus software will detect and remove the infection before the hacker begins to use the RAT. Depending on the infection and the antivirus software, the infection could be detected in real time when the infection occurred or in a scheduled or manually started virus scan. The interval during which the infection can be caught before damage is done can be short, which argues for frequent virus scans. Real-time detection will not always

---

[1] Apple, for example, has fostered an image of invulnerability. Linux is sometimes claimed to be invulnerable also. Security experts disagree. All platforms are vulnerable. For example, see Gary Davis, "Mobile Myths: Can My Apple Devices Get Hacked?" McAfee Blog Central, Feb 15, 2013. https://securingtomorrow.mcafee.com/consumer/consumer-threat-notices/mobile-myths-can-my-apple-devices-get-hacked/. Accessed March 2016. On the Linux side, see Paolo Rovelli, "Don't believe these four myths about Linux security," Sophos Blog, March 26, 2015. https://blogs.sophos.com/2015/03/26/dont-believe-these-four-myths-about-linux-security/. Accessed March 2016.

catch all infections; frequent virus scans in addition to real-time detection are an excellent idea. However, an infection cannot be caught if the antivirus software does not have its signature. Installing the latest signatures helps catch the latest infections, although there is always a chance that a new virus will not yet have a signature.

Aftermath of a Pwn

When the RAT is in place and the hacker has access, the real destruction can begin. An important point here is that the hacker's job is much more difficult, if not impossible, if the hacker does not have administrative privileges. Although the hackers may find a way to give themselves administrative privileges later, hackers inherit the privileges of the user account they use to enter the device, which is the user who triggered the initial infection. Therefore, avoiding assigning administrative privileges to the primary account on a device makes the device less vulnerable to attack.

One of the first steps of a sophisticated pwn is to make the infection harder to detect and remove. This includes mutating the infection software so that it no longer conforms to signatures known to antivirus software. That can mean making the signature unique to the device. If the antivirus program looks for certain file names, the names can be changed. If the antivirus program looks for patterns in the binary code, these can be disguised or moved around. The infection can be hidden off the hard disk or in areas usually reserved for the operating system. For instance, key virus code can be tucked into static memory in the Basic Input/Output System (BIOS) that runs before the operating system starts up. If the infection does this, a complete removal and replacement of the operating system will not eradicate the infection.

When the pwn is complete, the nasty fun begins. The infection can change filenames and modify file contents to suit the hackers' purposes. It can also change permissions on files so they cannot be opened or executed. Best of all, the intruder can change passwords and remove or change the privileges associated with accounts. When this happens, the victim has lost control of their own device. At that point, the victim has few alternatives. The device may still be recovered but a complete restore to factory defaults may be quicker and easier.

If the hacker remains in stealth mode, they avoid detection and allow the user to think they still own their device. The hacker can begin to mine the resources of the device. All the interesting data and passwords can be stolen. Data lockers, often called ransomware, can be set up. Webcams can be used to spy on users. Perhaps compromising photos can be sold or used for defamation or blackmail. Internet of Things (IoT) controls can be fiddled with, such as unlocking the front door for a burglar who has been informed that the house will be vacant for a few hours. The hacker may install a key logger, which will capture and record every keystroke from the keyboard in a log and send them to the hacker. A key log is a great source for information like bank account numbers and passwords that the victim was careful not to store on the device and only transfer through secure communication channels. And then there is the possibility of becoming a bot, hired out by the hacker to send spam or participate in denial of service attacks.

Stealing Your Data

You may expect that a hacker's prime target is payment card information, but this is not quite as attractive as it may seem. Most individuals have only a handful of payment cards, many only a single debit card and a single credit card. This is not a rich haul compared to 40 million cards taken in the Target heist. In addition, most people do not store their payment card information on their computers. Payment cards only sell for a few dollars on the black market. If the hacker decides to cut out the middleman and use the cards, they expose themselves in ways most hackers avoid, such as being caught with a stolen card in a store. Although a hacker will probably grab payment cards when they have the opportunity, they are unlikely to invade a personal computing device for payment cards.

Passwords

The passwords stored by browsers are an attractive prize for hackers. All browsers offer to memorize usernames and passwords. Browser stored and managed passwords are a great convenience that most users pounce on. After the browser has captured a password, the user does not have to think about it again. However, this is a mixed blessing because all a hacker has to do is bring up the browser, go to the stored passwords, and pick up the keys to your kingdom.

Browser developers have tried to make hacking more difficult. Firefox has a master password that users can set. Chrome uses a Google account password and Microsoft uses a Microsoft account to access passwords. There are advantages to both methods. By basing browser stored password protection on accounts that are used for many different things, those accounts become single points of failure. In other words, if OneDrive is hacked, so are the passwords in Edge. However, Chrome and Edge are more convenient because users are probably already signed into their Google or Microsoft account when they are asked for an account and password in their browser. The Firefox master password has to be entered each time Firefox is brought up, which is annoying, but a hacker has to work harder to get the password.

If the invader has installed a key logger, all bets are off. The key logger will record all passwords (and everything else) that are entered through the keyboard, including Microsoft and Google account passwords and Firefox master passwords. This underscores the benefits of detecting and removing malware as soon as possible.

The best prizes are passwords to sites like bank and stock trading accounts that offer opportunities to steal large amounts of money quickly. Access to a credit card site can be used for identity theft and help in crafting personalized social engineering exploits that might appear as emails to your friends that are made credible by personal information gleaned from your device. Purchases can be made from confederates selling on EBay and instead of sending the merchandise, the confederates forward money to the hacker. When the authorities investigate, the criminals have turned into phantoms and disappeared.

From your computer, a hacker can gain access to your cloud accounts, including your backups, your documents, and data in cloud storage (virtual systems running on cloud facilities like Amazon Web Services or Microsoft Azure).

Hackers are also looking for game accounts such as Steam and Xbox and entertainment accounts such as Hulu, HBO, and Netflix. Rumor has it that there is a thriving market in reselling stolen Netflix accounts. License keys for operating systems and applications are also nice lagniappes that a hacker may be happy to latch onto.

Email

Email account passwords are a special prize. By reading email, hackers obtain facts and details that they can use to make a person's life miserable for years to come. If they have not learned it already from Facebook, they can learn about the victim's family and friends and collect their email addresses, which opens all of them up for spam, harassment, and phishing, no doubt using the victim's name. They can develop a detailed profile the victim and use it for repeated identity thefts.

If the victim's healthcare and insurance providers use email to communicate with the victim, the hacker scoops up the victim's health information. Emailed bank and other financial statements are open to the hacker, as are receipts and invoices from vendors.

If the victim ever corresponds with their employer or customers, the hacker picks up inside information they can use to social engineer their way into those businesses. If security breaches are traced back to the victim, restoring trust may be difficult and time-consuming.

Documents

The documents stored on a victim's computer can also be valuable, although they are often individual and require more special knowledge to evaluate and exploit. Therefore, they are more likely to be taken in an attack that is directed toward a specific person rather than a blanket sweep of vulnerable devices.

There are many candidates for document theft. Business documents, tax filings, contracts, legal documents all might be used fraudulently. Health documents, appointment calendars, and to do lists are good materials for developing social engineering scams.

When a computer is hacked, documents or photographs that are in some way embarrassing or compromising are often publicized on public media. There is also potential for blackmail or other forms of extortion.

Other potential document losses are copies of reports, creative works, and photographs. EBook and music libraries can also be lost, although most of these are also stored in the cloud and are relatively easily replaced.

File encryption is a common strategy for protecting documents. Microsoft provides their BitLocker service on Windows. BitLocker encrypts and decrypts all the files on a device's disk automatically with only minor performance degradation on recently manufactured devices. There is some controversy over whether or not Microsoft has provided a backdoor for government agencies, but the encryption itself is considered secure. BitLocker is not available on home and student versions of Windows.

Threatware

Threatware attempts to extort money from its victims by making threats. Some of the threats are idle, others are chillingly real. A common threat is to render your data inaccessible to you.

Data lockers, often called ransomware, lock up the data and resources of personal computing devices so that their rightful owners can't get to them. Data locking amounts to an extortion scheme. The fundamental pattern is a message that pops up demanding money to restore access to your computer or to avoid some disaster. Sometimes the threat is real, sometimes not.

Data locking is probably the most direct route between a personal computer and a criminal's payday. And the criminals often succeed. A hospital in southern California paid out $17,000 to regain access to their data files. Criminals encrypted system and data files, then demanded payment for the decryption key. With their computer system effectively stopped, the hospital staff had to revert to pen and paper for record keeping and communications, which slowed operations and eventually may have affected patient care. The hospital administration determined that paying off the extortionists was the best choice. After paying in Bitcoins (see sidebar below), the hospital successfully restored their system. The entire episode took place over a weekend.[2]

---

[2]Richard Winton, "Hollywood hospital pays $17,000 in bitcoin to hackers; FBI investigating," Los Angeles Times, February 18, 2016, www.latimes.com/local/lanow/la-me-ln-hollywood-hospital-bitcoin-20160217-story.html. Accessed February, 2016.

BITCOIN

Bitcoin is a form of decentralized digital currency that relies heavily on encryption and cryptographic hash technology. Bitcoins do not correspond to any physical object. Instead, they exist as a record in closely guarded transaction histories called blocks.

The blocks are public, but an elaborate system of encryption and cryptographic hashes seeks to guarantee that the system remains secure. Maintaining blocks requires intense computing and it is time consuming. The time and expense required to defraud the system is a significant part of its security.

Users of bitcoins can pay out or receive the currency using private keys to sign the transactions. Transactions are effectively anonymous.

Bitcoins are kept in *digital wallets*, which are usually software applications that store keys, tracking numbers, and amounts of bitcoin for the owner. The wallet contains all the information necessary for bitcoin transactions. Bitcoin wallets can be portable USB flash drives or specially designed appliances. A bitcoin wallet can also be printed on paper for manually entered transactions.

The value of a bitcoins is more volatile now than traditional currencies. It may stabilize in the future, but at present the value of bitcoins sometimes varies rapidly. To guarantee a bitcoin's value, it must be exchanged for stable currency immediately after it is received.

Bitcoins have advantages as a currency. They reduce the cost of moving money from place to place and operate at electronic speeds, but the anonymous and decentralized nature of bitcoin has raised some skepticism because cybercriminals and other dealers in illicit goods take advantage of these properties.

Some of these methods involve little computer engineering. These scams can be as simple as a clickbait website. The bait is something like "Never before seen photographs of sexy top models and adorable kittens." Well, who could pass that up? But on clicking, the screen says "Child pornography download attempt. The FBI will be notified immediately unless a $1,000 purchase is made at the Mean Pirate Haxx web site using the coupon code X666X." No ugly child pornography was involved and nothing was done to the victim's computer. A surprising number of victims have been frightened by similar web sites into paying.

A scam like this is pure fraud. The perpetrator in this hypothetical case is vulnerable because PayPal, credit cards, and similar payment services are not anonymous. Recipients who do not carefully cover their tracks can usually be traced and the operators of most payment services are eager to prevent their services from being used fraudulently.

Anonymous digital currencies like bitcoin work better. They are designed to be as anonymous as cash transactions. That is a boon to cybercriminals because physically exchanging and transporting cash does not mix well with cybercrime.

Ransomware that threatens but does not damage is not as lethal as ransomware that modifies the victimized computer. This kind of ransomware changes filenames and permissions, modifies configuration files, or installs code that interferes with normal operations. There are many possibilities, and cybercriminals are creative.

Now, the most prevalent type of ransomware encrypts the files on the victim's computer and then demands ransom for the decryption key. The hospital attack described earlier is an example of this kind of attack. Antivirus tools are ineffective against this kind of malware, unless the tool detects and eradicates the infection before encryption starts.

CryptoLocker is a well-known example of effective and vicious ransomware. It has been very successful at extorting from its victims. In 2013, CryptoLocker's take was estimated to be in the hundreds of millions of dollars.[3] CryptoLocker was taken down in 2014 by global law enforcement.[4] However, malware as lucrative as CryptoLocker quickly comes back to life and there are now similar attacks occurring. CryptoWall, TeslaCrypt, and TorCrypt have all sprung up in the wake of CryptoLocker. Linux and Android are now targeted in addition to Windows systems.[5] The Apple OS X operating system for Mackintosh is related to Linux and is likely to be targeted soon, if not already.

A CryptoLocker-type infection typically begins with a targeted phishing attack with an attachment that infects the system when it is opened. The infection is dormant until the next time the affected computer is booted. The malware connects with its server. The server creates an asymmetric encryption pair of a public encryption key and a private decryption key, and sends the public key back to the infected computer. The infection works in the background, using the public key to encrypt files selected by extension. Targeted files include Word documents, Excel spreadsheets, photographs, and so on. The list is long

[3]Violet Blue, "CryptoLocker's crime wave: A trail of millions in laundered Bitcoin," ZDNet, December 22, 2013. www.zdnet.com/article/cryptolockers-crimewave-a-trail-of-millions-in-laundered-bitcoin/. Accessed February 2016.

[4]Brian Krebs, " 'Operation Tovar' Targets 'Gameover' ZeuS Botnet, CryptoLocker, Scourge," June 14, 2014. http://krebsonsecurity.com/2014/06/operation-tovar-targets-gameover-zeus-botnet-cryptolocker-scourge/. Accessed February 2016.

[5]Liviu Arsene, "Android Ransomware and SMS-Sending Trojans Remain a Growing Threat," Bitdefender Labs, January 2016. http://download.bitdefender.com/resources/files/News/CaseStudies/study/85/Android-Malware-Threat-Report-H2-2015.pdf. Accessed March 2016.

and the encryption process can take several days. When the encryption is complete, the ransom message appears. The message demands a payment for the private decryption key.[6] See Figure 4-1.

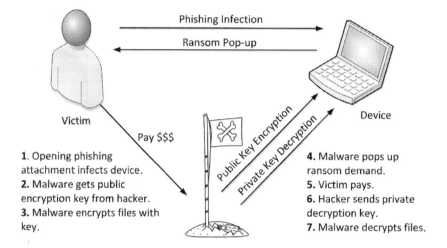

Figure 4-1. CryptoLocker infection communicates between the victim, the hacker, and the victim's device

The malware is insidious. It doesn't just encrypt the files on the computer; it also finds all network drives and attached drives such as external hard disks, flash drives, and memory cards. These too are encrypted.

Decryption is practically impossible without the private key. Some public services have collected sets of decryption keys that have been found on victimized systems. They attempt to use these keys to decrypt files, hoping that keys have been reused. This does not always work because the miscreants either assign public-private key pairs individually, or have a large number of pairs to draw on.

An antivirus tool can prevent this kind of attack under certain conditions but there are many limitations. The tool must have the signature for the infection. If the infection is new, or a recent variation, a signature is not likely to be available. If the tool has the signatures for the infection and the tool understands the modifications made by the infection, the antivirus can remove and reverse the changes, but it cannot unencrypt. Files that were encrypted before the infection

---

[6]For a more detailed technical description of what CryptoLocker does, see Octavian Minea, "Cryptolocker Ransomware Makes a Bitcoin Wallet per Victim," Bitdefender Labs. https://labs.bitdefender.com/2013/10/cryptolocker-ransomware-makes-a-bitcoin-wallet-per-victim/. Accessed March 2016.

was stopped remain encrypted. After files are encrypted, antivirus tools may not run in the normal fashion because the victim cannot execute anything on her computer. This can circumvented by putting the antivirus program on a bootable USB or DVD. After booting the system from removable media, the antivirus program can scan the hard drive to wipe out the ransomware, but that only prevents further encryption, it does not decrypt encrypted files.

Antivirus tools work best if they find the infection before encryption starts. This period can be a few minutes, or a few days. Usually, the ransom message does not appear until the encryption is complete or well under way.

Victims whose files have been encrypted have two practical alternatives: pay the ransom or restore from backup. The brutal fact is that most victims do not have adequate backups to restore their system. To begin with, unless backup systems are regularly checked, including trial restores, they can easily fail. In addition, ransomware is invidious in its encryption of attached and network drives, which many users rely on for backing up. Backups that are not touched by the attack can be still be ruined if the backup program does not keep successive snapshots of the system, because an automated backup that runs during the encryption can overlay readable files with encrypted copies, rendering the backup useless. The best defense against a CryptoLocker type attack is a carefully thought through backup strategy carried out and maintained meticulously.

In 2015, the FBI recommended that victims of ransomware pay the ransom.[7]

Sabotage

Some hackers are saboteurs whose goal is damage rather than material gain. Some are out to avenge some real or imagined slight. So-called *hacktivists* use hacking to support political positions. Teenage hackers vent adolescent frustrations with destruction and crime. Not a few cybersaboteurs try to show off their technical prowess at annoying others. Some are genuine idealists with impersonal goals. Yet others are extortionists.

Cybersabotage is unauthorized, intentional, and malicious interference with the normal processes and functions of a computer or system of computers. It can cause the destruction or damage of equipment or data. It can also prevent a system from fulfilling its purpose by interrupting or modifying processes. The implications for personal computer users and sabotage have grown as the IoT expands.

---

[7]The Security Ledger, "FBI's Advice on Ransomware? Just Pay the Ransom," October 22, 2015.
https://securityledger.com/2015/10/fbis-advice-on-cryptolocker-just-pay-the-ransom/. Accessed March 2014.

Supervisory Control and Data Acquisition

Industry has made progressively more use of supervisory control and acquisition (SCADA) since computerized control was introduced in the 1970s. During that time, the efficiency and capabilities of industrial processes have grown immensely due, in part, to SCADA. Understanding SCADA is important to personal computing because the IoT has extended the use of SCADA from industry to personal computing.

SCADA impacts many aspects of society. It prevents accidents like oil refinery explosions and nuclear plant meltdowns. Although these accidents still occur, many more are prevented by computerized control. Without SCADA, automobiles would be more expensive and less efficient. SCADA has made many industries more productive and safer. To implement SCADA, engineers place sensors at critical points in a process.

For example, sensors measure critical temperatures, pressures, and other aspects of processes in an oil refinery. The measurements are transmitted to a central computer and displayed to human managers. The human managers are able to respond to the measurements by operating controls through the same computer. In some circumstances, the computer itself responds to conditions faster and more accurately than human capabilities.

The net result of relying on SCADA is greater safety and efficiency. The production of some products would not be possible without the precise and instant control that SCADA provides. Industrial disasters are prevented by SCADA controls. Transportation, such as airlines and railroads, relies on SCADA for keeping passengers safe. Automobiles use less gasoline when SCADA continuously tunes the carburation. Skids are controlled by SCADA-assisted braking. Driverless cars are also an example of an application of SCADA.

The industrial benefits from SCADA point to a future with more efficient houses and appliances that will make lives easier and safer. As the IoT grows, SCADA will also make possible new services and capabilities that have not been thought of yet.

However, SCADA is not perfect. Every system, both human and computer, sometimes fails. Major disasters have been SCADA failures. Some of these failures have been attributed to cybercriminals.

In 1999, an oil pipeline ruptured and dumped over 200,000 gallons of gasoline into a creek flowing through Bellingham, Washington. The gasoline ignited over a 1.5-mile stretch of the creek. The explosion burned to death a fisherman and two young boys playing at the creek's edge.[8] The damage to property was

---

[8] I have lived in the Bellingham area all my life. I have a distant connection to the two dead boys. Reading between the lines as a software engineer, the NTSB report was tragic. The innocence of the victims was crushing.

in the tens of millions of dollars. The reasons for the rupture were complex, involving construction that accidentally weakened the pipeline, control errors, and administrative issues. The National Transportation Safety Board (NTSB) found that the disaster would have been prevented if the SCADA system had functioned properly.

The NTSB did not conclude that the disaster was the result of hacking, but they pointed out evidence suggesting that a hacker *could* have caused the disaster. A malfunctioning valve closed downstream from the rupture, causing a pressure spike. If the SCADA system had been functioning properly, the pressure spike would have been detected and the system would have compensated, preventing a rupture in a compromised section of pipe. The human operator did not react promptly. This may have been inattention or inadequacies in the user interface, but the SCADA system was sluggish at the time and likely prevented a quick response.

SCADA sluggishness may have been caused by a poorly timed or faulty software maintenance procedure, but the system was not well secured against unauthorized entry. The NTSB pointed out that as the system was configured, a hacker could have caused the sluggish responses although there was no positive evidence for an outside intrusion.[9]

Home SCADA

The IoT has introduced SCADA to the home. Our houses and our families are now subject to the same kinds of attacks and hazards that affect a petroleum pipeline or a hydroelectric plant. Unfortunately, IoT designers have often left security holes in their rush to convenience. These flaws have given hackers opportunities for a new range of malicious exploits. For example, some heating systems now have interfaces that turn the heat up or down in response to a message that arrives over the Internet or a cellular network. If a hacker breaks into the system and fiddles with the controls, they might be able to adjust the controls to overheat the heating unit and start a fire.

Alarm systems and webcams are also personal systems that are opportunities for interference. The hacker can break into the control mechanisms for the devices. Alarm systems can be disabled or set off false alarms. Webcams can be used for spying. This applies to all webcams, including those used for surveillance or nanny cams that are used to monitor babies and children. These security devices can themselves be insecure.

---

[9]National Transportation Safety Board, "Pipeline Rupture and Subsequent Fire in Bellingham, Washington June 10, 1999," www.ntsb.gov/investigations/AccidentReports/Reports/PAR0202.pdf. Accessed March 2016.

In the last few years, more and more automobiles are connected to the Internet while they are driven. If a car is connected to the Internet, hackers will eventually discover ways to break in. When they do, they will be able to compromise the vehicle's SCADA. Who knows what they will be able to do?

IoT has tremendous potential. Computerized remote control is efficient and convenient. Using SCADA technology can make life easier while consuming less energy to achieve more. Computerized control never daydreams and its reactions are never dulled by illness or a poor night's sleep. But computerized control is also a threat because it can be sabotaged remotely. An unsecured system can be pwned and twisted to the purposes of an invader. The results may not be the equal of the Bellingham pipeline explosion, but they can be devastating to an individual.

Personal Sabotage

Computer systems have improved since the Bellingham pipeline catastrophe, but the enormity of the damage cannot be forgotten and the evidence that cybercriminals could have caused the catastrophe is still troubling.

Hackers can cause disastrous physical damage when they attack industrial systems, but they can also cause damage when they attack personal computing devices. Even script kiddies know how to render a computer unbootable by deleting critical system files. With more skill, a hacker can stop the system cooling fans, force the processor into an overclocked mode, and overheat the processor to the point of destruction.[10]

Another way to damage a system is to replace device drivers, the software that communicates between an operating system like Windows or Linux and hardware such as keyboard or network interface cards. The keyboard driver could be modified to record keystrokes and the network interface could record network communications. For sheer annoyance, a derelict mouse driver could scramble messages causing the mouse to work in reverse or exhibit other strange behavior.

---

[10]Overclocking is running a processor at a greater speed than its specification, which causes the processor to generate more heat. Many processors have settings for overclocking, but the chip manufacturers warn against it. Computer game enthusiasts overclock their computers to improve performance, but they add extra fans and other cooling devices to protect the processor from overheating and burning out. Overclocked and undercooled processors can be served with nachos, although they are neither tasty or healthy.

The data stored on a computing device is a wonderful opportunity for destructive mischief. A subtle hacker might change file contents to do damage that would not surface until long after the break-in. One example is *logic bombs*. These are chunks of code that are designed to do something, usually malicious, under specified conditions. A mild example is a logic bomb that would trigger posting an offensive Facebook message. The trigger could be a date and time, a message from the hacker, or a complex combination of factors, like a call from a certain number on a smartphone, the outdoor temperature, the time of day, and a text from the FBI. Depending on the likelihood of meeting the conditions, a logic bomb can lie dormant for years.

Invasion of Privacy

Privacy is not a constitutional right in the United States. The United States Constitution does not contain the word *privacy* and there is no explicit right to privacy defined there. The current interpretation of the right to privacy is based on inferences from several amendments, including rights to free speech, due process, and strictures against unreasonable searches and seizures. It is also derived from statutes and common law.

Although privacy is not a constitutional right, it is well established. Today's legal concept of the right to privacy comes largely from an influential Harvard Law Review article written by Samuel D. Warren and Louis Brandeis in 1890.[11] Brandeis and Warren collected concepts and precedents and combined them into a statement of the right to privacy that has been accepted by the legal community, including the Supreme Court. The Warren-Brandeis article was written in response to new technology and business practices that were appearing at the end of the 19th century. They argued for extending traditional protections to provide protection from a new environment. They maintained that previous legal protection against trespass, libel, and other personal invasions would not adequately protect individuals from threats to privacy arising from business and technological innovations of the day such as sensation-seeking newspapers and predatory photographers.

Warren and Brandeis formulated several principles that underlie the concept of privacy. Privacy rules do not stop publication of material that is of general or public interest. This principle distinguishes private from public, but it can be difficult to apply. For instance, some facts of a public official's life may be of public interest, but the same facts of an ordinary citizen are not of public

---

[11]Samuel Warren, Louis Brandeis, "The Right To Privacy," Harvard Law Review, Vol. IV, No. 5, December 1890. http://faculty.uml.edu/sgallagher/Brandeisprivacy.htm. Accessed March 2016.

interest. Warren and Brandeis use the example of a private citizen who cannot spell. This, they say, is private and not of public interest, but the spelling skills of a member of Congress are of public interest.

Other principles include that when individuals publish facts about themselves, the facts, no matter what they are, are no longer private. Revelations made in court or other public bodies are also not protected by privacy rules. The truth or falsity of published material does not affect privacy rights, nor does the presence or lack of malice affect the right.

Although privacy has been established as a basic right, distinguishing public and private is still subject to controversy. Should the government have the right to peek into personal emails to identify terrorists? And what constitutes intrusion? One view says surveillance by a human is forbidden but a computer algorithm that scans email for suspicious patterns should be permitted. Others say that an algorithm is the same as a person. Others argue that viewing any aspect of information that is not explicitly public is a violation of privacy rights. Other questions revolve around due process. Is a search warrant adequate to allow law enforcement to examine any computer file? Are there circumstances under which officials may conduct secret searches of computer records without the knowledge of the owner? These are difficult questions that are still to be determined.

Statutes from several states define computer invasion of privacy explicitly as the intentional and unauthorized use of a computer or computer network to examine certain kinds of information. The information protected varies from statute to statute, but typically includes employment, health records, financial, and identifying information. The penalty for violation of the statutes also varies; some class the violation as a misdemeanor, other class it as a felony.

Identity Theft

Identity theft is using the persona of another person without their permission. It has many criminal uses, but it begins with collecting identity credentials for a victim and using them fraudulently.

Credentials can sometimes be obtained legally from public sources. Identity thieves can be creative and diligent in mining public sites for information. Social security and driver's license numbers are the two foundations for establishing a fraudulent identity. Payment card numbers are also used. An account name and password for a banking site may be all that is needed to set up a new credit card unknown to the real owner.

Personal details are useful secondary information. Posts on social media such as Facebook are one source. For example, birth dates are often part of establishing identity and these frequently appear in social media. Names of children, other relatives, and friends can all help build a convincing persona. Real estate purchase dates and prices often appear on real estate sites like Zillow. Public court records often contain useful facts for establishing credentials. Identity thieves also look through trash and paper mail searching for useful information.

Sometimes facts are stolen. Hacking into personal computing devices is one way of obtaining credentials; hacking into government and enterprise computers and stealing information wholesale is another. There is a ready market for stolen identity credentials. Often the identity thieves buy stolen credentials rather than steal themselves.

According to the Federal Trade Commission,[12] the most common use of identity theft is tax fraud, which soared from 2014 to 2015, increasing from 32% of identity theft crimes to 45%. Typically, a criminal will file a fake tax return for a large refund in a legitimate taxpayer's name using stolen credentials. When the victim files their legitimate tax return, it is rejected as a duplicate. At that point, the legitimate taxpayer is out their refund and the identity thief has cashed the refund check. Unchecked, the legitimate taxpayer could be penalized for the fraudster's unjustified refund. This kind of fraud was made easier by unintended consequences of efforts to speed refunds. To succeed, the thieves must file the fraudulent return before the victim or the return will be flagged as a duplicate and carefully examined. If the refund is prompt, the thief is likely to have cashed the refund check before the legitimate return is filed. Apparently, in the interest of prompt refunds, the IRS has also been less through in verifying the supporting documents such a W-2 forms before releasing the refund, which has reduced the likelihood that the thief will be caught. Getting the jump on the criminals and filing tax returns early is a useful defense against tax fraud of this kind.

A stolen identity has uses other than tax fraud. Opening a line of credit or credit card under a stolen identity is also common. In order to secure a new credit card, an applicant must convince an officer of the credit-granting organization that they are deserving of credit. That decision usually is confirmed by an authentication of identity and an adequate credit history. If the thief can authenticate himself as a person with a good credit rating using fraudulent credentials, the thief gets the line of credit, typically in the form of a new credit card. At that point, the thief charges the credit card to the limit and exits the scene. The person whose identity was used gets the bills.

This is different from using stolen payment card information and is potentially much more dangerous. Stolen payment card crimes are usually relatively easy for victims to resolve and the card holder almost always suffers little or no loss. Usually the organization extending the credit must pay the bill and the victims go on their way without much damage.

---

[12]Federal Trade Commission, "Consumer Sentinel Network Data Book for January to December 2015," February 2016. www.ftc.gov/system/files/documents/reports/consumer-sentinel-network-data-book-january-december-2015/160229csn-2015databook.pdf. Accessed March 2016.

A stolen identity is more difficult to prove and remedy. The process can go on for years and the victims are plagued with one sting after another.

Fortunately, access to credit ratings is controllable, although exercising the control involves phone calls and tedious paperwork. A potential victim can freeze or put a fraud flag on their credit record. A fraud flag or freeze will prevent the thief from getting new credit cards or other loans. There are only a small number of well-established credit rating agencies (four at the time of this writing). These agencies usually keep each other informed of freezes, but it is best to check whether a freeze has been propagated. When potential victims fear identity theft, they can contact the credit rating agencies and ask that their credit be frozen. No access is granted to a frozen account until it is unfrozen. A respectable credit granting agency will not grant credit without access to credit reports, so the thief is blocked from new lines of credit. Some states mandate free credit freezes when credentials are stolen; other states do not regulate fees for credit freezes. In most cases, credit freeze fees are worth peace of mind they bring.

Security experts say that freezing credit stops the consequences of identity better than the credit monitoring services that are offered as free compensation by breached organizations like Target in 2013.[13] Credit monitoring services inform the victim after suspicious activity in their name, but they do not stop the activity. The victim is still left with paperwork and hassle to recover their stolen identity. When victims are offered free monitoring, they should by all means take the free offer, but still get a credit freeze or fraud flag.

Some people who feel they are especially vulnerable to identity theft freeze their credit continuously, renewing the freeze each time it comes due. They unfreeze and immediately refreeze when they execute a transaction that requires a credit check.

Identity thieves use stolen identities for so many purposes: to avoid prosecution for crimes, to hide medical problems, to fraudulently obtaining medical care, and to falsify employment records or credentials. The list is long and after identity is stolen, each of these possibilities may require different actions to straighten everything out. Regaining a stolen identity is often a long hard path. The Federal Trade Commission provides some help on a website that helps victims of identity theft enter a report and formulate an individualized recovery plan, but executing the plan is left to the victim.[14]

---

[13]Bruce Krebs, "How I Learned to Stop Worrying and Embrace the Security Freeze," Krebs On Security, June 15, 2015. http://krebsonsecurity.com/2015/06/how-i-learned-to-stop-worrying-and-embrace-the-security-freeze/. Accessed March 2016.
[14]Federal Trade Commission, "IdentityTheft.gov." www.identitytheft.gov/. Accessed March 2016.

Sorting Out Data Loss

An inventory of the valuable data stored on a personal computer, laptop, tablet, or smartphone is an important aid in damage control after an invasion. You will need this information to plan for recovery. At the moment you are hacked, you should not scratch your head and wonder what your devices hold that can be exploited. Most people are busy enough eradicating the malware that has been planted on their computer. There is not much time or energy for working out a list of people and institutions to inform and countermeasures to take to avoid or minimize financial or reputation loss.

An inventory does not have to be elaborate to be useful. Prioritization is important. Everyone has their own priorities, but a few questions are crucial:

- What is on the device to be lost?
- How hard will it be to replace the loss?
- Can the loss contribute to identity theft?
- What damage could the loss do to reputation?

For most people, the first question will be about money: compromised bank accounts and other financial sites. A victim's best interest is to inform these institutions as soon as possible. They can activate their damage control systems and minimize the damage to you. What you don't want to happen is to forget to inform a bank or a retailer in the excitement. A plan for responding to a successful computer invasion can avert frustration and grief.

Surely the most difficult things to replace are personal photographs. Hackers are not likely to bother to permanently delete data like photographs, but it is possible in the aftermath of a ransom attack. Financial records stored in computer files may also be hard to replace. Documents such as building plans may also be important. Legal documents, such as contracts, may be nearly impossible to replace unless they are registered with the courts.

With all the use of online materials today, the inventory can be large. Recovering materials lost in an invasion can be impossible without reliable backups. By identifying the important materials in your inventory, you can quickly identify your losses and make sure your backup is safe. Also, a listing of irreplaceable or hard-to-replace materials ought to prompt you to verify that your backup system is backing up the right files.

In addition to losing dollars and cents, and treasured documents, losing identity, reputation, and self-esteem must be considered. We think of our computers as private, but hacking turns them public. You should have a plan for warning your friends and relatives that they might receive spam or strange emails that look like they came from you. You can let them know that they could be sent by a hacker and you can explain that they should neither believe or act on them. This will increase your chance of avoiding an embarrassing or damaging consequences.

For example, if you tell your boss about a break-in before the repercussions begin to fall from the sky, you may be able to explain away that the venting email using ill-chosen words that you sent to a friend and the hacker passed on to her. At least you could get some credit for stepping up to the problem instead of running from it.

The best strategy for controlling damage after an invasion is to act fast. If you know which credentials could be stolen, you can act faster. When stopping identity theft, even hours count, especially now that loans can be applied for online.

Computer as Target

Personal computing devices present a big target to cybercriminals. The virtues of computing devices are also their vulnerability. Most possessions have a single or only a few uses. A car is driven on roads and highways to transport us from place to place. We preserve perishable food in a refrigerator. Cars will not dig up your water pipes or clean your swimming pool. Refrigerators do not mow lawns.

Compare these with a personal computer. A moment ago, I checked if a prescription was ready at my pharmacy. Now I am typing a draft of this chapter. A few moments before that I downloaded a project management application to manage progress on writing this book. Yesterday, I ordered and paid for a book and a part for my tractor from an online retailer. My wife went online to our bank to transfer money to into a special account. Years ago, I built a system to run on a personal computer that turned on the lights based on the weather report and the time of sunset.[15]

Cars and refrigerators are comparatively easy to protect from accidents or crime. If you drive carefully, and keep your car locked, you have erected reasonable barriers to trouble. A refrigerator is even easier to protect because it doesn't venture outside your house or apartment, so the same steps you take to secure your living space takes care of your refrigerator.

In contrast, each task we do on a computer uncovers new vulnerabilities. Some of these vulnerabilities, like access to health records and banking, can be dangerous. And lucrative to criminals who try to take advantage of these weaknesses. Even the tasks that seem innocuous, like opening a document in a word processor, can be dangerous. Macro viruses are common viruses that live in the automatic macros used in documents with most word processors. An infected document can make changes to the computer and invite worse invasions.

---

[15]On cloudy days, the lights went on a few minutes earlier.

The project management application recently I downloaded had a nasty Trojan embedded in the installer. Lucky for me, my antivirus software detected it immediately and quarantined it. My computer could have been pwned. However, I don't think I was lucky. Catching that Trojan was the result of a plan and caution. The project management software was from an open source group that I was unsure of, so I scanned the installer before I ran it. That was being aware and taking action.

When you know that your personal computer, laptop, tablet, and smartphone are all targets, you can take steps to stop the criminals. They may still get you, but not nearly as often.

Misuse of Computers

When Personal Devices Break Bad

Computing itself can become a personal threat when it is misused. Some threats cannot be mitigated by following secure computing practices. This chapter discusses threats to our security that do not involve security breaches. These threats arise when computers are used to harm individuals and society. Computing is not unique in carrying both good and bad consequences, but the bad side of computing is now prominent and undeniable. The answers to these issues will not be found in better antimalware tools and firewalls. We can't stop child computer pornography with better backup practices or stronger passwords. However, with a better understanding of the problems we can change laws and plan for a better future.

We live in an age of information and communication. The technical revolution that promised to empower and entertain us has become a morass of unintended consequences. Both the information stored on our computers and the instant interaction provided by the Internet have been subverted for disagreeable purposes. Perspective is easily lost. For each bad, a more-than-counterbalancing good can be found, but the dangers remain.

© Marvin Waschke 2017
M. Waschke, *Personal Cybersecurity*, DOI 10.1007/978-1-4842-2430-4_5

A Tool for Mischief, Crime, and Mayhem

Why are computers a ready instrument for malice and crime? Fundamental world-changing innovations inevitably have unintended results. For example, innovations in medicine and sanitation have saved many lives and relieved suffering. No one intended it, but those same innovations are responsible for today's economic strains that derive from the burden of supporting growing populations of older people who outlive their retirement funds.

Computing is no different. Although computing has contributed heavily to the wealth of goods and services available today, the computer revolution has spawned many unintended consequences. Computers and high speed data networks do not fit well with traditional notions of crime and property because much of the value found in computing is abstract content rather than physical objects. Stealing a file of the magnetic stripe data from 1,000 credit cards is not the same as stealing 1,000 physical credit cards, although the consequences are almost identical. Law enforcement struggles to punish actions that are clearly malicious and harmful but do not fit traditional definitions of crime. Hazy enforcement, easy anonymity, and crimes that can be committed from great distance combine into a fecund breeding ground for criminal activities that were impossible a few years ago.

The breeding ground is continually fertilized and replenished by the rapid development of hardware and software that seems to accelerate exponentially with each year. There are more and faster processors each year producing more and more data. The growing volume of data is transmitted on faster and faster networks. As more data is produced, storage devices with increasing capacities are built to contain the data. Software advances to analyze the unprecedented quantities of data on the storage devices. Immense quantities of stored data combined with computing capacity and software analysis capabilities has streamlined commerce, tailored healthcare, and sharpened our knowledge of how society works, but the new stores of data and powers of analysis have also given criminals new opportunities for crime.

Misuse of Information

Information is misused for many purposes. It is used to attack individuals by digging up and exposing private information. It is stolen to gain a competitive advantage. It is used for fraud and false identities. Salacious texts and videos are purloined and sold as entertainment. Most of these misuses involve computers.

New Sources of Digital Information

Estimates say that Facebook alone generates many times the equivalent of the physical contents of the Library of Congress each day.[1] Records that have always been public have moved or are moving online. Not too long ago, researching court records required a visit to a court house and knowledge of the way records were stored in a each office. Now the records are online and records in distant places are easy to access. Libraries are rapidly digitizing their holdings and adding new digital resources.[2]

Our sources of information and the way information is generated has changed. Fifty years ago, the primary source for current events was a network of local, regional, and national newspapers, supplemented by news magazines and broadcast news organizations. Local newspapers are now struggling, as are regional newspapers. National newspapers like *The New York Times, the Wall Street Journal,* and *the Washington Post* now have websites that are at least as important as their press runs. Broadcast journalism shares television screens with cable news, and independent websites like Huffington Post and Politico rival newspapers and broadcast networks as sources for current events. These changes represent an enormous social change in the way information is dispersed.

These new online sources are interactive. Readers of *The New York Times* have opportunities to express their opinions and have them published in the *Times.* Unlike letters to the editor, comments are monitored for objectionable material, but not chosen or rejected for publication. All the news sources interact with their audience in a similar manner. News publication is not the one-way street that it once was.

In the past, developers had to limit the amount of information they stored from tracking the activity of running programs. They could not log too many details or retain logs for too long because logs were too large and grew too fast for the available storage. Since storage capacity has grown and cost has dropped significantly, especially for cloud storage, systems now have the resources to store much more and huge logs have become exploitable assets.

---

[1] See Pamela Vagata, Kevin Wilfong, "Scaling the Facebook data warehouse to 300 PB," April 10, 2014. https://code.facebook.com/posts/229861827208629/scaling-the-facebook-data-warehouse-to-300-pb/. Accessed April 2016. According to this article, Facebook stores 600 TB per day. As study in 2000 estimated the physical holdings of the library to be 10 TB. Peter Lyman, Hal Varian, "How Much Information?" School of Information Management and Systems, University of California, Berkeley, 2000. www2.sims.berkeley.edu/research/projects/how-much-info/how-much-info.pdf. Accessed April 2016. According to these numbers, Facebook takes in the equivalent of 60 Libraries of Congress per day.

[2] See Michael Agresta, "What Will Become of the Library?" Slate, April 22, 2014. www.slate.com/articles/life/design/2014/04/the_future_of_the_library_how_they_ll_evolve_for_the_digital_age.html. Accessed April 2016.

One of the consequences of the burst in online information is that digital information is subject to further processing. A few years ago, an investigator searching for personal history had travel to local libraries and read old newspapers. Investigators today can investigate from their local Starbucks, searching more newspapers faster than their earlier counterparts could imagine. This powerful sword cuts both ways. The job of a legitimate investigator is much easier, but the job of a criminal searching for details from a person's past to use for extortion is also easier.

Tools for analyzing data have grown in capacity and sophistication to take advantage of new data. *Big data* refers to methods of identifying patterns and extracting significant information from large quantities of data that were not possible when computers were less powerful. Developers harness the power of many computers to process a mountain of data. Each computer processes a small chunk of data, then combines its results with other computers, processing and combining over and over until they reach a usable result. The outcome is information about the ways in which people, businesses, and natural phenomena act that was unavailable before.

The burgeoning of information and ways of analyzing it have produced a new world of knowledge and possibility, not all good.

Privacy

The information that is now stored in private and public datacenters and computers and the access provided by the Internet have resulted in an assault on privacy. The assault comes from more than one direction. Governments, businesses, and other enterprises have increased capacity for entering areas that were once considered private. Individuals also have greater opportunities for intruding on the affairs of others by mining the vast quantities of information now available online.

Businesses

The online buying, searching, and browsing habits of computer users are all recorded and stored. Most computer applications on desktops, laptops, tablets, and phones also record some user activities. Operating systems also record activities. Social media contains enormous repositories of information on their users. Streaming services track the preferences and habits of their subscribers.

Most of these businesses have privacy policies that describe the data collected and how it will be used, but these policies are often tucked away out of sight and described in legal language that many users have difficulty understanding and most would prefer not to read. Some policies include opt out choices that give users a measure of control over the data recorded and how it is used. However, these options are often overlooked.

Businesses like Amazon use the information they collect to deliver a user experience on their site that many users appreciate. Online businesses have an advantage in collecting information on their users because each transaction is tied to an identified user account. A physical store has more difficulty tying transactions to individuals. The need to tie to individuals is one reason many retailers have discount savings cards or similar programs to encourage users to identify themselves when making purchases.

One of the more troubling customer data practices is sharing or selling data to other businesses. As an example, telecommunications providers have a wealth of information on the location of the cellphones they support. This information can be used to extrapolate home addresses, workplaces, and commute routes. Retailers can use cellular location information to determine if their customers are spending time in competing stores. Software is available to link location information with web browsing history. A retailer could place the items a customer has browsed into online ads for a store on the customer's commute route. Many customers would appreciate the convenience of these ads, but perhaps not realize how the trick was done. Other customers would find using cellphone location data in this way intrusive. Nevertheless, location data is potentially a significant source of revenue for the telecommunications industry. In Europe, where privacy laws are much stricter than the United States, this practice is prohibited.[3]

The information that can be obtained through data analysis can be amazing. Target Corporation is one of the leaders in analysis of customer transaction data. One of their interesting achievements is to identify their pregnant women customers, sometimes before the women know it themselves, from their buying patterns. This has led to at least one embarrassing case where Target's directed ads revealed to parents that their teenage daughter was pregnant.[4]

Governments

The challenge to government is to balance the need of government to protect its citizenry against the citizenry's legitimate demands for privacy and freedom from intrusion. For most of the 20th century, privacy was perceived to be adequately protected by the courts. Telephone and government mail

---

[3]Joel Hruska, "How telcos plan to make billions by selling and combining customer data," ExtremeTech, October 28, 2015. www.extremetech.com/extreme/216988-how-telcos-plan-to-make-billions-by-selling-combining-customer-data. Accessed April 2016.

[4]Charles Duhigg, "How Companies Learn Your Secrets," The New York Times, February 16, 2012. www.nytimes.com/2012/02/19/magazine/shopping-habits.html. Accessed March 2016.

were the primary means of communication. Government mail is protected by statutes enforced by the courts. Phone taps were possible from the beginning of the service, but, again by statute, law enforcement could only implement a tap with a search warrant issued by a court. Without a warrant, evidence obtained through the tap was not admissible in court and law enforcement was exposed to civil action.

Thanks to high-speed computer networks and computer-based computer communication—such as email, messaging, voice over the Internet, websites, and social media—the technology has become more diverse and the rules less clear. Mass data gathering has become easier and analyzing vast quantities of data is now possible. Unlike telephone calls, most computer-based communication is persistent—the communications process preserves the message in storage until it is deleted. Unlike a telephone tap, which must be authorized before the data can be gathered, copies of emails can be seized after the need is identified. The next step down the slippery slope is to seize copies in anticipation of the need. Further down the slope, all emails are seized just in case a need appears. Computer and cellular voice and messaging are like email and subject to the same kind of government scrutiny.

Governments have also been the beneficiary of the enormous pools of information that businesses collect and the technical potential for gathering and analyzing even more. The goals of governments differ from the goals of businesses. A primary goal of governments is to identify and find criminals and other miscreants. This can be done using techniques like those used by retailers to identify and direct ads to persons in specific life-phases such as pregnant women. For instance, the government could, and probably already has, developed methods to identify terrorists with some degree of accuracy. Thus, everyone is safer. But are terrorists the only targets of this kind of analysis? Analysis like this could also be used to identify individuals who hold beliefs that are merely unpopular but not threatening (like a terrorist).

The question is, when is it appropriate to apply these methods? And what data can they be properly applied to? Many feel that the government has over-reached; they frequently cite Edward Snowden and the National Security Agency surveillance documents he leaked to the press in 2013.[5] Snowden's revelations show that the NSA has been collecting far more information than most Americans suspected and it engages in operations, such as advanced hacking expeditions, tapping into major communications links, and surveillance of foreign leaders; many citizens were suprised by its willingness to operate near or beyond the limits of the law.

---

[5]See Lorenzo Franceschi-Bicchierai, "The 10 Biggest Revelations From Edward Snowden's Leaks," Mashable, June 5, 2014. http://mashable.com/2014/06/05/edward-snowden-revelations/. Accessed April 2016.

The specter of abuse of power such as that attributed to J. Edgar Hoover arises. Generally, historians agree that Hoover abused his position as head of the Federal Bureau of Investigation to collect dossiers on many innocent citizens and officials, and used the dossiers to bully his victims.[6] Today, an official with an inclination toward abuses like those of Hoover has a more powerful set of tools for building his dossiers.

Doxing

Collecting public information on a victim, assembling it into a dossier, and using the contents of the dossier to embarrass, harm, or extort from the victim is called *doxing* (sometimes spelled *doxxing*). Like pwning, the word doxing arose from hacker slang. Apparently, the first use of the term came from one hacker revealing the "documents" of another to publicize his genuine identity.

Interrupting the daily life of a celebrity or political figure by publishing their private telephone number and street address of is a form of doxing. Sometimes the target is an entire organization. The names, telephone numbers, and addresses of members of controversial organizations have been published. If the information is public but hard to find, there may be nothing illegal about publishing this information; the doxer may have ferreted out the information from public sources that most of the public are not aware of. A skilled and persistent searcher can often find information that the owner may have thought to be private.

The distinction between innocent curiosity or research and doxing is malicious intent. When someone googles the name of a celebrity out of curiosity and follows up by clicking some of the links that come back, they indulge their interest, but they have done nothing wrong. The celebrity may even be pleased with the interest. The searcher may continue to dig, following up on references, using uncovered data to make further searches. The follow ups break no laws. This activity would also be acceptable to most people, but some might raise their eyebrows a bit and begin to wonder.

But somewhere there is a line between an interested fan and a doxer who pushes on with the intention of collecting personal information and using it to salve an unhealthy obsession or indulge in questionable or malicious activity. Such a person might start searching court records, prying into semi-private

---

[6]The extent of Hoover's vagaries may be exagerated, but his abuse was clear. The view is this article seems to be fairly well-balanced: Kenneth D. Ackerman, "Five myths about J. Edgar Hoover," The Washington Post, November 9, 2011. www.washingtonpost.com/opinions/five-myths-about-j-edgar-hoover/2011/11/07/gIQASLlo5M_story.html. Accessed April 2016.

entries in social media such as Facebook or LinkedIn, searching for embarrassing photographs and personal information. Personal information that is available by mistakes in privacy settings are special prizes. If non-hacking doxers stay with publicly available material and do not commit some form of criminal harassment, they have not broken laws. Even when they break harassment laws, the crime is usually only a misdemeanor with a small fine and little or no jail time. Often the punishment is minor compared to the damage done to the victim.[7]

At some point, the doxer may turn into a hacker and attempt to access email accounts, personal computing devices, cloud storage, and social media accounts, all in search of information they can use for their purposes. Crossing the line into hacking is clearly illegal, but up to that point, ambiguity reigns.

Doxing is an effective tool for harassment and extortion. There are horror stories about teenagers encouraged to perform sex acts on video. Then the encouragement turns to harassment when the videos are placed on public sites with names, addresses, and phone numbers. For these extreme cases, the child pornography laws can be applied, but law enforcement is not always prepared to find the perpetrators.

Plagiarism and Piracy

Digitized data differs from conventionally stored data in many ways, but the ease with which digital data can be copied and recombined with other data inspires some important misuses. Plagiarism is one of these. Cutting and pasting a sentence or paragraph happens in an instant. Students and writers take notes this way constantly. Applications such as Microsoft OneNote and Evernote make this style of working easy and quick.

This practice can easily be misused or abused by copying text fragments into other works without attribution or consent from the original author. This is an act of plagiarism. Plagiarism is unethical but not a crime. However, unauthorized use of copyrighted material is unlawful and often part of plagiarism.

Students are sometimes found guilty of turning in papers that contain unattributed copied material. Search engines like Google play a double role. Students can easily find material to copy, but their plagiarism is also easy to detect with the same search engine. Students both plagiarize more often and are detected more often. Careers and reputations have been ruined when the

---

[7]This article chronicles a particularly disturbing example of doxing among many. *Swatting*, maliciously directing a SWAT team to a victim's resident, frequently accompanies doxing. Jason Fagone, "The Serial Swatter," The New York Times Magazine, November 24, 2015. www.nytimes.com/2015/11/29/magazine/the-serial-swatter.html?_r=1. Accessed April 2016.

results of these temptations and mistakes have been revealed. Reputable journalists, scholars, and authors have been found to have committed plagiarism through intentional or unintentional copying and pasting.[8]

Wholesale copying of entire pieces—blog posts, articles, essay, books—is a more blatant form of intellectual theft made easy by digitized text. One form of this theft is electronic publications that simply substitute the original author's name and title for another and then are sold as a new publication. Stealing the entire content of a work approaches piracy, but differs because the thieves steal the content and substitute their own names and reputations, while pirates steal everything.

Piracy also thrives on the easy duplication of digital materials. A pirate copies an entire work. The pirated material could be an electronic book, a computer game, software, or an audio or video recording. Pirates not only steal the content of an item; they steal the value of the reputation of the author whose name remains on the work. The crime is the same as pirating paper books, wrist watches, or other goods. The pirate sells a copy of the original work as the original and pockets the price without permission and without compensating the true owners.

Misuse of Computing

The increase in the availability of computing capacity since the turn of the 20th century has powered many achievements. Some, such as decoding DNA, have been desirable; others, such as improving the odds of success of income tax fraud, are not so desirable. In the hands of well-meaning technologists, the powers of faster and cheaper processors and the aggregated capacity of cloud installations are a force for efficiency and innovation. But criminals are also able to take advantage of computing capacity.

Big Data and Cybercrime

Big data analysis is a brute force operation that applies aggregated computing capacity to discover connections and patterns among elements in large quantities of data. Prior to the rise of big data, a large data set might be several billions (gigabytes) of characters. What is considered big data changes every year, but large data sets are now measured in trillions (terabytes), quadrillions (petabytes), quintillions (exabytes), and sextillions (zettabytes) of characters.

---

[8]For an example, see Lloyd Grove, "Malcolm Gladwell's Plagiarism Problem," The Daily Beast, December 11, 2014. www.thedailybeast.com/articles/2014/12/11/malcolm-gladwell-s-plagiarism-problem.html. Accessed April 2016. As this article points out, plagiarism is often complex and ambiguous.

Big data has some characteristics other than the size of its data sets. Big data is usually unstructured. Traditional data management almost always means relational data management. Relational data is organized in orderly rows and columns that have precise meanings. The meaning of the data is determined by the position of the data in the table. The way the table is organized is called the *schema* and it is stored separately from the data. In Figure 5-1, "Boston warehouse" is Fred's location because it is in the Fred row and the Location column. Relational data can be manipulated using operations that are mathematically predictable and consistent.

Big data is seldom as orderly as relational data. It is freeform, often as attribute-value pairs. The attribute, such as "Elizabeth's location" in Figure 5-1 determines the meaning of the value "Louisville plant." The pairs are stored in a jumble as the data is added in no special order.

Attribute-value pairs are more flexible than relational rows and columns because new attributes can be added easily. In Figure 5-1, Fred's hire date was added because the data happened to be available. In a relational database, the table must be modified when a new attribute is added. In this case, a new column would have to be added to the Personnel table. This is a time-consuming operation that usually requires the intervention of a database administrator.

Relational Table   Attribute-Value Pairs

Figure 5-1. Relational data structure is more rigid that attribute-value pairs

When an attribute value database is analyzed, relationships between pairs must be found. In relational databases, relationships are conveniently defined in the schema. This is fast, but the relationships that are usually most interesting in big data sets are the ones that were not known when the data was written. Because new data can be incorporated easily and relationships do not have to be defined before the data is stored, big data uses unstructured data, like attribute-value pairs.

Because big data is huge and unstructured, processing big data requires much more processing than traditional data. Even the largest single computer is seldom adequate for practical big data processing. Many computers must be harnessed to work in parallel to process all that data. The algorithms for parallel processing unstructured data tend to be more challenging than relational data algorithms. This also increases the computing load.

All this computing effort is worth it because big data techniques can discover relationships between entities that would be unknown without it. These discovered relationships are as useful to cybercriminals as they are to marketers.

Phishing, for example, is a perverse form of marketing. Tricking a victim into executing an attachment to an email is not that much different from convincing a consumer to purchase an item they had not thought of buying. Marketers use interests and habits inferred from big data to urge the consumer to buy. Phishers use account information and friends' names from big data to convince a victim that an email attachment is legitimate.

Cybercriminals also use big data-derived information to commit scams like tax fraud. Using big data-collected information, they can construct plausible applications for tax refunds to get money from the IRS. They can also use it to fabricate credible demands for tax penalties from innocent victims. The penalties are delivered to the criminal's account, not the IRS. The same information can be used to construct fake identities for many purposes.

Encryption and Password Cracking

Encryption and password cracking are basically power games. All encryption and cryptographic hashes can be broken, given enough time and computing capacity, but the required time and capacity often renders cracking effectively impossible. An algorithm that uses more computing time to complete the encryption generally requires more time to decrypt. An encryption algorithm that takes too long to encrypt hinders performance, but an encryption that requires more time to decrypt than a hacker can practically devote to cracking the code has defeated the hack.

This is the power contest between hackers and encryptors. A hacker who can muster enough computing power to crack an encryption in a workable time has beaten a previously uncrackable encryption. As available computing power increases, both encryption and encryption breaking get faster. This makes more complex and resistant encryptions practical, but it also makes breaking the encryption more practical for hackers. If you accept that the typical hacker does not have the computing resources available to established enterprises, encryption has the upper hand. But there are several circumstances where that is not the case. Government agencies and military organizations have unlimited resources when breaking an encryption is a priority. Hackers can be exceptionally innovative in putting together specialized devices and using them efficiently.[9] As faster and more efficient processors become available for breaking encryption, the balance of power shifts to the code breakers. As encryptors make use of greater computing capacity to develop stronger encryption, the balance of power shifts back to the encryptors. It is a never-ending battle.[10]

Misuse of Communication

Most people today use their computing devices as communication tools rather than computing tools. Facebook, Twitter, LinkedIn, Reddit, Instagram, and Flickr are all communications tools that use computing to enhance the communications experience. A service like Uber relies on smartphones for communication between passengers and drivers. Much of the utility of business-to-business and business-to-consumer applications is derived from communications abilities.

The Internet itself is the most important computer communications tool. The communications that we have come to value in the 21st century are two-way communication, which has often replaced one-way communication. Print media communicates one way: from authors to readers. Sometimes the author is an individual; in other cases, it is an agency such as a newspaper editorial board. Regardless, the reader has no convenient means of broadcasting to the rest of the audience through the medium. Radio and television also only support communication from stations to audiences, not the reverse.

Internet communications go both ways. Reader comments have become a staple of the Internet. Publications such as *The New York Times* or *The Washington Post* attach comments to almost every news item. In these comments, readers can step up to the newspaper's podium and broadcast their own opinions. For many readers, the comments are as important as the item itself. Two-way communication gives readers a new stake in the popularity of the publications they read because the publication's audience is now the reader's audience when the reader comments.

---

[9]In this example, also cited in Chapter 3, a specialized machine has been built up from standard components for password cracking. Dan Goodin, "25-GPU cluster cracks every standard Windows password in <6 hours," Ars Technica, December 2012. `http://arstechnica.com/security/2012/12/25-gpu-cluster-cracks-every-standard-windows-password-in-6-hours/`. Accessed February 2016.

[10]Computing capacity is not the only factor in the battle, but it is an important one. Clever encryption algorithm and equally clever encryption breaking techniques are also critical, but increasing computing capacity always changes the encryption landscape.

Unlike previous means of mass communication, the Internet is a forum in which everyone can participate. The kind of interaction that was previously limited to relatively small gatherings or meetings now can take place anytime and attract a large audience. In some Internet forums, such as scientific groups, participants exchange carefully crafted and thought out documents and respond with equally careful replies. In other forums, the exchange is shot from the hip and is spontaneous, sometimes raucous. Participants are not constrained to be in the same place at the same time. Although Internet forums are not likely to completely replace humans gathering in the same room, they provide a useful addition to the pool of communication alternatives which did not exist before the Internet became ubiquitous.

Free access has added a dimension to communications that some find problematic. Journalists are typically trained in research and putting forth a coherent news story. They are trained in journalistic ethics of accuracy and fairness. Typical readers are not. Consequently, their contributions cannot be judged on the same basis as those from trained journalists. The typical reader's lack of journalism training is not inherently bad. There is much to be said for opening the doors to new opinions, but at the same time, the nature of communication has changed.

Internet Fraud, Spam, and Trolls

Fraud is the most common computer crime and it also the computer crime that is the least dependent on computers. Romance-related fraud is one of the most common computer frauds, but it certainly did not begin on the Internet. A slick and romantic stranger who convinces an innocent victim to part with money, virtue, or whatever is a stock figure that has been around as long as stories have been told. The scam works face-to-face, through traditional mails, over the phone, and in cyberspace. Computers and the Internet are not needed for successful romance fraud.

Nevertheless, computers and the Internet do offer advantages to all kinds of fraudsters. In email, a chat room, or social media, everyone can control their persona. Young can be old, old can be young and it all only depends on talent at dissembling. In a chat room or on a website, there is no way to judge whether a person is down-and-out or prosperous, well-dressed or wearing dirty sweats. This is obviously helpful in romance scams, but it also helps with other varieties of fraud such as confidence games in which the fraudster convinces the victim to send money for a faked purpose.

Face-to-face scams in the physical world may be easy to execute for a person with the right talents and skills, but evading law enforcement may not be easy at all. Physical addresses, credit card charges, driver's licenses, and many other artifacts can be used to trace fraudsters.

On the Internet, tracing can be difficult. In this realm, the tools of traditional law enforcement do not apply. Physical addresses, for example, can be checked by visiting the location. Email addresses, on the other hand, are easy to obtain without authenticating the identity of the owner and effectively vanish into nowhere when the owner abandons them. Unlike anonymous post office boxes, email addresses that conceal their owners are indistinguishable from email addresses used by genuine persons. False names, fake photographs, and fictional biographies are easily attached to made-up personas.

The unfortunate result is that the characteristics of the Internet and computing make fraud easier to execute and harder to apprehend.

Spamming and trolls are other examples of computing and the Internet facilitating activities that are not dependent on either computing or the Internet.

Spam is a simple extension of direct mail advertising. Sending out spam is cheap. Direct mail advertising is also cheap, but not nearly as cheap as spamming. Unlike direct mail advertising, sending out a million emails is not much more expensive than sending out a hundred. If only a tenth of a percent of a million emails respond, that's a thousand hits, which can be a respectable business proposition. Shady operations prefer the economics of spam to direct mail. If the shady operation's spam happens to be fraudulent, as they often are, tracing and prosecuting an off-shore spammer can be difficult or impossible.

Trolls are a pain to everyone. There is nothing new about annoying naysayers who show up at all sorts of meetings to argue with anyone and all. They don't seem to care if their arguments have truth, value, or even make sense. They feel free to accuse anyone of anything. Like romance fraudsters, they appear as stock characters in both history and literature. However, there is often no agreement on who is a troll and who is a bold speaker of the truth. Punishing one person's troll is often punishing someone else's hero.

The openness and two-way communication fostered by the Internet provides opportunities for trolls. Forums can be poisoned by trolls who single out participants for attack or generally attack everyone in the discussion. The disgruntled and malicious trolls are protected by forum rules designed to protect reasonable members of the forum. Sometimes, moderators can eject the troll, but that usually only happens when the forum agrees that the troll should go. Consensus is not always possible, and the troll must be tolerated as a cost of an open forum.

The Darknet

The *darknet* is a collection of networks of websites that are not visible without special software or hardware. The darknet is dark because it is unseen and hard to detect, not because it is inherently bad. There are legitimate purposes for invisible networks. Journalists protect their informants by communicating over dark networks. Whistleblowers avoid scrutiny by the employers over dark networks. Diplomats and government officials communicate secretly over invisible networks. The victims of stalkers use darknets to avoid being spied upon. Ordinary people who want privacy while surfing the Web also use the darknet. The darknet was developed for legitimate privacy, not criminal purposes.

But there are less legitimate uses. Darknet sites offer anonymity and reduce the traceability of their members. These qualities protect criminals as well as legitimate users. There are darknet sites that specialize in protecting their members in pursuit of illegal trade and other crimes. These criminal darknet sites allow or encourage trade in illegal drugs, money laundering, weapons, stolen or forged credentials, sex trafficking, or anything banned from legal commerce. There are unsubstantiated but credible rumors of murder for hire on the darknet.[11]

Access to Darknet Sites

The most important darknet protocol is *onion routing*. The network that uses onion routing is called the Onion Router or, most commonly, Tor. Like the Internet, Tor was developed by the United States military and is still supported by the United States government.[12] The relationship between Tor and the U. S. intelligence organizations is complex. Various agencies have been active in both developing Tor security and breaking it. Paradoxically, Tor is a tool for both criminals and law enforcement.

Regular Internet communications use packets of information that have both a source and a target address. When a message is sent, the network routing equipment reads the target address and passes the packet on to the target computer. The receiving computer reads the source address and replies. When packets are encrypted, the payload, not the addressing, is encrypted. Consequently, both the source and the target address are available to network sniffers, tools that can read packets as they traverse the network. Tor uses a more elaborate routing scheme that also encrypts addresses. The packets

---

[11]"The disturbing world of the Deep Web, where contract killers and drug dealers ply their trade on the internet" Daily Mail, October 11, 2013. www.dailymail.co.uk/news/article-2454735/The-disturbing-world-Deep-Web-contract-killers-drug-dealers-ply-trade-internet.html#. Accessed March 2014. This article describes several sites that appear to be murder for hire. However, there have not been any murders attributed to a darknet site. The lack of verified murders may show that the sites are effective or that the idea is a hoax.

[12]Yasha Levine, "Almost Everyone Involved in Developing Tor was (or is) Funded by the US Government," Pando, July 16, 2014. https://pando.com/2014/07/16/tor-spooks/. Accessed April, 2014.

hop between multiple intermediate Tor routers, which are run by volunteers. These volunteers include government agencies, businesses, non-profit organizations, and individuals. Combining encryption with complex and variable routes, Tor is is much more difficult to trace than conventional routing and has therefore become the foundation of the darknet.[13]

Criminal Darknet Sites

Criminal darknet sites are almost always for members only. The site administrators vet account applications carefully and require endorsements from existing members. Some require evidence of past crimes before granting membership. The admission procedures are intended to keep out law enforcement. They are also to enforce "honor among thieves." Even a criminal trading exchange must have reliable trading rules, and most sites police their rules.

Although admission policies are important for maintaining the darknet, illegal commerce could not exist without protocols like Tor that foster anonymity and make messages difficult to trace and invisible to the ordinary Internet, even though these networks use the same communications infrastructure as the ordinary Internet.

Estimates of the number of sites on the darknet vary. It is probably considerably less than a million and likely more than 100,000. These sites for illegal trade are crucial to the cybercrime ecosystem. Forty million credit cards (the take from the Target heist) cannot be effectively exploited by a small group of hackers. *Carding*, turning stolen payment card information into cash, requires feet on the street making fraudulent payment card purchases and fencing the loot. Carding requires skill at face-to-face deception and the logistics of disposal of stolen goods, not technical hacking skills. Without convenient darknet intermediaries managing the division of labor between technical and street criminals, hacking would be far less lucrative.

The trade on these criminal sites parallels the development of online commerce by firms such as eBay and Amazon. Online commerce has proven to be far reaching and effective. Drug sellers or dealers in any kind of stolen or illegal goods and services reap the same advantages. Anonymity of transactions, including payments using crypto-currencies such a bitcoin, are added attractions.

The criminal sites do more to facilitate cybercrime. They also act as an exchange for technical information useful to other hackers, Sometimes the information is freely published. In other cases, the information is sold; often

---

[13]The Tor website describes a collection of applications and tools for working with Tor. www.torproject.org/index.html.en. Accessed April 2016.

this information is a description of an exploitable weakness in an operating system or application. These exchanges also sell prepackaged code that less-skilled or unskilled hackers use to launch attacks.

These sites are usually developed and maintained by technically oriented hackers, but the participants include less-technical criminals trafficking in illegal goods and services such as stolen art, extreme pornography, illegal or restricted drugs, and weapons. If it is illegal, it is probably sold somewhere on the darknet.

Law enforcement, lead in the U.S. by the FBI, have been working to take these criminal sites down. In 2008, a large site was taken down through the efforts of an undercover agent who became an administrator of the site. The FBI estimated that the site, Dark Market, had approximately 2,500 registered users. Fifty-six arrests were made in the takedown. The FBI estimated that 70 million dollars in potential losses were prevented.[14]

In October of 2013, The Silk Road site was taken down and the operator, the so-called Dread Pirate Roberts, was arrested. Per the prosecutors, Silk Road had taken in 214 million dollars in sales and 13 million in commissions when it was shut down. Silk Road was an anonymous bitcoin based operation. In February 2015, Dread Pirate Roberts was found guilty of charges including drug trafficking, money laundering, and computer crimes.[15] He was later sentenced to life in prison.[16]

Relatively recently, the Darkode site was taken down by a multi-agency investigation team with partners in 20 countries. Darkode has been called the most dangerous site on the Internet, perhaps because it was an active forum for exchanging hacking methods. Unfortunately, the site appears to have regenerated itself shortly after being shut down.[17]

---

[14]Federal Bureau of Investigation, "'Dark Market' Takedown," October 20, 2008. www.fbi.gov/news/stories/2008/october/darkmarket_102008. Accessed April 2016.

[15]Nate Andersen, Cyrus Farivar, "How the feds took down the Dread Pirate Roberts," Ars Technica, October 2, 2013. http://arstechnica.com/tech-policy/2013/10/how-the-feds-took-down-the-dread-pirate-roberts/. Accessed April 2016.

[16]Benjamin Weiser, "Ross Ulbricht, Creator of Silk Road Website, Is Sentenced to Life in Prison," New York Times, May 29, 2015. www.nytimes.com/2015/05/30/nyregion/ross-ulbricht-creator-of-silk-road-website-is-sentenced-to-life-in-prison.html?_r=0. Accessed April 2016.

[17]Alastair Stevenson, "It only took 2 weeks for the world's most dangerous hacking forum to get back online after the FBI shut it down," Business Insider, July 28, 2015. www.businessinsider.com/darkode-admin-returns-with-new-and-improved-hacking-site-2015-7. Accessed April 2015.

Silk Road and Darkode illustrate two issues that complicate dealing with criminals on the darknet. Dread Pirate Roberts was apparently convinced that he was doing a service to humanity by providing the freedom to buy and sell anything that people wanted to trade in. When he was arrested, and during his trial and sentencing, his supporters declared that he had done nothing wrong and that taking down Silk Road was a violation of rights even though it supported traffic in dangerous and damaging substances. You may agree or disagree with that position, but it is important to notice that sites like Silk Road have support from idealists as well as criminals.

Darkode illustrates another issue. These criminal sites can be a whack-a-mole game. Knock one down and it pops up somewhere else. The technology for these sites is not dependent on a specific set of physical hardware or location. A sophisticated criminal site uses something like an enterprise failover system. In a well-prepared enterprise IT department, a disaster will trigger a failover system, which is a combination of software, hardware, and human intervention that establishes a replica of the system in a safe location. After the alternate system is up and running, the continuation of a business following a successful failover is still dependent on the people who provide and consume the products the system. For instance, a business badly damaged by a catastrophe such as a fire or flood may never recover even though the IT system was reproduced perfectly because employees, customers, and suppliers may not be able to recover.

Law enforcement can extinguish a criminal enterprise permanently by neutralizing enough of the operators and customers to break the criminal community even though the site reappears. This may be the case with Darkode. Although it has resurfaced, its organization and clientele is much weaker than before and may be on the way to oblivion.[18]

Manipulation of Markets

When prices in a public commodities or securities exchange are artificially lowered or raised, it is called market manipulation. Using computers to manipulate markets involves taking advantage of both computing power and high-speed networks. Market manipulators rely on communications that are fast enough to keep them ahead of the humans in the market. A lead of a few milliseconds is sufficient to gain the edge.

---

[18]Loucif Kharouni, "Darkode is down again, don't call a Sp3cial1st!" Damballa, July 29, 2015. www.damballa.com/darkode-reloaded/. Accessed April 2015.

Pump and Dump

One way to manipulate a market is to surreptitiously acquire a large block of cheap stock, then broadcast rumors that push up the stock's low price, and then sell the overvalued stock back on the exchange at the artificially increased prices. This scenario is called *pump-and-dump*.

A similar scenario occurs when a seller sells shares at a market price and then promises to deliver the shares at a future date. If the market price goes down, the seller profits by delivering shares purchased at the dropped price. This is *short selling*, a legitimate practice that becomes manipulation when the seller acts to force the price down through rumors or other illicit means. This scenario is called *short-and-distort*.

Pump-and-dump and short-and-distort are the patterns for many market manipulation schemes and Internet-based communications are helpful in all of them.

Spam email is an efficient method for spreading rumors and misinformation. Hackers use the same methods as they use for phishing expeditions. Big data analysis and stolen email addresses identify vulnerable targets, and botnets send out barrages of spam in staggering quantities.

Pump-and-dump stock or commodity scams have advantages over other spam attacks. Unlike phishing, the source of the misinformation is untraceable because there is no direct link between the victim and the scam. The victim sells or buys on a public exchange rather than transacting with the source of the scam. There need be no contact between the manipulators and their victims in a stock scam. If the manipulators can avoid being traced as the source of the spam, which is relatively easy, investigators are hard-pressed even to connect the manipulators to the misinformation.

High Frequency Trading

Another form of market manipulation is tied to high frequency trading. A computer can execute transactions much faster than humans. In the time it takes a human to buy or sell a block of shares, a computer can execute thousands of transactions.

Algorithms bridge this speed gap. A simple algorithm might direct the computer to purchase a block of stock whenever the price drops below a threshold, and then sell when the stock price exceeds another threshold. Operating on a powerful computer, an algorithm can execute thousands of transactions while a human sits at a console adjusting thresholds and transaction speeds of the algorithm without being involved in any specific transaction. In real life, the algorithms are more complicated than this example and consider more complex factors and relationships, like the cash available for trading, the price and direction of similar stocks, and so on, but it remains a powerful machine controlled by a human master.

Like most things cyber, high frequency trading is neither good nor bad. High frequency trades can make investing cheaper by reducing the expensive human element on the trading floor and it can reduce the spread between asking prices and offers to buy. This shifts the influences from traders on the market floor to investors on the exchange. Some economists believe that high frequency trading reduces market volatility by trading against outlying highs and lows and forcing them back to the mean.[19] However, some believe that high frequency trading has caused sudden wild variations in share prices, such as the Flash Crash of 2010 when prices dropped 10% in a few minutes, then rapidly rebounded. Immediate assessments tended to blame the crash on high frequency trading.[20] However, later evaluations do not assign as much responsibility to high frequency trading.[21]

High frequency traders can intentionally manipulate markets for gain. In 2014, a high frequency trading firm was fined one million dollars for manipulating shares on the NASDAQ exchange. The firm placed storms of high speed trades in the last two minutes of the trading day, manipulating closing prices, and taking advantage of special conditions as markets close to execute favorable trades.[22]

---

[19]See Antonya Allen, "High Frequency Trading Cuts Volatility: Professor," CNBC, August 31, 2011. www.cnbc.com/id/44337362. Accessed April 2014. Not everyone agrees that high frequency trading is positive in every circumstance. For a more nuanced and somewhat more difficult to follow report, see Marvin Wee, "Market volatility is here to stay, but high-frequency trading not all bad," The Conversation, September 15, 2015. http://theconversation.com/market-volatility-is-here-to-stay-but-high-frequency-trading-not-all-bad-46615. Accessed April 2015.

[20]The Economist Online, "What caused the flash crash? One big, bad trade," The Economist, October 1, 2010.

[21]Andrei Kirilenko, Albert S. Kyle, Mehrdad Samadi, Tugkan Tuzun, "The Flash Crash: The Impact of High Frequency Trading on an Electronic Market," Commodity Futures Trading Commission, May 5, 2014. www.cftc.gov/idc/groups/public/@economicanalysis/documents/file/oce_flashcrash0314.pdf. Accessed April 2014. This paper does not blame high frequency trading for the initiation of 2010 event, but it does say that it exacerbated the event.

A similar event occurred in the US Treasury market. A report on this event does not assign blame to high frequency trading, but does recommend further attention to the markets. U.S. Department of the Treasury, Board of Governors of the Federal Reserve System, Federal Reserve Bank of New York, U.S. Securities and Exchange Commission, U.S. Commodity Futures Trading Commission, "Joint Staff Report: The U.S. Treasury Market on October 15, 2014" July 13, 2015. www.treasury.gov/press-center/press-releases/Documents/Joint_Staff_Report_Treasury_10-15-2015.pdf. Accessed April 2016.

[22]U.S. Securities and Exchange Commission, "SEC Charges New York-Based High Frequency Trading Firm With Fraudulent Trading to Manipulate Closing Prices," Press Release, October 16, 2014. www.sec.gov/News/PressRelease/Detail/PressRelease/1370543184457#.VEApEfnF_pU. Accessed April 2016.

The Dilemma

Computers and computer communications have proved to be both a blessing and a curse. Many of the same features enable both legitimate and illegitimate activities. The catalog of misuses is long, and policing computing and computer communications challenges law enforcement. Much of the challenge stems from the dual nature of the technology that is misused. If, for example, high frequency securities trading was an unmitigated swindle, prohibiting it and enforcing the prohibition would be relatively easy. However, in many cases, the experts can't decide if a high frequency trading practice helps or hinders trading. This makes formulating a reasonable computerized trading policy difficult. Without policy, policing is haphazard, to say the least. The same applies to the darknet and Tor. They are used both legitimately and illegitimately. Privacy and encryption present a similar augment. We want it both ways: unbreakable privacy but not for the criminals whose communications we want to see.

This is the dilemma of the misuse of computing and computerized communication: the same technology has both good and bad uses. And the extent of the good and the bad are limited only by the ingenuity and industry of their proponents.

Cloud Threats

Clouds Are Good, But Not All Good

Clouds are a long way from the personal computer that appeared in the mid-1980s and took over the industry. Home personal computers were thought of as private, just another standalone appliance like a vacuum cleaner or an electric coffee pot. A personal computer was a personal possession. Their owners controlled all access. Owners bought software and installed it on their computer in the same way they bought a new dishwasher and installed it in their kitchen. Both the software and the dishwasher was theirs and theirs alone. Anyone who wanted to use either the software or the dishwasher had to enter the owner's home with the owner's permission. An intrusion into a private personal computer was housebreaking or trespassing, an occasion for the classic work that police have performed for many decades.

Networks, especially the Internet, connect home computers to the outside world. Laptops, smartphones, and tablets unleash computer users from their desktop machines and free them to ramble outside the home.

Now, via networks, individual computers of all kinds use resources that are in physically distant clouds. This arrangement offers important benefits. Although our devices are much more powerful than the devices of a decade or two ago, our expectations from our devices far exceeds their capacity.

For example, laptops today often have multi-terabyte disc drives. Ten years ago, 500 megabytes were considered adequate for a laptop. Like many others a decade ago, I stored a dictionary on my laptop. I no longer do that. Instead, I use the Internet to access a much larger and continuously updated dictionary that is stored in a cloud. Although I have a hard drive on my laptop that is

© Marvin Waschke 2017
M. Waschke, *Personal Cybersecurity*, DOI 10.1007/978-1-4842-2430-4_6

orders of magnitude larger than the drives of 10 years ago, the online diction-ary I access is larger and more frequently updated than anything I could host locally. Wireless Internet connections are everywhere and so convenient, the requirement for an Internet connection is not a bother.[1]

It's the same for most everyone. You could not even consider storing on your private hard drive the data that Google scans or Wikipedia contains. We now use smartphones, tablets, and laptops in addition to desk top PCs, and they are all connect to clouds, each of which supplies services that we could not duplicate with our own local resources.

Clouds have increased the usefulness and entertainment value of our personal devices, but not without a cost. There are now a host of security threats and concerns that are not easily addressed with old-fashioned police work.

What Is the Cloud?

Clouds are all over the place. Often, everything seems to be on its way into the cloud. As much as the term is used, people frequently have a misconcep-tion of what a cloud is. Perhaps surprisingly, a cloud is both a business and a technical concept, and both aspects of the cloud have a direct bearing on individual cloud security.

Cloud Business

Clouds are a business arrangement between a consumer and a provider. The provider agrees to provide certain computing services to the consumer and, unless the service happens to be free, the consumer agrees to pay the provider at some agreed upon rate. The service may offer the use of simulated com-puters and other computing resources in remote data centers, or the service may be an application like an accounting program that runs on the provider's servers, or the provider could offer storage services on their remote storage devices. In all cases, the provider supplies the equipment for generating and delivering the service and maintains the service. In most cases, the consumers pay for the services in proportion to what they consume.

For instance, a music service provider stores recorded music on disk drives and other devices in their system and makes sure the music is available to their consumers. The consumer pays for the service, not the equipment for producing the service. The service is different from buying a CD or DVD at a music store. After a customer buys a CD, the customer owns the CD that stores the recording of the music. If the CD is damaged, the customer has to

---

[1]Wireless connections offer their own security issues, but that is a discussion for another section.

buy another CD. Subscribing to a music service, the consumers have rights to the music they have subscribed to, but not the physical devices that store the music. The subscribers do not care what happens to the equipment that stores the music they listen to. Equipment issues are the provider's problem.

This business arrangement offers benefits to the consumer. In the case of a music service, they probably have access to more music at lower cost than they did when purchasing their own CDs and DVDs. Media storage no longer takes up space in their homes, they no longer have to box up heavy media and lug them around when they move, and they don't have to worry about damaging their CDs or insuring them against accidents. However, subscribers usually can't sell their music to someone else when they get tired of it like they can sell a CD.

The business behind these marvelous services can be confusing or worse. The agreement between a cloud service provider and consumer is complex compared to an ordinary purchase. Buying and selling has been going on for a long, long time and the rules have been worked out and embodied in customs we all know. The common law and statutes of buying and selling are thoroughly understood by the legal system. Most people have an intuitive idea of the rights and responsibilities of buying and selling.

Cloud service consumer-provider relationships are not as clear. The exchange is abstract. There is nothing like a CD to see or touch. Most people do not have a clear notion of what it means to have rights to the music, but not physical media. For example, they do not have an immediate understanding what happens when their music provider goes out of business. Do they have any rights to the music they once had? Or do their rights terminate with the departure of the provider?

Commonplace rules for buying and selling physical objects are often unclear when applied to abstract rights. Rather than rely on bewildering legal arguments to sort out rights and obligations, cloud providers and consumers usually agree on explicit agreements that spell out the rights and obligations. These are service contracts. These contracts spell out the rights and obligations of the provider and consumer. They often contain provisions that specify the guaranteed performance and reliability of the service, and incentives and penalties to encourage compliance. Most importantly, the agreement will spell out the limits on the liability of both the consumer and provider. For example, the agreement may stipulate that the provider is not liable for performance degradation due to network issues. These agreements are documented in a service contract that is binding on both parties.

Service contracts are often sources of contention. When a large enterprise enters into a contract with a cloud provider, they have some leverage and the possibility of negotiating a mutually acceptable agreement. Individual consumers and smaller businesses do not have leverage and the provider calls the shots and writes a *click-through contract* that the consumer must agree to before they can access the service. Consumers can easily agree to the contract without reading it. Thus, consumers often do not fully understand what they have signed up for and are later surprised that the service was not what they thought, to the point that they feel they have been treated unfairly.

Cloud Technology

Technically, "the cloud" does not exist. There are many clouds. When someone says "the cloud" they either mean the collection of all clouds, or, more likely, the cloud they happen to be using at the moment. A cloud is a pool of computing and storage resources. These resources are linked together to run *virtual machines* for parceling out resources to consumers. A virtual machine is a software program that imitates a physical computer in such a way that other software can be run on this software imitation computer as if it were a real physical computer. Virtual machines are created and taken down as needed by cloud consumers. See Figure 6-1. This has proven to be a flexible and efficient way to support the business side of the cloud concept.

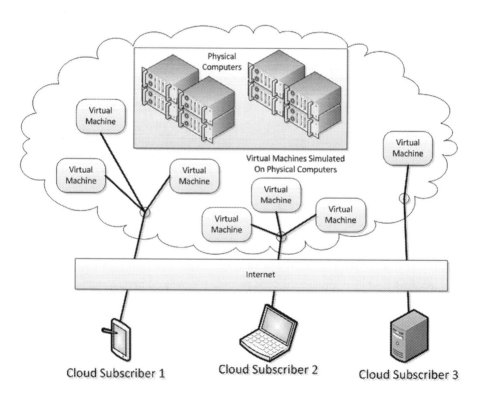

Figure 6-1. Cloud subscribers connect to private virtual machines that run on physical computers

Virtual machines break the binding between software and hardware. From a datacenter that pools together large numbers of computers, a cloud provider can offer to create as many virtual computers with as much capacity as a consumer wants and the consumer can increase or decrease the capacity when they want, limited only by the total physical capacity of the entire datacenter. The provider can offer virtual computers to many different consumers simultaneously.

When an underlying physical computer breaks down, the virtual computers it supported are moved, almost always automatically, to other physical computers. The cloud datacenter is in continual flux with virtual computers starting, stopping, and moving from physical computer to physical computer, responding to consumer requests and changes in the computing environment. Cloud technology has advanced to the point that a single public cloud may be implemented in several geographically dispersed datacenters. Often data is copied to each datacenter. If a power outage disables one datacenter, the load is transferred to datacenters in other regions unaffected by the outage. Constantly adjusting to circumstances, a cloud datacenter can be more reliable and safer than a traditional system.

These computers are all virtual, but to the consumer, they are almost indistinguishable from a physical computer. Ordinarily, software does not need to be rewritten to run on a cloud, but it is often changed to optimize performance on a cloud. The consumer usually pays in proportion to the number, size, and running time of the virtual machines they use. The consumer can tailor their capacity to their needs to an extent that is impossible with physical machines they purchase or lease. The ability to adjust capacity and costs has led many businesses to replace all or part of their computing hardware with off-site public cloud services that are offered by providers like Microsoft and Amazon Web Services. Personal consumers usually are not aware of the virtual machines behind the services they use, but they are there.

Clouds are implemented in many ways. Some clouds are private, owned and used by a single enterprise that manages their IT equipment as if it were deployed on an external provider cloud. Other clouds are public, offering cloud services to all comers. There are also variations in which clouds are shared among several users, private clouds may offer some access to external entities, and so on.

Providing raw computing power rather than a service implemented on a cloud is called infrastructure as a service (IaaS). IaaS replaces a computer or a group of computers and storage resources with similar devices running in a cloud. Most individuals are not exposed to this type of cloud service. Instead, another party implements a service on a cloud and then offers services publicly.

Virtualized cloud technology enables many companies to offer services, like Dropbox, Google Docs, or Intuit QuickBooks Online, that run in remote cloud datacenters and use remote storage rather than the consumer's physical computer and disk storage. Cloud applications are usually much more powerful than an individual's desktop, laptop, tablet, or smartphone could support although they may be hindered by a draggy network. These cloud-based applications are maintained by the provider, not the consumer. This is another reason cloud-based applications are attractive.

Cloud Exposures

Although the cloud confers many benefits, it is also a relatively new paradigm for computing. This paradigm has security issues that conventional computing does not have. Some of these issues have greater implications for business than individuals, but many apply to individuals as well. Some of these differences stem from the business aspect of clouds; others are technical.

A service running on virtual machines in a cloud has most of the security vulnerabilities of an application running locally on an individual machine. However, instead of a non-technical home user, the security of an application running in a provider's well-run datacenter is the responsibility of a security professional and the application runs on well-maintained hardware placed in an optimum environment in a highly secure datacenter. Security breaches are still possible, but they are less likely than a breach to a casually maintained application running on an unsecured laptop left on a table at Starbucks.

Services executing in a cloud datacenter are subject to another kind of issue that is not a security breach. Mistakes made by datacenter operators can lead to interruptions or degradations in service. For example, the operators may fumble maintenance on the system, which results in a slowdown or complete interruption. Although a non-technical user is more likely than a trained professional to cause maintenance issues, expectations for the professional are higher. Users can take cold comfort in blaming themselves for the problems they cause for themselves, but that may be more satisfactory than a mysterious interruption that was not supposed to happen.[2]

A few years ago, the biggest obstacle to cloud adoption among government agencies and large enterprises, particularly in the financial industries, was security. These questions have not gone away, but many have been answered. Both businesses and government are used to security risks and regularly

---

[2]For example, a maintenance mistake at Amazon Web Services caused a significant loss of service for Netflix in 2012. Steven Musil, "Amazon apologizes for Netflix's Christmas Eve streaming outage," CNET, December 31. www.cnet.com/news/amazon-apologizes-for-netflixs-christmas-eve-streaming-outage/. Accessed April 2014.

accept risk, but they avoid what they call *unmanaged risk*. Risk is deemed to be managed when the business has a clear estimate of the probability and magnitude of a loss and have taken steps to mitigate the loss. Early cloud implementations were often considered to be unmanaged risks and therefore avoided. Decisions on the manageability of business risks are usually made by auditors. Corporate and government auditors have subsequently developed methods for assessing and mitigating the risks in cloud deployments. These have included auditing standards and security certification for cloud providers. Although some uncertainty lingers, the hesitancy has diminished substantially. Amazon Web Services, for example, offers a cloud implementations tailored to government risk requirements.[3]

Cloud Attack Surfaces

The attack surface of a service is the set of points where the service is vulnerable to attack. All other things being equal, a service with a small attack surface is more secure than a service with a larger attack surface. A traditional application is vulnerable to attack on the computer where it runs. There are a limited number of points where an intruder can gain access to the system, such as the Ethernet adapter, the Bluetooth radio, the wireless radio, the keyboard, etc. These vulnerable points can each be identified, watched for intrusions, and protected.

Services implemented on clouds have larger attack surfaces than traditional applications that run on the user's device. Traditional applications are contained; an invader must gain access to the user's device to affect the application. Personal devices certainly have considerable attack surfaces that have often been penetrated, but the tools for fending off attackers, such as antivirus tools and frequent system updates, are well known and generally used.

Cloud attack surfaces include the interfaces that are used for managing and interacting with cloud application, the network connection to the consumer, and the internal operations of the provider, not to mention the vulnerabilities of the consumer's personal devices. Some of these attack surfaces are proprietary implementations, others are standard, but they are not as well known and subject to wide public scrutiny as personal device interfaces.

Cloud services are supported by trained and experienced professionals who are much better prepared to protect their systems than a typical individual user. Nevertheless, their attack surface is larger and less well known, which means more opportunities for criminals to develop new threats.

---

[3]See AWS GovCloud (US). https://aws.amazon.com/govcloud-us/. Accessed November 2016.

Hypervisor Vulnerability

Virtualization implementations have an important vulnerability that could seriously affect cloud implementations. This potential weakness is important because with the current state of technology, virtualization is unavoidable. Cloud implementations depend on virtualization to deliver services that are dynamically tailored to the varying needs of their consumers. There is really no alternative to virtualization available or on the horizon today. However, virtualization implementations are vulnerable to a chilling exploitation.

In a cloud, virtual machines are popping up and down and transferring from one physical machine to another all the time. These virtual machines are controlled by a process, often called the *hypervisor*. The job of the hypervisor is to supervise the frenzy of activity in a virtualized environment. The hypervisor starts each virtual machine and then supervises it from start-up to shut down. The hypervisor maintains contact with each virtual machine and maintains basic control. Communication is always supposed to be from the hypervisor to the virtual machine, never the reverse.

Virtual machines can communicate via a network, actually a virtual network that can connect with a physical network, just like physical computers. This network communication is vulnerable to attack in the same way that any network connection is vulnerable. Data must be protected and unauthorized use of the network must be prevented. The protective measures such as firewalls, encryption, and other defenses are effective in protecting virtual systems.

However, virtual machines have an additional vulnerability: communication through the hypervisor. If the hypervisor has a defect that allows virtual machines to access the hypervisor, one virtual machine could affect another virtual machine through the hypervisor rather than the known and controlled network connection.

This vulnerability is especially insidious. An attacker who gains access to one virtual machine and exploits a hypervisor vulnerability could gain access to many other virtual machines, including those owned by other consumers. A bad-guy subscriber, or an innocent subscriber with weak security, could become a platform for invading all the subscribers to a compromised cloud. If the cloud were from one of the large cloud providers, the results could be disastrous. See Figure 6-2.

Network Exposure

A cloud-based service depends on the provider's equipment and implementation, the connecting network, and the end user's computing device. Dependency on three parties instead just the end user increases the attack surface and makes identification of the source of vulnerabilities more difficult. In addition, pointing out which party is responsible for each vulnerability can be confusing.

Network Vulnerability

Unlike traditional applications that use only the resources on the user's computer, cloud services are remote and rely upon transmission over a network, usually the Internet, to connect the consumer to the cloud implementation of the service. This presents a new set of security issues and vulnerabilities.

The provider is responsible for what happens in the cloud; the consumer is responsible for what happens on their device. The responsibility for the successful transmission of data depends on the network providers. A failure at the provider, the network, or the user's own software and hardware can cause the service to malfunction. In addition, data is sometimes transferred from network operator to network operator on its route between consumer and provider, adding further complications.

The consequences of this distribution of responsibility appear when an individual customer of a cloud service, say a music service, calls the provider's customer service to say that their music is coming in bursts with gaps of silence. The service rep checks the situation out and says "Everything is fine here, call your ISP." The poor user barely knows what an ISP is (an Internet Service Provider) and when they call their ISP, they don't know how to articulate their problem in a way that a network engineer can understand and the best the user gets in reply an unsatisfying suggestion to wait and try again later.

There may have been an issue like a denial of service attack or a host of other things, such as a satellite transmission garbled by solar emissions, a overloaded router somewhere in the Internet, a broken connection that had to circumvented. The possibilities are endless, but the point is that finding the source of the disturbance involves many participants. If the cause is hacking somewhere in the system, finding and stopping the hacker may be difficult.

Denial of Service Attacks

All cloud services are subject to denial of service attacks, perhaps the most serious network vulnerability. These attacks are directed at the service provider, but affect the consumers of the service. I've talked about denial of service in other chapters. A denial of service attack is a flood of messages directed at a provider site that is intended to overwhelm the provider, and block service to the provider's legitimate consumers.

As a consumer, there is little you can do to prevent denial of service attacks, other than avoid being an unknowing contributor to attacks by allowing your devices to become bots used to launch attacks. Consumers experience a denial of service attack as a slowdown or interruption in service. Sometimes, the service does not respond when brought up in a browser, or the pages populate slowly, or jerkily. Although these are symptoms of denial of service attacks, they can be caused by other issues. Often, services have service sites that post messages to explain what is going on. For instance, Amazon Web Services provides their Service Health Dashboard[5], which offers up-to-the-minute status information. The AWS dashboard is the place to check if any AWS service were undergoing a denial of service attack. Other cloud services provide similar dashboards.

During an attack, the provider is inundated with bogus requests and messages that take away resources from responding to legitimate transactions. Denial of service attacks, especially those that are coordinated attacks from many sources, called distributed denial of service attacks, are an issue that providers have taken seriously. Some denial of service attacks can now be squelched effectively, but hackers are innovative and attacks still occur. Hackers continually come up with new methods. The latest ploy is to use devices in the Internet of Things as bots. Like so many things in security, the latest innovative attacks succeed until the providers find an effective defense.

The good news is that denial of service is disruptive but seldom destructive. The attacks are launched for harassment or coercion rather than theft. For consumers, a provider under denial of service attack may be unreachable, or the service provided is slow and erratic, but the damage is limited to the unavailability of the service.

Man-in-the-Middle Attacks

Another network based cloud attack is the man-in-the-middle attack. This type of attack affects cloud consumers directly. The attack interferes with the connection between the consumer and the cloud provider. A man-in-the-middle attacker hijacks the network connection between the consumer and cloud and places himself in the middle so he can manipulate communication between consumer and provider.

Men-in-the-middle have several opportunities for mischief. They can log consumers' data as it travels over the network wire as they forward it on to the provider. These logs are mined by the hacker for prizes such as passwords, payment card data, guarded intellectual property, and the like. The men-in-the-middle can also divert the stream of traffic from the provider to their own

---

[5]http://status.aws.amazon.com/

server and send fake responses to the consumer. This places the man-in-the-middle in a position to do great damage. For example, a man-in-the-middle attack could fake, or spoof, a banking site. The consumer may think that they are dealing with a legitimate bank, but in fact, they are dealing with a criminal hacker who steals credentials, creates bogus accounts, or executes any number of fraudulent schemes.

Man-in-the middle exploits are similar to some phishing expeditions that divert unwary victims to spoofing sites. In a phishing attack, the hacker will try to trick the user into clicking to an address that is a spoof of a legitimate site. Some man-in-the-middle attacks achieve the same goal, but they do it in a more insidious manner. The victim clicks on a legitimate address, but the hacker has rigged the addressing system so that the legitimate address takes the victim to an illegitimate site. A man-in-the-middle attack like this requires greater technical knowledge and is more difficult to pull off, but it can be effective. The phishing style attack can usually be warded off by vigilant inspection of network addresses. No amount of address inspection will help if the address itself has been diverted.

The basic defense against man-in-the-middle attacks is well maintained TLS (or SSL) connections. Personal users should take care that the connections with their services use https rather than http and pay attention when a browser says a certificate is invalid. For a TLS connection to succeed, the target must supply a valid certificate of identity issued by a verifiable certification authority. A hacker attempting to hijack a secure connection often shows up as an invalid certificate. Too often, users will order their browser to ignore the bad certificate, defeating TLS man-in-the-middle defense and leaving encryption of data in transit also vulnerable. However, an invalid certificate does not always signal a man-in-the-middle attack. The invalid certificate flag is also raised when a provider neglects to renew their certificate on time. A check with the provider support site can dispel doubts.

Interruptions

Everyone experiences network interruptions at one time or another. The Internet architecture assumes the network is unreliable and is designed to be resilient to network lapses. For this reason, when an interruption occurs, the network can often heal itself by routing traffic around the interruption; traffic slows, but does not stop. The Internet is surprisingly redundant and resilient, but sites still lose contact with the rest of the Internet. Entire countries are sometimes dependent on a single undersea cable that can be severed by an underwater earthquake or other mishaps such as shark bites.[6] Communities often depend on suspended cables that fall in windstorms. Excavation damage to buried cables can also bring down communities. Network operators continue to improve the reliability of their systems, but network interruptions will probably never be eliminated.

Network interruptions can have important implications for data storage as well as the consumer experience. These implications are discussed below in the "Cloud Data Repository" section.

Service Contracts

When consumers use a cloud, they trust the cloud provider to take proper care of security and other interests that they have entrusted to the provider. The interests delegated to the provider can be data that consumers expect to be kept private and protected from corruption or loss. They also include processes that the consumer expects to behave as promised and perform reliably and well. In a traditional personal computing environment, users of a computing device have complete control. They choose the software products. They can install the latest antivirus software, keep their applications and operating systems patched, even disconnect the Internet when they feel it is needed. They can make sure their laptops, tablets, and smartphones are in safe places. They can put locks on the door to their desktop computer and they have many options for securing their environment.

A cloud computer user can and should take similar precautions, but their cloud applications remain in the hands of their cloud providers. The user has delegated responsibility to the provider, which has benefits. The user's responsibility for updates and maintenance goes to the provider. The provider takes care of a large share of the security of the cloud service and the provider is responsible for deploying adequate hardware to support the application and the day-to-day necessities of keeping the service up and running.

All this is great, but there is a big *if* here. It's great if the provider does their job, and it's a nightmare if the provider slacks off. Delegation of responsibilities like these happens often in business. Contracts are negotiated to ensure each party fully understands their role and expectations for the transaction and see that the expectations set in the contract are legally enforceable.

The multimillion-dollar cloud service contracts signed when a large corporation engages a cloud provider are often the detailed product of lengthy negotiation. The service contracts that individuals agree to when they subscribe to a cloud

---

[6]Really. See YouTube. "Shark Bites Optic Cables Undersea 15.8.2014," August 15, 2014. www.youtube.com/watch?v=XMxkRh7sx84. Accessed April 2016.

service are seldom the product of negotiation. Instead they are click-through agreements that must be accepted in order to access the service. Users accept the agreement or they don't. One size fits all, whether you like it or not. U.S. courts have generally enforced reasonable click-through agreements.[7]

However, reasonability depends on who is doing the reasoning. The provisions in these agreements invariably limit providers' liability and often specify a process for dispute arbitration. Since the consumer has no role in formulating the agreement, it is not surprising that the provisions in these agreements are usually stacked heavily in the provider's favor. A cynic might say that click-through agreements are written by reversing the service contract provisions that are demanded by powerful corporate consumers with the economic muscle to stand up to the provider.

The individual usually is given little protection by a click-through service contract. Typically, the provider will accept no liability for malfunction or interrupted delivery of the service. They also seldom accept responsibility for loss of data stored on the service. Furthermore, the consumer often agrees not to take the provider to court or to participate in class action suits against the provider. Instead, the dispute may be taken to an arbitrator chosen by the provider and the consumer may be required to pay the costs of arbitration.

After lamenting the state of click-through service contracts, I must say that I personally use a number of cloud services and find them quite satisfactory. Individual consumers are better off in some ways than big enterprises with iron-clad service contracts.

Although cloud service providers use their contracts to protect themselves zealously from the dissatisfaction of their users, in another way, the providers are at the mercy of their customers, no matter what their contract says. Their profits and corporate interests depend on the good will of their customers. If an individual has a month-to-month license to use an office service, they can drop the service whenever they please. Dropping a service may cause an individual some inconvenience, but large corporate service consumers often find switching providers to be too expensive to even think about.

Often, enterprises with carefully negotiated contracts slide into dependency on their providers and become stuck with their provider. The provider's services become so deeply embedded in the enterprise business process that switching providers becomes an expense that can threaten executive careers. The cost of retraining for a new service can easily prohibit switching service providers.

---

[7]Wilmer Hale, "Are 'Click Through' Agreements Enforceable?" Publications & News, March 22, 2000. www.wilmerhale.com/pages/publicationsandNewsDetail. aspx?NewsPubId=86850. Accessed April 2016.

Clearly, the enterprises have some advantages in dealing with cloud service providers, but possibly not as much advantage as appears on the surface. By all means, individual users should read click-through agreements before they accept them. Annoyingly, the best products can have the worst agreements. The dismal truth is that the alternative to a one-sided service contract is usually no service.

Without the protection of an equitably negotiated service contract, individual users must rely on the reputation and integrity of the provider. Not all providers are reputable, but most are, and bad reputations are hard to hide on the Internet. A draconian click-through agreement is a sign of an aggressive legal team, not necessarily poor service. One-sided contracts are often over-ridden by the desire to avoid a bad reputation with potential consumers.

Potential cloud service consumers should ask questions. Does the service have satisfied consumers? A service that has been available for a substantial period but has few users is certainly suspect. Look at reviews and user comments. Does the service have known technical deficiencies? These are often reported in blogs and trade publications. Is the service frequently down or slow? Does the provider offer a service health dashboard? Do customers complain about the provider's customer service? Is a stable company behind the service? Services that are acquired or go out of business may abandon their consumers or show a marked decrease in the quality of the service. In fairness, an acquisition or merger can also improve services from a struggling company.

Credential Compromise

Stealing passwords is a basic attack vector that applies to every aspect of computer security, including cloud services. Clouds are vulnerable to stealing passwords in the same way that any account is vulnerable. Phishing, keyboard logging, man-in-the-middle attacks, and peaking over someone's shoulder as they type in a password work just as well with cloud passwords as with anything else; cloud credentials have the same vulnerabilities as smartphone PINs and tablet and laptop passwords.

Cloud service credentials are critical in direct proportion to the importance of the service itself. Locally installed applications are only accessible from the machine on which they are installed; cloud services are available from anywhere on the Internet.

Consequently, cloud services depend more on strong credentials to prevent unauthorized access. These credentials are the keys to important resources and should not be treated trivially. Both individuals and enterprises should take care with their cloud credentials, following the basic rules of password hygiene: long passwords, preferably random or phrases—not individual words, frequently changed, not duplicated, and kept secret. Use multi-factor authentication when available.

Cloud service vendors that offer multiple services often present users with a single account for accessing all their services. This is convenient and saves memorizing a handful of passwords for all these services. However, users must keep in mind that these passwords are of a great value to hackers because they unlock many treasures. Keep these passwords strong and change them often.

Cloud Data Repositories

Cloud data repositories are like personal hard drives that are accessible anywhere the Internet reaches and have larger data storage capacity than that of a personal device such as a smartphone, tablet, laptop, or desktop. A cloud repository is slower than direct storage, especially solid state storage, but is adequate for many purposes. Many people use cloud storage for bulky data such as audio files, photographs, and video. The data is slower to retrieve than data on an internal disk, but much faster than alternatives like carrying around a set of DVDs.

Besides increased data capacity, cloud repositories share data easily. For example, before cloud repositories, a team or group of friends with data that they all want to access could each keep copies of the data and email changes to each other. However, that method is slow and it is hard to keep track of who has what version of the data. If one person misses an email, the whole collection of data can turn into a mess of compounding errors.

Sharing via a cloud can be much easier and efficient. A single copy of the data can be stored in the cloud and each member of the group has access. There is only ever one copy of the data. This is less error prone and avoids the effort of exchanging data. Placing the data in a central repository is also a more efficient use of network bandwidth than transferring data to members who may not use it.

Another related use is for synchronizing data between devices. People who have several devices—a desktop, laptop, tablet, and smartphone—may want to access their data from each of these devices. Storing the data on a cloud repository fills the bill. Each of their devices can access the same data in the cloud. Some data repository services like Dropbox or OneDrive will store copies of the data locally on each of the devices and manage synchronizing them. This can be very convenient when the devices are not always online.

Cloud repositories are also useful because they are remote from personal devices. When data is only stored locally, it is subject to local disasters. A cautious user may store backups from the office at home and from home at the office, but when a hurricane wipes out the whole town, caution did them no good. Typically, cloud repositories store data redundantly in widely separated data centers, providing protection from even regional disasters. Cloud repositories also provide some protection from ransomware attacks that render local data inaccessible with a key which the criminal offers for ransom. Storing files in a cloud data repository can help recover from ransomware attacks, which have become a frequent threat.[8]

Cloud Repository Risks

A reputable cloud provider can store data more securely than an individual. Cloud datacenters can be physically secured and guarded more effectively than most individuals are able to protect their personal devices. In addition, cloud administrative teams are usually better prepared to defend against malicious hackers than most individuals.

Data Loss

Data loss from cloud repositories is possible, but not as likely as many people fear. Cloud providers usually store data redundantly so that more than one storage device has to fail before data is lost. Often, copies of data are stored in geographically remote locations to guard against disasters like fires or floods that take down all storage in a single area.

Temporary Loss of Access

Data repositories are subject to all of the risks that apply to all cloud services, such as denial of service attacks and network interruptions.

Maintenance and System Issues

Maintenance or other system issues can interrupt service. The length and frequency of these interruptions depends on the quality of the provider's internal practices. Enterprises protect themselves from these interruptions with service level agreements in their service contract that call for penalties on the provider when service interruptions exceed a threshold. Individual users ordinarily do not have service level agreements. Fortunately for individuals, when providers strengthen their processes and equipment to avoid service level penalties, service is often improved for all users, not just the enterprises that pay for service level agreements, because most improved practices usually apply to the entire service, not specific accounts. This is because clouds are architected as pools of physical resources that are allocated by the hypervisor to individual virtual machines. Any account may, at any given time, be assigned any available resource from the pool by the hypervisor. If any resource is less

---

[8]Be cautious. Using a cloud data repository will not always help in a ransomware attack. See Chapter 10 for more detail on combatting ransomware.

reliable or the pool is not adequate to meet the demand, the account may not get their contracted level of performance. The practical solution to this is to design the cloud to support all users at a moderate level and expect to absorb some premium customer service level penalties. This, of course, benefits personal accounts that are not likely to have any service level agreements at all.

Denial of Service

When a cloud repository provider is undergoing a denial of service attack, users will see the attack as a degradation of access to their data. Slow or stopped downloads and uploads may halt activity on the user's device when the repository is under attack. The disruption may last a few minutes or a few days, depending on the provider's defenses and the attacker's resources. The good news is that denial of service attacks rarely destroy data. When the attack is over, the user's data will be intact.

Network Interruption

Another issue that arises with cloud data repositories is a break in the network that blocks access to users' data. Network interruptions are technically called network partitions because they partition the network into groups of computers that cannot communicate with other groups. Partitions are unavoidable and frequent enough that they must be anticipated and ways found to maintain reliable network communications even when partitions occur. Partitions are most serious when they interrupt activity that must complete, such as accounting transactions.

Elaborate methods have been developed to deal with network interruption of transactions. These methods aim at insuring that transactions always complete satisfactorily. Some methods assure the user that a transaction is either complete or totally rejected. This form of assurance is considered the gold standard for transaction integrity. However, enforcing this approach is resource intensive and the "make or break" policy halts business during an interruption, which can mean losses for an active online business. Often today, methods guarantee that all transactions will eventually complete correctly when the partition is removed rather than halting transactions until the interruption is over. Using this approach, an order submitted by a customer may not immediately arrive at the vendor, but the system guarantees that it will be delivered and recorded accurately when the interruption is over. Businesses often operate this way because they prefer to stay open for business while the network is misbehaving rather than force their customers to wait and possibly change their mind.

Data handling policies that ensure transactional integrity contribute to the security of cloud-based repositories. These policies give users confidence that their data will arrive at the cloud storage site and be distributed correctly to the cloud providers' redundant sites, and the user will be able to retrieve the data consistently.

Privacy

The primary tool for keeping data private on cloud data repositories is encryption. Unencrypted data in cloud storage is subject to intrusion in several ways. Government authorities may demand access with search warrants, subpoenas, or other forms of legal authorization. The provider's system may be hacked into and data taken. A rogue employee of the cloud provider may access data and expose it. An operations or administrative error in the service may unintentionally expose data. Some form of business disruption—a bankruptcy or hostile takeover, for example—can cause business and operational chaos that exposes data, renders it inaccessible, or destroys it.

Security experts often distinguish between data in transit and data at rest. See Figure 6-3. Data must be secured in both states.

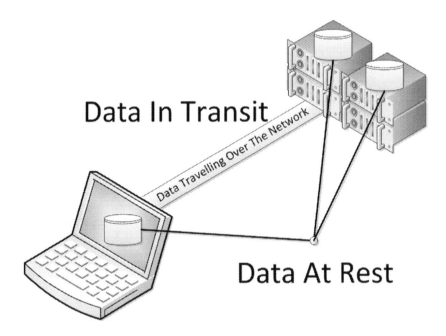

Figure 6-3. To be secure, data must be protected both in transit and at rest

DATA IN TRANSIT AND DATA AT REST

Data in transit and *data at rest* are important concepts when talking about cloud security. Data at rest is data that is stored at least semi-permanently and possibly permanently. Data in transit is data that is being transmitted over a network, often the Internet.

For individuals, data at rest is usually data that has been stored on a disk or solid state storage on a personal device or a storage unit at the data's destination in a cloud. Data in transit is on the wire, on its way between a cloud location and a personal device.

Both data at rest and data in transit must be protected to be secure. Data at rest is usually protected by encrypting the data. The key to decryption has to be accessible on the individual's computer, and may also be accessible to the cloud provider. The encryption can be symmetric, where the provider and consumer share the same key, or asymmetric, where the provider and consumer have different keys.

Protecting data in transit has additional challenges. Data must be encrypted as for data at rest, but there is an additional vulnerability: the encrypted data may be hijacked, sent to the wrong destination, and accessed by the hijackers. Even if the data is encrypted, the hijackers can crack it at their leisure. A widely used protocol verifies the target through cryptographic signatures and encrypts the data being sent. This is called Secure Sockets Layer (SSL) or Transfer Layer Security (TLS). SSL is an older version of the protocol that has been declared insecure and superseded by TLS. SSL is seldom used now, but the name is still often used. When you see https rather than http in a browser address, it is using TLS to protect data in transit.

Keep in mind that no matter how strong an encryption, given time and resources, the encryption can be broken. Eventually, every encryption becomes insecure as the industry evolves. The point of encryption is to make the cost in time and resources to break the encryption prohibitively greater than the value of the encrypted data. Keep in mind that you can reasonably expect that at any moment in time, data encrypted 10 years before is now easily decrypted.

Currently, the Advanced Encryption Standard (AES) is the most generally accepted algorithm for secure encryption. It was developed by the United States government and published by the National Institute of Standards (NIST) in 2007.[9] AES is used by the United States government to encrypt classified documents. Although it has critics, it is generally accepted as the strong encryption standard. There are encryptions other than AES, but AES is best known and a safe choice.

The standard supports keys that can be 128, 192, or 256 bits long. These are referred to as AES 128, AES 192, and AES 256. The U.S. federal government requires AES 256, but most experts feel AES 128 is now practically as secure as AES 256.

---

[9]National Institute of Standards and Technology, " Announcing the Advanced Encryption Standard (AES)," Federal Information Processing Standards Publication 197, November 26, 2001. http://csrc.nist.gov/publications/fips/fips197/fips-197.pdf. Accessed May 2016.

The number of possible 128 bit keys is a 39-digit decimal number, the number of possible 256 bit keys is a 78-digit decimal number. Theoretically, AES 256 is much, much stronger that AES 128. However, the practical difference in strength is negligible because cracking AES 128 with the best current technology would take more than 13.7 billion years, the age of the universe. AES 256 would take much longer, but who cares?[10]

Most, if not all, cloud data services encrypt. Anyone with any concern whatsoever for data privacy should choose a service with encryption. Data should be encrypted both at rest and in transit. Most cloud storage products encrypt data resting in the cloud and use TLS to protect data in transit from snooping and man-in-middle attacks.

Where encryption keys are stored is also important. Some cloud repository providers keep the encryption keys on their system. This is convenient because they manage and protect the keys for you. It's sort of like the old hotel system where you left your room key at the front desk, which was convenient but the desk clerk could give your key to the wrong person. Similarly, a cloud repository provider may be compelled to give the key to someone you may not authorize, such as a government agent, to view your data. If the consumer holds the only key, the provider is unable to reveal your data under any circumstances, including under a subpoena or warrant. On the other hand, a key managed by the provider will probably be well-chosen and will not be lost or forgotten.

Probably the most significant weakness in AES encryption, or any encryption, is not the algorithm, but faulty implementations of the algorithm, which is always a danger everywhere in computing. If a weak algorithm is substituted in the code by mistake, the AES algorithm not coded correctly, the encryption keys not managed well, or many other potential flaws, the encryption is vulnerable.[11]

An alternative to ensure absolute privacy is to encrypt data before it is handed over to the cloud repository service. There are several products on the market that support independent local encryption. They are more trouble for the user, but the data is more private and secure.

---

[10]Mohit Arora, " How secure is AES against brute force attacks?" EETimes, May 7, 2012. www.eetimes.com/document.asp?doc_id=1279619. Accessed May 2016.
[11]From decades of experience in development, I can say that bonehead mistakes happen. Sound quality assurance testing eliminates many issues, but humans are always human. Cutting edge technology remains bleeding edge technology.
An example of a faulty implementation is documented here. In this case, the faulty implementation was in ransomware attack malware. Steven J. Vaughan-Nichols, "How to easily defeat Linux Encoder ransomware," ZDnet, November 16, 2015. www.zdnet.com/article/how-to-fix-linux-encoder-ransomware/. Accessed April 2016.

Cloud Backup

Although cloud backup is subject to all the risks and limitations of any cloud service, it has many advantages, both in security and convenience. They are a specialized form of cloud data repository services.

Usually, a simple cloud repository acts as an overflow for data that exceeds local capacity or is used to share data between physical devices. A complete system backup is more difficult than simply copying a few files. Experts use backup programs that are designed to copy every system and data file, and store them in a way that the backed-up computer can be restored efficiently and accurately after a disaster. A simple cloud data repository can be used to back up data and complete systems, but doing it without a backup system is an error-prone process, which is exactly what you don't want in a critical process like restoring a backup.[12]

Cloud backup services automate the backup process. The expertise to reliably manage backup and restoration is built into the system. The backup software chooses the correct system files and data to back up after a relatively simple set of configuration steps. Backups are usually scheduled automatically, or backed up as they change, so backups are not inadvertently skipped. The service automatically copies only files that have changed since the last backup, which shortens the backup and decreases the amount of network traffic. The system will probably periodically schedule a total backup of all files in case a changed file was somehow missed. The service also manages restoration from backups stored on the cloud. Often, restoring a file is handled with a click on the file directory display and system restores are quick and error-free.

An important benefit of cloud backup services is convenient remote and redundant storage of backups, which a well-implemented cloud backup service will do in the background without the user being aware. See Figure 6-4. Most people know that they should store a copy of their backups outside their house or office so the backup will not be destroyed by a fire or other disaster. But who has the discipline and motivation to keep up that effort week after week? A common problem with including any manual step in backup procedures is that after months or years of no need for a restoration, discipline fails and steps are neglected. Then disaster strikes, and there is no recourse.

---

[12]I cannot tell you how many times I have helped restore systems after a backup failed to restore a damaged system. Faulty backups prolong and magnify damage after a catastrophe.

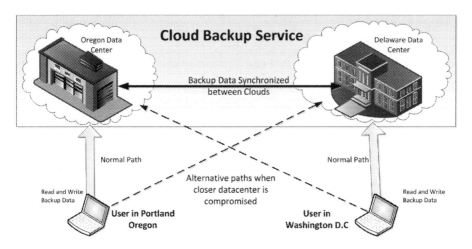

Figure 6-4. Cloud backup systems store backups redundantly to ensure they are always available and the failure of one datacenter will not bring down the service

Some people worry that cloud backup services are unreliable because they don't trust the network and the provider's implementation of the service, but the deciding question is this: is the person is more reliable than the cloud service? All I can say is that I use a cloud backup service.

Email

Although email is seldom thought of as a cloud data repository service, email was the first widely available cloud service. Most large email services provide remote cloud storage of emails. If the email service is small, such as a private email server, email may be stored on a single disk on a single server, but larger services, such as Google Gmail or Microsoft Outlook (formerly Hotmail) make use of cloud architecture for storing email.

An email service is similar to a cloud backup service in that it requires more software than a generic data repository, but essentially, sending an email is copying a file to storage on the email server. Receiving an email is copying a file from the email server to storage on the local device. However, email gets special handling for addressing, formatting and so on.

Even a very small email service is subject to the same cloud risks as a huge email provider. Email services all depend on network reliability and security and they depend on the integrity of the provider's implementation. The service can fail, from issues on the server or from issues in the network. A well-run and prepared small service may be as capable as a mega-service in mitigating risks. Mega-services usually have the staff and expertise to deal with issues, but smaller services may pay more attention to the issues of an individual subscriber and they are a smaller target for hacker attacks.

Some email services protect email in transit with TLS (also called SSL) encryption and authentication, making it unlikely that emails will be snooped on or subjected to a man-in-the-middle interception. However, it takes a partner to tango or use TLS. Google Gmail, Yahoo Mail, and Microsoft Outlook (Hotmail) services all support TLS, but only when communicating with other services that support TLS. Thus, security of emails is somewhat variable because it depends both the sender and recipient using TLS. Most services provide some flag to indicate when the email was transmitted using TLS. Some services also encrypt email data at rest, just as simple cloud data repositories encrypt.

Another, more secure but more onerous, approach places the responsibility on the sender and receiver rather than the sending and receiving services. This approach encrypts emails before they are sent and the receiver decrypts the message. Asymmetric private-public key encryption works well for this. The sender encrypts with a public key and the receiver decrypts with a private key, all independent of email services. The drawback is the sender and receiver have to agree to use encryption and receivers distribute their public keys to senders. There are various add-on packages available that manage the encryption and decryption and more or less manage the keys.

These packages increase the security of email considerably. The email is protected both in transit and at rest in the service repository and the sender and receiver do not depend on both the sending and receiving email services supporting TLS, nor can the provider provide access to email contents in court proceedings (electronic discovery) or when requested by government authorities.

Privacy Intrusion

Users should keep in mind that there is no free lunch in cloud services. Many services, such as cloud storage, are offered for free. Cloud-based Internet search appear to be free. The cloud service providers who offer these services are not charities. Their stockholders expect them to produce profits; companies either turn a profit, convince their stockholders that they will turn a profit in the future, or disappear. There is always a motive behind a free service.

Free cloud data storage is probably the most benign. Cloud data storage costs very little. A few gigabytes of storage costs only pennies and the storage provider can offer a free service as a *loss leader*, expecting the free user to eventually convert to a paying user. Free users should always look carefully before jumping in but, generally, there are some great deals available. Remember that the provider always has the option of converting a free service to a paying service. You may be forced to discontinue the service and move your data off the service or begin to pay.

When a user opens a browser, they will almost always eventually engage with a cloud service of some type. Bringing up a remote page, they reveal something about themselves, if only that they have some level of interest in the page they opened. If they go to an online retailer, they reveal their interest in the products they browse. If they perform an Internet search, they reveal their interest in the object of the search. Their smartphone reveals their location. The pattern of smartphone locations reveals where they live, work, shop, and where they go for entertainment. Social media sites are also sources of information on their users' likes, dislikes, friends, and relatives. When all this information is connected, which can now be done using big data techniques, a remarkably detailed profile of a person emerges.

If this profile is used for targeted advertising, the targeting can be precise. If the profile shows that a person goes out to dinner every Tuesday evening, on Tuesday afternoons, they might be targeted for special offers from restaurants close to their route home on every web page they open. Look up nasal allergies on a health site and receive ads for nasal spray at local drugstores. Look up something you are not interested in by mistake and get ads for things you don't want.

Targeted advertising may be intrusive and annoying, but still as innocuous as tasteless ads on traditional television. Targeting can even be desirable. A restaurant discount on your day to dine out may be a welcome surprise—and a boon to a restaurant owner who wants your business. If you need nasal spray, you may appreciate the ads. Being barraged by ads for something you looked up by mistake may not be pleasant, but it is not terrible either.

But target marketing profiles can also become sinister when they are used for other purposes. Some patterns may suggest that a person is an alcoholic or drug abuser. This inference may be correct, or it may not. If the inference is correct, facts are facts and might lead to beneficial intervention. However, if the inference is wrong, the effects could be horrible for an innocent victim. False inferences in a profile can silently affect vital aspects of life such as employment, insurance rates, and credit ratings. Although these profiles can usually be accessed with some effort, an affected person may easily be unaware of a malignant profile and unknowingly suffer from it. When the victim is aware of the profile, it may be time-consuming and expensive to correct.

Disturbingly, a target marketing profile compilation system is successful if the inferences are correct frequently enough to support increased purchases. A system that is wrong 25% of the time may still be a roaring success at generating sales. However, if the same profiles were misused for something like employment screening or criminal investigation, errors in 5 out of 20 cases are likely to seriously damage individuals. With all good intent, conclusions from these profiles may be a tempting shortcut replacement for a more expensive personal investigation and result in serious injury.

Clouds are a critical part of this kind target profiling. They have the capacity to pool vast quantities of data. These data pools are rich sources for big data analysis that connects the dots to form a profile of the individual. The profiles are often the price paid for free cloud services. On the one hand, they offer desirable free services and streamline the connection between buyers and sellers, but they also offer opportunities for abuse.

Are Clouds Worth the Trouble?

Enterprises use clouds as an extension of their datacenters and as an alternative for delivering computer-based services to their customers. Most individuals consume services offered from clouds rather than use them as a direct extension to their personal devices. These uses are different, but the security issues overlap. When enterprises and individuals use clouds to manage and extend their own capacity for data processing, they trust their data and processes to their cloud provider. Enterprises use service contracts and service audits to protect themselves.

Individuals do not usually have these tools. They are offered take-it-or-leave-it click-through contracts that are seldom read and often absolve the provider of almost all responsibility. Audits are expensive and providers are unlikely to submit to an audit for a single consumer. Consequently, individual users are left on their own.

After these negatives, there are many vendors that offer reliable, secure, and economical services. Cloud datacenters are generally more secure than all but the most fortified home systems. Typically, they are manned by security and IT professionals who are trained to deal with invaders and equipment failures and are more likely to defuse a dangerous situation than any individual. Although click-through service contracts tend to be slanted in the provider's favor, the providers still have strong incentives to provide good and reliable service because they compete on the cost and quality of their services in a robust marketplace.

However, users are still obliged to follow basic security practices like good password management. Most important, users should take the time to be aware of what the service will and will not do. For instance, users should be aware that a storage service can recover specific files or groups of files, but it usually will not restore a complete system like a backup service. If you have privacy concerns, as most people do, find out if your privacy expectations match the provisions the provider offers.

Finally, the basic security tradeoff, more secure equals more hassle, applies to cloud services as much as anywhere else. Strong passwords and multi-factor authentication are bothersome, but they buy a more secure service. Encryption and decryption slow processing but they increase privacy. Consumers have to choose products that satisfy their preferences for safety and convenience.

Why Doesn't Somebody Stop It?

Where Are the Authorities?

When we read or hear about cybercrime, crimes such as hospital records held for ransom, fraudulent sports ticket sales, theft of millions of payment cards, stolen trade secrets, or outing personal documents, we inevitably wonder what the authorities are doing about it. Crime rates in general have been going down dramatically for the last decade, but cybercrime is rampant.[1] Why can't the law enforcement resources that have been effective against conventional crime also take down cybercriminals? If law enforcement has to change, how should it change?

---

[1]For a look at the decline in conventional crime, see Neil Howe, "What's Behind The Decline In Crime?" Forbes, May 28, 2015. www.forbes.com/sites/neilhowe/2015/05/28/whats-behind-the-decline-in-crime/#3a3a8eec7733. Accessed August 2016. For the rise in digital crime, see Steve Morgan, "Cyber Crime Costs Projected To Reach $2 Trillion by 2019," Forbes, January 17, 2016. www.forbes.com/sites/stevemorgan/2016/01/17/cyber-crime-costs-projected-to-reach-2-trillion-by-2019/#31b8dad13bb0. Accessed August 2016.

© Marvin Waschke 2017
M. Waschke, *Personal Cybersecurity*, DOI 10.1007/978-1-4842-2430-4_7

The answers are not simple. The reasons for the decline in conventional crime rates are not clear. Shifting age distributions may be as significant as cultural changes and policing techniques. Cybercrime, compared to conventional theft, fraud, and violence, is a new thing for law enforcement. It presents new challenges and requires new tactics. Not all agencies are prepared and in many cases the new tactics don't yet exist. In some cases, what many people think ought to be criminal is legal under current laws. In areas such as privacy, factions contend over what should be illegal. The obstacles to cybercrime enforcement are many.

The Problem Is New

The problem is new and not so new. In the 1960s, stories of cybercrime already circulated but they differed from what we usually think of as cybercrime today.

Mainframe computers were only accessible to a small group of scientists and engineers. Most mainframes connected with their peripherals but not with other computers. There was no Internet; networks were a vision and hope, not a reality. Therefore, cybercrimes were almost always the action of an insider, typically an employee, who used the computer to commit some form of theft, embezzlement, or fraud. Most of these crimes were schemes that took advantage of lack of understanding of computing among the public and the management responsible for the computer system.[2]

Insider computer embezzlement still goes on but an interconnected, ubiquitous network provides many more opportunities for cybercrimes. New mechanisms for cybercrime are invented continuously. The most prominent cybercrimes today are invasions. An outside criminal invades a computer system and steals its resources or subverts its processes to the criminal's advantage.

Network and the Internet

Today, isolated computers are rare and verging on non-existent. Almost any computer can connect with any other computer on the planet. Only computer security prevents me sitting in my office from connecting to computers in the Pentagon in Washington D.C., the Kremlin in Moscow, or the Chinese Military Commission in Beijing. The physical connectivity is labyrinthine, but it exists. If you know how

---

[2]The story of the programmer who wrote code to snatch the fraction of a cent discarded when dollar amounts are rounded down to the nearest cent has grown to an urban legend. Whether it actually ever occurred is open to question, although I have heard more than one loquacious old-timer deliver an eyewitness account of the crook being marched out in handcuffs. Real or not, there is a kernel of truth. An insider with access to code can modify complex systems to skim resources in ways that even a detailed audit could miss. This is always a danger.

to navigate around and through the security, you can access any computer on the planet. The security is tough, much tougher than it looks in the movies, but the underlying connectivity exists, and patient and persistent researchers and criminals have repeatedly shown that the connectivity can be used illicitly.

All computers are affected by this connectivity. Even systems that appear to be completely isolated are actually susceptible to unauthorized access over the network. A personal desktop without wireless and without a wired network connection, or an isolated military network that has no external connections to the Internet or any other network are both still vulnerable. These are so-called *air-gapped systems*. Air-gapping is possibly the ultimate protection, but even air-gapped systems can be invaded (see the sidebar.)

AIR-GAPPED SYSTEMS

An *air-gapped system* has no physical or electromagnetic connection to other computers. A standalone local computer with no wired or wireless connections, direct or indirect, to external networks, especially the Internet, is air-gapped. Such devices seem safe from unauthorized intrusion.

But even air-gapped systems are reachable with patience and know-how. USB storage devices, like USB drives (thumb drives), can be used to introduce malware. A device like a laptop temporarily connected to an air-gapped network for data transfer or some form of maintenance can be a vehicle for inserting or extracting information and code.

Computers emit information in unintentional ways. Those who want to know and are able to muster adequate resources have developed surprising methods of eavesdropping. Computer chips and circuitry emit electromagnetic radiation that can be detected and interpreted. The sound of typing can be recorded and interpreted. Infected devices can send sonic or ultrasonic messages through computer speakers and receive messages through microphones. The yokes on old-fashioned cathode ray displays emit signals that can be captured from outside office buildings and used to reconstruct the content displayed. Well-heeled intruders develop technology to peer over the shoulder of any user they target.

Air gaps are inconvenient when the users of the system need to communicate through the air gap. The inconvenience offers ripe opportunities for social engineering that often lead to air gap failures. The famous Stuxnet exploit against Iranian nuclear fuel refineries infiltrated an air-gapped system, probably via infected USB drives.[3] Failures like this can be avoided by following a protocol that prohibits such connections, but it is easy to imagine someone in a hurry to make a quick change ignoring the protocol "just once," and breaking the entire system.

---

[3]See Kim Zetter, "An Unprecedented Look at Stuxnet, the World's First Digital Weapon," Wired, November 3, 2014. www.wired.com/2014/11/countdown-to-zero-day-stuxnet/. Accessed August 2016.

Air gaps are perhaps the ultimate barrier to cybercrime, but a patient criminal with ample resources and sufficient motivation can get through. Even a disconnected home computer is susceptible.

Before the Internet began to reach everywhere, the world of computing was a patchwork of semi-hostile walled communities. Each company, institution, or person had their walled community. Travel to and from the communities was difficult. Crime was confined within walls and law enforcement was a local affair that seldom involved reaching outside the local community.

The Internet has replaced the physical walls with arbitrary lines painted on the ground. The lines are not difficult to cross but crossing them breaks rules and laws. Even moderately savvy users can jump on a jet-power motorcycle to race over the lines. And, most of the time, the cops have to get permission to follow. This is the architecture of Internet crime and law enforcement.

New Opportunities for Crime

Opportunities for cybercrime are on the rise for a combination of reasons. Computers are used more often and for more purposes each year. The spread of the smartphone is one cause. People walk around today with computers in their hands that are far more powerful than the mainframe installations that directed the moon missions of the mid Twentieth Century. A decade ago, around 200 million personal computers were shipped per year.[4] The first iPhone was not sold until 2007. The number of smartphones in use worldwide is expected soon to be over 2 billion.[5] That is 10 times the number of personal computers 10 years ago. Each one of these smartphones, in addition to the servers, desktops, laptops, and tablets that fill our lives, is as much a target for cybercrime as a desktop or laptop.

The smartphone explosion is not the only source of new cybercrime opportunities. We are at the beginning of the Internet of Things (IoT) that is extending the reach of cybercrime in startling new directions. Smartphones, tablets, laptops, and desktops are all variations on a pattern: processing capacity, storage, and

---

[4]"Total unit shipments of PCs worldwide from 2006 to 2015 (in million units)," Statistica, 2016. www.statista.com/statistics/273495/global-shipments-of-personal-computers-since-2006/. Accessed June 2016.
[5]"Number of smartphone users worldwide from 2014 to 2019 (in millions)," Statistica, 2016. www.statista.com/statistics/330695/number-of-smartphone-users-worldwide/. Accessed June 2016.

network connections, and human interfaces. These devices come in many shapes and sizes, and their human interfaces vary from keyboards to microphones and back-lit screens to speakers and printers, all designed to interact with different human senses.

With the advent of the IoT, computers attached to the Internet are no longer limited to this basic pattern. Many elements of the IoT are not intended to interact directly with humans. They have other tricks. Industry uses devices in the IoT to monitor and control equipment and processes that vary from nuclear reactors to sewing machines. Fitness monitors track our steps, our global position, and our heart rate and communicate directly with our computers. More sophisticated medical monitors track blood pressure and blood glucose. Smart thermostats in our living rooms are attached to the Internet and can transmit the temperature in our houses to smartphones or tablets on the other side of the globe. The phone or tablet issues commands to adjust the temperature up or down. The elements of the IoT greatly increase the number of points on the network ready to be invaded by enterprising hackers. These elements of the IoT cluster around us. Sometimes we are aware of them and interact with them; other times we are unaware.

In 2016, at any given time, there are estimated to be 3.5 billion Internet connected users.[6] Each of these users is a candidate victim of cybercrime. Some estimates place the number of IoT devices connected to the Internet at 50 billion in 2020.[7] These statistics are related, but users are not the same as devices. Currently a single Internet user is likely to have several IoT devices in use. In the future, this number will certainly rise. Some IoT devices may not be assignable to a specific user, but many devices will be.

Owning a laptop and a smartphone offers criminals two routes into your electronic domain. A fitness monitor, a home security system, and a front door you can unlock from your phone offer three additional opportunities for a creative criminal. Your automobile may already be attached to the Internet. The electric utility that supplies electrical power to your house may be planning or already has IoT sensors that monitor your electricity usage.

---

[6]"Internet Users," Internet Live Stats. www.internetlivestats.com/internet-users/. Accessed June 2016.
[7]Staff, "Fifty billion internet nodes predicted by 2020," Electronics Weekly, January 8, 2013. www.electronicsweekly.com/news/business/information-technology/fifty-billion-internet-nodes-predicted-by-2020-2013-01/. Accessed June 2016.

As we are all caught up in the trend to attach more and more of our personal infrastructure to the Internet, we offer more opportunities for criminals to attempt to use the Internet to victimize us. The IoT promises to make lives better. An intelligent power grid combined with alternative energy sources is designed to reduce the cost of electricity and dependence on foreign energy sources while decreasing the total energy used by each individual. The control and instrumentation offered by the IoT network increases the comfort and ease of our lives.

But the benefits come with a cost. Complex systems take time to perfect and they increase vulnerability to both technical flaws and criminal exploitation.

Not only have we increased the ways that criminals can attack us, we have made attacks more lucrative with the activities we increasingly perform on our highly portable computers. Much of our business-to-customer and business-to-business commerce now takes place online. Not only are we expanding our attack surface by increasing the ways we are attached to the network, we are making the attachments more attractive by offering more things to steal. We shop more online for a wider and more diverse range of goods and services. More of our banking and other financial transaction are over wires. We use electronic notifications and documents instead of paper, and our primary message delivery service is the Internet, not the post office. Much of the technology is decades old, but the technology has become more accessible and used more often. Instead of robbing the till, shoplifting, and breaking and entering, cybercriminals steal payment card information, purchase goods with stolen credentials, and hack into home security cameras. Data is intercepted to be used against us and there is more of it to intercept.

The entire economy is increasingly run on a digital infrastructure. Some countries are already planning a transition to an all-electronic economy that does not use physical money. The smart electric grid mentioned earlier increases national dependence on computer networks. Increasingly, industrial supervisory control and data acquisition puts the lifeblood of our transportation and manufacturing onto the Internet.

A few years ago, for the first time, the majority of adults in the US were banking online.[8] Most people now bank using payment cards and direct funds transfer, and manage their financial accounts online. Hackers rob banks by hacking into servers and financial communication systems, and come away with millions of dollars. Gun-toting bank robbers are left with slim pickings at bank branches holding little cash in their vaults. The days of Willie Sutton packing a gun and robbing banks "because that's where the money is" are over.[9]

---

[8]Susannah Fox, "51% of U.S. Adults Bank Online," Pew Research Center, August 7, 2013. www.pewinternet.org/2013/08/07/51-of-u-s-adults-bank-online/. Accessed June 2016.
[9]Apparently, Willie Sutton did not say this, but he has often been quoted as saying it. For general background, see "Willie Sutton," Wikipedia. https://en.wikipedia.org/wiki/Willie_Sutton . Accessed August 2016.

With both the number of computers and the uses of computers rising rapidly, the opportunities for cybercrime have increased, and with the rise in opportunity for crime, the number of crimes has risen.

New Kind of Criminal

Cybercriminals are not beetle-browed thugs lurking in dark alleys; in other words, they are not stereotypical criminals. Even the stereotype of the disgruntled and wild-eyed hacker surrounded by greasy take-out wrappers and hunched over a glowing screen is not accurate. The attendees at hacker conventions, such as Def Con or Black Hat, are hard to distinguish from the attendees at any other engineering conference. Certainly, these convention attendees are there as computer security professionals, but realistically, the criminal engineering elite have the same interests as the white hat professionals and are likely to be there to join in the conversation.

Top tier cybercriminals must have expertise and knowledge of computer engineering including software and hardware and in-depth understanding of business practices. Without technical knowledge of computers and networks, criminals can't gain access. Without knowledge of business practices and systems, the criminals do not know what to do when they get access, where the money is, or how to extract it. A successful large scale exploit is likely to require knowledge of several software systems, networking, hardware vulnerabilities, and detailed knowledge of the business transacted on the system. Acquiring this knowledge and skill is not easy. It requires intelligence, discipline, training, and practical experience. Often, advanced academic training and insider experience is also necessary. These skills are all in demand both for legitimate employment and crime. One consequence is that cybercriminals are able to switch from one side of the law to the other with relative ease. Expert cybercriminals are probably indistinguishable from other technical workers.

Cybercriminal: Dread Pirate Roberts

Ross Ulbricht, who called himself "Dread Pirate Roberts," was the owner of the Silk Road anonymous trading site. He is an example of a cybercriminal with a high order of expertise. The Silk Road site was taken down by the FBI in 2013. Ulbricht is now serving two life sentences and several other sentences for charges including narcotics trafficking, money laundering, murder-for-hire, and computer hacking.[10] With the exception of hacking, Ulbricht's charges sound like the charges levelled at traditional organized crime boss.

---

[10]For details on his charges, see United States District Court, Southern District of New York, "United States v. Ross William Ulbricht, Indictment," Department of Justice, February 4, 2014. `www.justice.gov/sites/default/files/usao-sdny/legacy/2015/03/25/US%20v.%20Ross%20Ulbricht%20Indictment.pdf`. Accessed June 2016.

But Ulbricht was far from a traditional criminal. He had no criminal record, no history of advancement from minor offenses to misdemeanors to felonies. He had no known criminal associates. His friends, relatives, and the people he lived with did not suspect he was involved in illegal activity.

Ulbricht was a solar energy researcher and co-author of scientific papers, but at some point he abandoned research and began building an anonymous merchandise exchange that encouraged illegal trade. He has said that he built the exchange to support libertarian economic principles.

While operating Silk Road he acquired tens of millions of dollars in the form of bitcoins from commissions on the Silk Road site, but, unlike typical drug dealers, he apparently was not motivated by greed and showed no interest in spending on luxuries.

His lifestyle was remarkably low key. He sublet a single room in a house and lived quietly, spending most of his time in solitude, working on his laptop computer. He spent little money, travelled seldom, and did little that would have drawn the attention of a typical criminal investigation.[11] Eventually, he was captured while using his laptop in the science fiction section of a public library through a combination of painstaking online research and sophisticated cyberforensics.[12]

Ulbricht's case highlights the challenge in finding cybercrooks who do not act like traditional criminals. Investigations of drug traffickers and users of murder for hire services are usually quite different from the Silk Road takedown. More and more investigators are being trained to capture the next Dread Pirate Roberts, but it is still a new direction for law enforcement, and the methods used by the criminals to evade detection are also improving rapidly.[13]

---

[11]Ryan Mac, "Living With Ross Ulbricht: Housemates Say They Saw No Clues Of Silk Road Or The Dread Pirate Roberts," Forbes, October 9, 2013. www.forbes.com/sites/ryanmac/2013/10/09/living-with-ross-ulbricht-housemates-say-they-saw-no-clues-of-silk-road-or-the-dread-pirate-roberts/#344e84c764f2. Accessed June 2016.

[12]Nate Anderson and Cyrus Farivar, "How the feds took down the Dread Pirate Roberts," Ars Technica, October 2, 2013.
http://arstechnica.com/tech-policy/2013/10/how-the-feds-took-down-the-dread-pirate-roberts/2/. Accessed June 2016.

[13]Jim Edwards, "This Is The Physics Student And Used Book Seller Who Allegedly Ran The 'Silk Road' Market For Drugs And Assassins," Business Insider, October 2, 2013. www.businessinsider.com/meet-ross-ulbricht-the-brilliant-alleged-mastermind-of-silk-road-2013-10. Accessed June 2016.

Cybercriminals and Law Enforcement

The traditional tools of law enforcement are not well-suited to catching cybercriminals. A traditional crime investigation is usually performed by a coordinated team. The police are the first to a crime scene. Their job is to come to the rescue of victims, catch criminals still on the scene, do an initial assessment of the nature and gravity of the crime, and secure the scene. Crime scene investigators collect and evaluate evidence; detectives interview suspects and witnesses; representatives of the district attorney advise on the legal intricacies, such as applicable laws, required evidence, and warrants.

Almost none of these roles apply to investigation of cybercriminals, and when they do apply, the expertise needed to execute the roles is far from traditional. The local computer crime scene is seldom a tangible building or a plot of ground to be cordoned off. There may be a device, like a hacked laptop or smartphone, but in many cases, the only evidence of the crime is the report of the crime and buried in records that are stored all over the Internet. Computer criminals do not leave footprints, fingerprints, or DNA samples. There are no blood spatters to analyze, no firearms or bullets to trace. The detectives have no witnesses to interview.

Criminals like Ross Ulbricht seldom have criminal records. They probably don't have criminal associates, nor are they likely to have violent tendencies that cause them to brush periodically with law enforcement. They don't have identifying fingerprints or DNA samples in law enforcement files. They are not likely to show up on security cameras. Because conventional methods and tools of law enforcement do not apply to cybercriminals, law enforcement has been forced to evolve new techniques for solving these crimes.

Although there are no footprints in the sand to photograph and preserve, cybercriminals do leave traces. The crime investigator may have nothing more than a few emails stored on an Internet service provider's server, lines in the log from an anonymous chatroom, and some entries in the victim's bank record, but these may well be all the clues an experienced cyberinvestigator needs to track down the perpetrator.

The successful capture of Dread Pirate Roberts was accomplished by careful and arduous undercover work, but not the kind of undercover work we usually see on television. The undercover agents may never have seen Dread Pirate Roberts or any of his lieutenants or customers. Instead, many hours were spent in chatrooms establishing trust among the criminal community, discovering rivalries and vulnerabilities. The undercover detective probably did his undercover work seated in a cubicle in a police lab, not hanging out in seedy nightclubs. From that cubicle, fragments of information were pieced together that could eventually be used to infer the pirate's real identity and location. The final arrest was an undramatic anti-climax in the science fiction section of a public library.

New Kind of Crime

Cybercrime is technological crime. Traditional criminals rely on force and guile to extract gain from their victims. The traditional relationship between criminal and victim is usually direct and personal. Cybercriminals use their knowledge of computing technology to victimize remote victims whom they have never met or communicated with directly. The victim may be unaware of the crime until long after the act.

Cybercrimes Are Local, Cybercriminals Are Global

The locations of the victims of a cybercrime are seldom a clue to the location of the criminals who executed the cybercrimes. For example, an intrusion into banking systems in the third world that affected banks in the US was executed remotely. From October 2015 through February 2016, banks in Bangladesh, Vietnam, and the Philippines were attacked. The attacks were directed at a highly secure electronic funds transfer system referred to as SWIFT. The attacks were directed toward third world banks with vulnerable security practices. Reports say that attackers transferred $81 million from Federal Reserve Bank of New York accounts. Investigators traced the attacks to North Korea. Detecting and tracing the attacks is a formidable technical and investigative challenge, but resolving the case enters the realm of foreign relations, diplomacy, and military strategy—a situation that goes far beyond the limits of typical law enforcement.[14]

Finding The Perpetrator

A rapid search for a perpetrator in the vicinity of the crime is basic police procedure that is part of every police officer's training. The equivalent search for a cybercriminal is tracing the network address and location of the cybercriminal's computer, which is actually both a location and a point in time because cybercriminals change network addresses and move quickly and physical location is not tightly tied to address. See the sidebar below for some of the complications involved in tracing perpetrators using network addresses.

---

[14]Nicole Perlroth, Michael Corkery, "North Korea Linked to Digital Attacks on Global Banks," New York Times, May 26, 2016. www.nytimes.com/2016/05/27/business/dealbook/north-korea-linked-to-digital-thefts-from-global-banks.html?_r=0. Accessed June 2016.

FINDING THE PERP: IP AND MAC ADDRESSES

A device connected to the Internet has two addresses: an Internet Protocol address (IP address) and a Media Access Control address (MAC address). Both are essential for communication using current network protocols and both provide basic clues for identifying cybercriminals. They are similar to fingerprints and DNA for finding physical criminals.

MAC addresses are less well-known than IP addresses. They are a sequence of letters and numbers (actually a 48-bit hexadecimal number) manufactured into physical hardware. Every device designed to connect to a network has a MAC address, also called a *physical address*. Devices that can connect to a network via more than one interface (by both wire and wireless, for example) have a different MAC address for each interface. MAC addresses stay with an interface until the hardware is changed. MAC addresses are theoretically unique throughout all space and time. Virtual systems, manufacturing errors, and hackers can violate the MAC uniqueness rule, but it is valid most of the time. Therefore, a MAC address identifies a physical computer unambiguously, with rare exceptions.

Uniqueness and stability make MAC addresses useful forensically. Find the laptop with a MAC address that matches a MAC address found in the network logs of an invaded computer, and you are likely to have found the laptop that did the deed. However, MAC addresses are not much help in physically finding the criminal, much like a fingerprint confirms the identities of culprits, but the investigator still has to find the culprit attached to the fingerprint.

IP addresses are also unique, but they depend on where the device connects, not the identity of the device itself. You have one IP address connecting from home and another when you connect from a coffee shop. At each connection location, IP addresses are usually assigned only temporarily to a device. When your tablet connects to your home Wi-Fi, your router assigns an IP address from its pool of IP addresses. When your tablet disconnects, the address goes back in the pool, where it might be assigned to your laptop or some other device when it connects. Your home Wi-Fi system router probably has a single IP address that your Internet Service Provider (ISP) has assigned to your home Wi-Fi network, but it may change over time depending on your ISP's policy. Your ISP may periodically change it, or you might get a new IP address each time your router connects to your ISP. Nevertheless, at any point in time, the IP address assigned to your Internet connection is theoretically unique over the entire Internet, although it will change as you physically move around the Internet.

Because IP addresses can change often, they are usually not useful for identifying computers. The exception is servers, which are often assigned IP addresses that do not change (static IP addresses). However, IP addresses can be used to track down physical locations. An IP address is a set of directions to the Internet routing system, which uses the IP address to guide messages through a series of hops that eventually lead to a local service provider, which directs the message to the computer assigned the IP address. Therefore, if investigators know the time that a message was sent to or from an IP address, they can get the location of the device at the time the message was sent from the service provider. They may also have the MAC address of the device, providing confirmation that the identification is correct. The investigator will then know that the message was sent from a device connected to the Wi-Fi network of a certain coffee shop at a certain data and time.[15]

Cybercriminals disguise their identity and location when they attack to make the search for a perpetrator as difficult as possible for police, not unlike a physical criminal dons a hoody and dark glasses to rob a convenience store. The search for an evasive cybercriminal is a job for a trained specialist. Although this training is becoming more common, cybercrime specialists are still scarce and they must concentrate on the most significant crimes. Successfully finding a cybercriminal is not easy. The search may lead to a public wireless network like a coffee shop. When it leads to a residence or office, the criminal may have temporarily hijacked the Wi-Fi Internet connection and may have no permanent connection with the location (see the following sidebar). The search could lead through a Tor network, a way of using the Internet that is intentionally difficult to follow. They can disappear without a trace.

WAR DRIVING

War driving is the practice of driving around with a portable Wi-Fi device (laptop, tablet, smartphone, or custom device) searching for insecure wireless networks. War drivers often use specialized antennas to extend their reach. Software is available for download that automates the practice. Combined with global positioning systems, war driving software can automatically generate maps that locate Wi-Fi network sites.

War driving is legal in most places, although some local laws outlaw it. The step usually taken after finding available Wi-Fi sites is illegal. Open networks discovered on a war drive that are not encrypted and secured with a password can easily be accessed without authorization from the owners. This is illegal. Criminals war drive, or use maps produced by war drivers, to gain unauthorized access to Wi-Fi networks. They may do this to steal Internet access, gain illicit access to passwords and data by hacking into devices on the Wi-Fi network, or hide their identity by communicating from a location that cannot be traced to them.

---

[15]This sidebar is not for network engineers! It is only a sketch of what goes on with IP and MAC addresses. I have intentionally simplified by leaving out some major complications, like network address translation, static addresses, and IP versions.

The obstacles to these searches do not mean that a search is pointless, but they are challenging. Cyberforensic specialists use combined methods. For instance, they can cross-reference network records with credit card records to generate a list of who was in a coffee shop while the suspect was using the coffee shop network address to access the Internet. Similar correlations can be made with security camera records. Cellular phone records are another source. The combination of information may narrow the suspects or target the criminal.

These techniques are powerful, but determined criminals can circumvent them. Criminals that use technologies designed for anonymous communication, such as the Tor browser, may be traceable, but tracing is requires a concerted effort with specialized expertise, equipment, and a planned, prolonged effort. Some organizations, such as the National Security Agency, have the resources to trace, decrypt, and otherwise track criminals who use advanced evasive technology, but most law enforcement agencies don't have those resources (see the following sidebar).

TOR

Tor (The Onion Router) was developed to offer privacy, confidentiality, and anonymity on the Internet. In the mid-1990s, United States Naval Research Laboratory scientists and engineers generated the Tor concepts and architecture for protection of online secret communications. The Tor project continues to be developed and maintained through grants from various agencies of the U.S. government, contributions from individuals, and other organizations.

The basic principles behind Tor are a network of volunteer servers and repeated encryption of the information associated with the message. Messages are routed and repeatedly encrypted on random paths through the Tor server network. It is called "the onion router" because pealing back one layer of encryption reveals another layer, like pealing an onion. Although Tor has proven to be penetrable with sufficient resources and effort, the exceptional effort required makes Tor-protected network traffic much more private than normal Internet traffic.

The Tor browser is a free download. A moderately savvy computer user can be up and running on Tor in a short time.

Tor leads a double life. It preserves privacy and prevents intrusion into both legitimate and illegitimate activities. Tor protects both foreign correspondents and terrorists who threaten them. Individuals use Tor to protect their privacy from intrusive business interests and Tor prevents criminals from spying on law enforcement communications. Tor also protects intellectual property from prying by competitors and foreign nations. At the same time, Tor prevents law enforcement from spying on criminals, terrorists, and antagonistic foreign nations.

Ironically, using evasive technologies is easy and cheap; catching a criminal who uses evasive technologies is difficult and expensive.

Extradition

After perpetrators are found, they must be apprehended and taken to court. Identifying the courts and enforcement agencies that govern a conventional crime or dispute is usually one of the easier parts of conventional law enforcement. Conventional crime is almost always local. The victim of the crime, the execution of the crime, and the perpetrator of the crime are all in the same geographic location and the courts and law enforcement agencies of the local area have jurisdiction over the crime. Choosing between a civil or criminal court or a more specialized court like a family court follows well-understood rules.

In contrast, even determining the location of a cybercrime can be challenging. The victim of a cybercrime may be located thousands of miles from the perpetrator. The execution of a cybercrime, such as a denial of service attack, can be launched from thousands of servers spread over all the globe. Which location has jurisdiction? The attacked site? The locations of the hacked servers that sent the attack messages? The locations of the command and control servers, of which there may be many? Or the coffee shop where the perpetrator sat for a few minutes while he started the attack? Without a specific locality, prosecution is perplexing. Resolving the perplexity is difficult and expensive.

If the jurisdictions can be determined and the perpetrator of a cybercrime can be found and a solid case established, the difficulties are not over when the perpetrator is not in the same jurisdiction as the victim. In that case, the perpetrator must be extradited to be prosecuted.

Extradition is a complex and expensive process. Extradition is necessary because a law enforcement authority can only prosecute a suspect within in their jurisdiction. Although conventional criminals certainly flee across jurisdictional boundaries, most conventional crimes are performed in the same jurisdiction as their victims and don't require extradition. A burglary victim complains to the local police. The police identify the criminals, apprehend them, and bring them to trial. If the criminals have fled the area, the criminals must be extradited. The victim's jurisdiction must convey a request for an arrest to an authority with jurisdiction over the criminal and the criminal's jurisdiction must agree to the request. After the agreement has been made, officers in the criminal's jurisdiction perform the arrest. Then it is up to the victim's jurisdiction to get the prisoner and transport him or her to the victim's jurisdiction and bring the criminal to trial.

In most cases, extradition only occurs when the act is criminal in both the jurisdiction of the victim and the jurisdiction of perpetrator. If not, a request for extradition is likely rejected. Extradition for cybercrimes tends to be more difficult than conventional crime because conventional crime laws tend to be more consistent across jurisdictions than cybercrime laws. This is a problem within national boundaries, and an enormous problem when jurisdictions cross international boundaries.

The laws governing cybercrime are not always consistent across jurisdictional boundaries. In the U.S., for example, the CAN-SPAM Act of 2003 is U.S. federal anti-unsolicited commercial email legislation. Prior to CAN-SPAM, many states had some form of anti-spam legislation. The federal act preempts many, but not all, of these state laws. Consequently, some spam practices are illegal in some states but not others.

Washington State, for example, prohibits hiding the point of origin of commercial emails by disguising the email address. Other states do not.[16] Spammers tried in Washington State courts can be convicted of cybercrimes that would be ignored in some other states. The question of jurisdiction in such a trial is important. The Washington law declares disguised addresses are illegal when either sent or received on Washington computers. Under Washington State law, a prosecutor could attempt to prosecute a spammer sending disguised addresses from a state where disguised addresses are legal. When that happens, the accused spammer would have to be extradited or voluntarily travel to Washington State to stand trial. However, since states are not obligated to extradite an accused person who has not committed a crime under their laws or federal law, the spammer could be immune to prosecution.[17]

The entire extradition process is slow, expensive, and somewhat risky. A long-distance investigation requires long-range inquiries into unfamiliar territory. If the investigation succeeds in finding a likely suspect, the remote jurisdiction may refuse to extradite the suspect. Also, there is little margin for error because extraditing the wrong suspect is an expensive and highly visible mistake.

Due to the expense and risk, local law enforcement may only have funds to pursue and extradite the most egregious cybercriminals. Less extreme crimes that involve smaller sums of money often have to be ignored. Crooks can take advantage of this weakness. For example, a ransomware ring might keep ransoms low enough to avoid extradition and prosecution. A fraudulent online sports ticket racket might keep their prices below the bar for extradition and only prey on out-of-state victims.

---

[16]Cornell University Law School, "U.S. State Anti-Spam Laws: Introduction and Broader Framework," LII, undated. www.law.cornell.edu/wex/inbox/state_anti-spam_laws#. Accessed June 2016.

[17]Fortunately, the spammer is not likely to get off. Spamming is illegal under the federal law and would probably be extradited for spamming, not the disguised address. Once the spammer arrives in Washington State, they are subject to local law and they can be nailed for the disguised address as well as spamming.

These problems become worse when the crime is international. Not all countries are equally distressed by cybercrime. Although it may not be a publicly declared policy, some nation states are tolerant of international cybercrime and make no effort to prosecute cybercriminals. In extreme cases, such as the North Korea example above, the criminal act appears to be an instrument of government policy. When cybercriminals hide behind practices like this, prosecuting the criminals requires foreign diplomacy in addition to police action. That means the prosecution not only has to make its case, they have to contend for a place on a diplomatic agenda.

The prospects for local victims of remote cybercriminals are not good. Finding the criminal is difficult, requiring skills that may not be available, and expensive. Extraditing and prosecuting the criminals once they are found is also difficult and easily more expensive than finding the criminals. Local law enforcement budgets are never unlimited and often severely limited, meaning that expensive-to-solve, low-dollar, non-violent crimes will not be given high priority.

Realistically, a victim reporting a small cybercrime to the local authorities is likely to get sympathy, but little more. This is most unfortunate because it gives certain types of cybercrime a free pass. A ransomware operation that keeps ransoms low and avoids victimizing near jurisdictions is almost guaranteed to prey on their victims with immunity. Email fraud scams and many other cybercrimes that spread their illegal gains over many victims are similarly skipped over by prosecution.

For crimes that occur entirely within national boundaries, legislation could help by simplifying jurisdictional issues and streamlining the extradition process. Unfortunately, exactly how to simplify and streamline the process is a difficult problem in itself. For example, in the U.S., if criminals could be prosecuted in their home state for cyber fraud on victims in another state, the cost of prosecution may decrease, but what would motivate prosecutors to expend local resources on crimes that do not affect their local constituents?

More extensive federal cybercrime laws may be a solution, but federal officials are already consumed with big ticket crimes. In addition, without substantial changes in the federal legal infrastructure, running low-dollar-amount cybercrimes through the federal court system would be cumbersome and not likely to satisfy many victims.

The international arena is not better. The situation has improved with the establishment of international cybercrime treaties. The most prominent treaty is the Convention on Cybercrime, also known as the Budapest Convention, which was adopted by the Council of Europe in 2001. After 15 years, 49 nation states have ratified it, mostly in Europe, but non-European states such as the United States, Australia, Canada, Israel, and Japan have also ratified it. Signatories to the convention must agree to align local laws with the Convention's policy on unauthorized computer access, data theft, child pornography trafficking, and several other areas. This greatly simplifies prosecution and extradition.

Ratification has been wide, but not universal. Non-signatories protest that the convention intrudes on their national sovereignty. North and South Korea, Russia, China, and India are notable non-signatories.[18]

Despite the Convention, there are still locations that are relative safe havens for cybercriminals. In addition, cross-border extradition and prosecution are more expensive and difficult than extradition and prosecution within national boundaries. Consequently, international cybercriminals who keep the damage to each victim low enough can often get a free pass.

Somehow this knot must be untied or we will have to resign ourselves to high cybercrime rates.

Hidden and Under-reported

Although lack of privacy on computers is troubling, cybercrimes are often less public than conventional crimes. When a person is assaulted on the street, the event is public. Uninvolved witnesses may call 911 for the victim. If the police arrive on the scene soon enough, they may arrest and charge the perpetrator without the participation of the victim.

Cybercrimes seldom take place in public. A crime like pwning, illicitly seizing control of a computer, and turning the computer into a remotely controlled bot takes place inside the victimized computer and over the Internet. The effects of the pwning may be public, such as using the seized computer as part of a denial of service attack, but even the rightful owner of the computer may never be aware that the computer has been effectively stolen.

Other crimes such as identity theft are similar. The victims of the theft may go for years without realizing that their identities are being used by the criminals.

In other cases, such as cyberbullying or harassment, the victim knows they are victimized, but the damage is private. Schoolyard bullying is in sight of the teachers and other school authorities, but a cyberbully's acts are invisible to others if the victim does not speak up.

If a crime is visible only to the victim, the victim must report the crime to someone, if only to a confidant who goes to the authorities. If the victim is unwilling to report the crime, or unaware of the crime, the crime is not reported.

Too often, victims do not report cybercrimes. There are a number of reasons for this.

---

[18]For the text of the convention, see "Convention on Cybercrime," Council of Europe, November 23, 2001. www.europarl.europa.eu/meetdocs/2014_2019/documents/libe/dv/7_conv_budapest_/7_conv_budapest_en.pdf. Accessed August 2016.

For current status of convention ratification, see "Chart of signatures and ratifications of Treaty 185," Council of Europe. www.coe.int/en/web/conventions/full-list/-/conventions/treaty/185/signatures?p_auth=UQvnS5gj. Accessed August 2016.

The victims of cybercrime often feel they have brought the crime upon themselves and are unwilling to reveal their poor judgement. They might think they should have known not to open that suspicious email attachment or follow that clickbait link, and they don't want to publicly admit to their mistake. A business may have been waiting for a profitable quarter to invest in upgraded security systems and training, and is ashamed to admit that its parsimonious strategy backfired.

A business may also hesitate to report that it has been hacked because it fears adverse publicity. Not only does it risk a reputation for backward practices, its customers and partners may be afraid to do business with it. Therefore, a hacked department store might prefer to quietly deal with stolen payment card data themselves rather than call in the FBI or other law enforcement and risk losing customers.

The indirect victims of crimes like payment card data theft have little incentive to report thefts because the bank or the credit card company is required by law to make good the loss. When the authorities are called in, finding the crooks is difficult and time consuming. In addition, prosecution is likely to be complicated by jurisdictional issues and extradition. By the time a conviction occurs, recoverable assets may have disappeared and there may be no compensation forthcoming. It is not surprising that companies that are hacked may see few advantages in reporting the crime to the authorities.

Similarly, an individual who falls for an Internet too-good-to-be-true used car scam that accepts his money and neglects to deliver the car may not be eager to make his humiliation public, and the local law enforcement agency may brush him off because the agency does not have the skills or the resources for an investigation and extradition. The likelihood that the individual will report the next crime sinks fast.

Reporting of traditional crime is often driven by insurance. When my laptop was stolen in an airport several years ago, I missed my flight because I went to the airport police and filled out a theft report. I did not expect the thief to be caught or the laptop to be returned. I was tempted to skip reporting and catch my flight, but I knew that if I did not fill out the report and submit a copy with my claim, my insurance company would not honor it. Many property crimes are reported to meet insurance requirements, rather than from civic duty or expectations that property will be returned. Cybercrimes seldom have this incentive to reporting because few individuals have cyber-risk insurance. However, cyber-risk insurance is becoming more common, as one would expect with rising cybercrime rates.[19] Perhaps this trend will drive more extensive reporting of cybercrime.

---

[19]See "Early NAIC Analysis Sheds Light On Cybersecurity Insurance Data," National Association of Insurance Commissioners, June 30, 2016. www.naic.org/Releases/2016_docs/cybersecurity_insurance_data_analysis.htm. Accessed August 2014.

Cybercrimes are sometimes a "death by a thousand cuts," which is another reason they are not reported. Each crime may be insignificant, but may become significant when the crime is repeated many times. A single spam email is a criminal act, but the victim can delete it in an instant and the event is hardly worth the trouble to mention. If the criminal is perspicacious enough to send out their spam to a million victims, but only two pieces a month to each individual victim, they may never be reported. Although two spam emails a month from a single source is only a minor annoyance, most people get spam in their inbox from enough sources to make managing it a significant issue. In addition, some of that spam is likely to contain phishing malware that is downright dangerous. Nevertheless, a hundred spam emails in your inbox from a hundred different spammers is more hassle to report than most people are willing to undertake and the spammers slip by.

Reporting cybercrime is important because underreporting impedes accurate measurement of the impact of cybercrime and the criminals who perpetrate unreported crimes cannot be prosecuted. When the real impact is underreported, the resources assigned to address the problem will not be sufficient. Fortunately, the individual victim is not the only point to begin the attack on cybercrime. For example, many enterprises are built around online business and Internet activity. Internet retailers and Internet media providers are two examples among many. If consumers are driven away from online activity by cybercrime, these enterprises suffer, which is a powerful incentive to act against cybercrime. One action is to help authorities identify and prosecute under-reported crimes (see the following sidebar).

HOW TO REPORT CYBERCRIME

Reporting crimes, any kind of crime, is an important step any citizen can take to reduce crimes. Enforcement officials cannot prevent crimes they don't know about. This is especially true for cybercrimes because the victim is likely to be the only witness and the only person aware of the damage or loss.

The US Department of Justice has a website with advice on reporting Internet-related or intellectual property crimes.

www.justice.gov/criminal-ccips/reporting-computer-internet-related-or-intellectual-property-crime

Several federal agencies, including the FBI, the Secret Service, and Homeland Security, take reports. In most cases, the Internet Crime Complaint Center (IC3) (ic3.gov) is the best starting point. The IC3 is an FBI-run clearing house that takes complaints and refers them to the appropriate local, state, and federal agencies. Reporting directly to law enforcement agencies may be more direct, but an IC3 complaint is available to all jurisdictions and can help find and convict the criminal. Adding a complaint to the IC3 data base increases the effectiveness of all cybercrime law enforcement agencies.

In the European Union law enforcement agency, Europol, also has a site with advice for reporting cybercrime:

`www.europol.europa.eu/content/report-cybercrime`

Cybercrime Law Enforcement Agencies

Progress is being made. In the US, on the national level, the Department of Justice, through the FBI, has taken the lead in establishing regional computer forensic centers and training programs for local law enforcement agencies. The FBI also actively investigates and enforces federal and international cybercrime. Some types of cybercrimes are investigated by the Bureau of Alcohol, Tobacco, and Firearms. The Department of Homeland Security investigates cyberterrorism through the Secret Service and provides additional training and support to state and local law enforcement.

The National White Collar Crime Center (NW3C) is a non-profit organization funded by its members and federal agencies, mainly the Department of Justice. The NW3C provides cybercrime training and support to state and local law enforcement.

The FBI established a national clearing house for reporting cybercrime. This clearinghouse, called the Internet Crime Complaint Center (IC3), accepts reports on all forms of cybercrime. The FBI pursues the subset of these reports that are fall into its jurisdiction. The rest are dispatched to an agency with jurisdiction. Sometimes the appropriate agency is Homeland Security or the Secret Service, but more likely, the report will be referred to a state or local agency.

The IC3 can bundle together reports as well as dispatch them. Criminals who commit large numbers of small crimes that each fall below the practical bar for prosecution may rise above the bar when their crimes are bundled together. If victims consistently report crimes to the IC3, even small crimes, the chances of seeing some of these criminals prosecuted will increase and the number of cybercrimes will decrease. The IC3 encourages anyone to report cybercrimes without regard to the size of the crime or the jurisdiction.[20]

A central clearinghouse also raises the level of awareness of the need for regional and national task forces that bring together resources to deal with cybercrime. A task force can supply experts and equipment that individual agencies would not ordinarily be able to access. For example, tracing a distributed denial of service attack requires specialized software and hardware

---

[20]Lest anyone get sporty, filing a false or intentionally misleading report is a felony. See the sidebar, "Reporting Cybercrimes," for more detail on reporting.

and the skill to use the resources. Most local enforcement groups do not have the resources to undertake such a project, but a task force combining the resources of several jurisdictions may be able to accumulate the resources and expertise needed to be successful. In addition, task forces provide for coordination and cooperation across jurisdictional boundaries that often impede investigation and prosecution of cybercrimes.

In the European Union, the European Police Office (Europol) pursues international crimes by coordinating the law enforcement authorities of the members of the EU. Europol opened the European Cybercrime Centre (EC3) as a center of technical expertise that provides coordination and support to member states' anti-cybercrime operations and investigations.[21]

Interpol is distinct from Europol. Interpol was formed in the first half of the 20th century to facilitate international police cooperation. Although its headquarters are located in France, it is a global organization with only a few states that are not members, unlike Europol, which is limited to European Union membership. Interpol provides support and coordination to cybercrime law enforcement agencies on a global scale. Interpol opened a research and development center for cyber expertise in 2014.[22]

Where We Are Today

Today, cybercrime is affecting a growing number of institutions and individuals. The conventional crime rate has gone down substantially in the last decade for several reasons, including changing demographics and improving police techniques, but cybercrime has been soaring. The police techniques that been effective in reducing crime are not effective against cybercrime. Local and state police are stymied. Their police academy training simply does not apply to a denial of service attack on a business, ransomware at a local hospital, or victims of Internet fraud.

The federal authorities are better prepared, but they concentrate on large cases involving many thousands of dollars and affecting hundreds and thousands of people, not five-hundred dollar fraudulent Internet sales of fake football tickets.

In fact, five-hundred dollar cases are properly the realm of local enforcement, but local enforcement seldom has the tools and skills to identify the fraudster, and if they could, the culprit is probably in another state or country. The cost of investigating, extraditing, and trying the distant criminal is probably

---

[21]For more information on EC3, see "Combating Cybercrime in a Digital Age," Europol. www.europol.europa.eu/ec3. Accessed August 2016.
[22]For more information on Interpol's anti-cybercrime activities, see "Cybercrime," Interpol. www.interpol.int/Crime-areas/Cybercrime/Cybercrime. Accessed August 2016.

much greater than the sum stolen and more than local budgets can bear. Cyberharassment crimes are often similar. The actions of local enforcement are restrained and the criminals can carry on with impunity. Consequently, the closure rate for local cybercrime cases is less that one in ten.

The situation is bad. Although those $500 dollar frauds, $800 ransoms, and $1,000 car sales frauds are small when compared with the theft of millions of payment cards or millions of dollars stolen in attacks of bank wire transfers, for the persons who lost their money and did not get to go to the game, these are not trivial and the aggregated cost of these crimes is large.

Enforcement is improving. Federal programs are training local police in cyber-forensic methods and local officers are trading on their own local pockets of expertise. Regional enforcement centers pool resources and apply them where they are most needed. Local enforcement is working with local private industry and universities to deepen their expertise. The FBI is acting as a central cybercrime reporting hub for the entire country and helping connect the dots to link together small frauds into large operations that justify national and international resources and will finance extradition to a jurisdiction where the crimes can be prosecuted.

International organizations are making it more difficult for international criminals to slip through the net.

Realistically, despite the advances, a victim of cybercrime is lucky to get anything more than sympathy from the authorities. Banks, payment card companies, and merchants are all likely to help the victims of the business' compromised systems, but the cyber equivalent of car theft or home burglary is not likely to be treated as thoroughly or as competently as a physical theft or burglary. There are certainly exceptions, and the number of exceptions is likely to increase, but the prospects are not good.

Fortunately, there is another side to the problem. Law enforcement struggles to apprehend and convict cybercriminals, but avoiding becoming cybercrime victim is getting somewhat easier. The computing industry is much more aware of cybercrime today than they were even 10 years ago and systems today are designed to be more crime resistant and have become more secure. Of course, the cybercrime business is booming, as criminals are busy devising new ways to steal and defraud using computers, but the vendors are also aware that their business depends on secure and reliable systems. In the next chapter, I look in more detail at what the industry has done and is doing to improve prevention and detection of cybercrimes.

What Has the Industry Done?

Have They Made Any Progress?

When we read about half a billion passwords stolen from a sophisticated Internet service, it might hard to believe, but software is more secure today than it ever has been before. The industry has come a long way.

The Security Legacy

The first commercial software project I worked on in my software career did not have a quality assurance program. When sales sold a copy of the system, the development manager went around to the developers' desks gathering a handful of eight-inch floppy disks containing the developer's current best work. The handful of disks went to the new customer. Often, a developer went out to the site with the floppies to put the code together and get it running.

When a customer had an issue, a developer was likely to go back on site to diagnose the problem and write code to fix it on the spot. Consequently, no two customers were certain to have the same code. A defect fixed for one customer was not always fixed for other customers. Learning to use the software often amounted to learning to dodge the pitfalls and landmines of the implementation.

© Marvin Waschke 2017
M. Waschke, *Personal Cybersecurity*, DOI 10.1007/978-1-4842-2430-4_8

After I had worked there for about a year, management asked one of the technical writers to take on product testing after she complained that the software was difficult to document because it often did not work. I remember developers grumbled about fixing things the tester found: little nit-picky things like a miskey that would erase critical data files without warning or the system inexplicably dying and forcing the user to start over. Today, defects like these would be called *show stoppers* and would be instantly escalated to the highest level. In those days, users were just grateful to be able to process their accounts receivable in a few hours instead of working weekends to get the bills out on time. A few bugs were nothing compared to the days of drudgery that the computer eliminated.

I cringed while writing the paragraphs above because the practices at my old employer were so far from current software development management practice. Yet, this was a successful software business that still flourishes where others have failed. At that time, they produced well-respected products, which delighted their customers, despite deficiencies in development methodology and what we would today call dismal product quality. Good customer service compensated for the many flaws and defects in the products, but more than anything else, expectations were much different. Customers were willing to put up with almost anything to get the productivity jumps they craved, and a few bugs were an acceptable price for the productivity gain.

Of course, the practices of my former employer have evolved with the industry. Today, a product built in the old cowboy style would be considered amateurish and impossibly expensive to support, falling far below customer and investor expectations.

Software development and customer expectations of reliability and consistency have changed. Practices that worked when expectations were limited and customer bases were small are not even close to acceptable now.

The same has happened to computer security. In the days of isolated personal desktops and limited networks, security did not have to be built into software. Locks on the doors and windows were enough. And when the locks were broken, the intruder probably did not know what to do with the computing gear anyway. As devices became connected and computing became more exposed to outsiders, security became more important, but old habits change slowly and security was slow to receive proper attention in many mainstream products.

As the importance of security began to be acknowledged, engineers still tended to think of it as an add-on. When a project began, security would be given a prominent place in project plans. But as the project progressed, strange things would happen. Security is often a hindrance to rapid development. Much of development consists of making a small addition, testing it, observing the effect, correcting it, and making more additions. This cycle is repeated many times, often many times an hour, in developing a product. A little thing like entering a password, updating a security token, or the like, are irritating time sinks in the cycle. Developers are always impatient and canny. They find ways avoid these annoyances. They might add a backdoor to bypass security, or a switch that turns off security. Or, most dangerous of all, decide to put off writing security checks until the module is working properly without them.

Of course, typical software projects all begin to slide, that is, get behind schedule. Usually, to bring the project back on schedule, unnecessary features are trimmed and the project is streamlined. At this point, the temptation to scale back security plans and leave in temporary security holes is strong. Often security features are relegated to the next release, which could be a long time coming. After all, the customers are clamoring for functionality. Only a minority care about security. Until a breach occurs, security is an annoyance, not a feature. Given a choice, most product managers will choose a feature that might capture customer attention and garner sales, and they pass on boring, annoying, security checks. Consequently, products, especially consumer products, were often released with weak or no security built in.

These products, utilities, and operating systems become sitting ducks for criminal hackers. These products are the legacy we have today.

The Turning Point

As you saw in the last chapter, prosecution of cybercrime is becoming more effective, but the challenges are still tough. Too many clever cybercriminals get away with their crimes. On the other hand, today's hardware and software has been made more resistant to intrusion and more resilient to attack, so that the cybercriminal's job has become more difficult.

It's hard to pinpoint a date or name an event, but, around 2000, the tide began to turn. The industry began to realize that cybersecurity was not being taken seriously enough to keep up with the increasing penetration and criticality of the role of computers in almost every aspect of culture and society. At the same time, cybercriminals were becoming more active and visible. The computing industry became aware that cybercrime and lack of security could be a significant deterrent to current and future business.

It is no surprise that security consciousness grew as the Internet began to be a necessity in homes and businesses. Some of the contradictions between a free and open Internet and safe and reliable computing had become evident. Networked computers had become the norm, and criminal hackers were building steam. And it was becoming evident that enforcing cybercrime laws is demanding and requires training and resources that are not easy for law enforcement to obtain.

The industry has stepped up. Like traditional crime, cybercrime can be controlled in two ways. You can catch more housebreakers when the police have more personnel, better 911 service, faster patrol cruisers, and more effective crime scene investigation tools. Alternatively, you can make house breaking harder to commit and easier to prevent by designing better locks, more secure windows, and motion detectors.

The industry has invested heavily in tools and techniques that make computing more secure and private. Cybercrimes have become harder to commit and easier to stop.

The Microsoft Security Development Lifecycle

Microsoft is a representative of the changing attitudes in the software industry. It was certainly a prominent software vendor at the turn of the millennium, and it was also quite typical. Software and hardware companies realized that old practices that ignored or downplayed vulnerabilities would simply not do. On January 15, 2002, Bill Gates sent an email to Microsoft employees that would be called the "Trustworthy Computing Memo."[1] In the memo, Gates stated that security, availability, and privacy were the new priorities for Windows development. Issues in these areas would be fixed first, before anything else, and would be the first considerations in all designs. Shortly thereafter, in an astonishing assertion of the seriousness of the directives in the memo, the Windows development division shut down while developers received training in secure and reliable coding and design practices.

Later, Microsoft developed a set of security guidelines, in the form of a documented development process, which it published as "The Microsoft Security Development Lifecycle (SDL) Process Guidance."[2] It also made publicly available many of the tools it uses for testing. With few exceptions, all Microsoft development teams are required to follow the guidance. In addition, other companies in the industry, such as Cisco and Adobe, have chosen to adopt the Microsoft SDL.

The choice of a process rather than a set of security features or rules was an important and wise choice. Security practices and mechanisms change as the industry progresses. Processes change also, but their most important property is the ability to adapt to evolving technology while preserving core goals.

---

[1]"Memo from Bill Gates," January 15, 2002. https://news.microsoft.com/2012/01/11/memo-from-bill-gates/. Accessed September 2016.
[2]The latest version can be downloaded at www.microsoft.com/en-us/download/details.aspx?id=29884. Accessed September 2016.

The SDL is a classic feedback cycle (See Figure 8-1) that begins with security training for the development team. All participants are required to participate in continuing security training and maintain adequate levels of certification for their role in the project. Next, security requirements are established, including plans for testing and assessment. The design stage includes analysis of attack surfaces and models of potential threats. During implementation, approved tools and components are used and best coding practices are followed. Code is reviewed by peers. The completed code is verified through various forms of testing and analysis, including *tiger team* or *white hat testing* in which professionals play the part of hackers and attempt to invade the product. After the project is released, the behavior of the product and user issues are recorded and classified in preparation for the next round of the cycle.

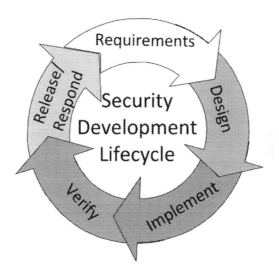

Figure 8-1. The Microsoft Security Development Lifecycle is a classic feedback loop

The original SDL was formulated as a *waterfall model* in which each stage is separated from the next as the development flows over an irreversible waterfall from one stage to the next, often over two or three years. This development methodology is not used as much today as it once was. Now, developers prefer use *agile development*. They break projects down into smaller efforts called *sprints* that are completed and released in a few weeks. Each sprint results in a working product with more features than the previous sprint. As features are added, the design is adapted to the requirements revealed by the results of the sprint. The SDL has been adapted to more rapid development by performing the entire SDL for each sprint. Tailoring the SDL to the precise features added in the sprint reduces the overhead of repeating the SDL many times.

The details of the Microsoft SDL are important to software developers because they define a set of best practices for developing secure software. SDL is not the only such guideline. Most established software companies have similar processes. Often, the Microsoft SDL is the model for security processes, but it is not the only model. Groups and agencies such as the Software Engineering Institute, the Federal Aviation Agency, and the Department of Homeland Security have all published guidelines for secure software development.[3] These guidelines have different emphasis and details, but they are all similar.

For personal computer users, the guidelines themselves are dry stuff and not of much interest. However, the guidelines are crucially important to computer users in one way: SDL and similar guidelines have made the life of hackers and cybercriminals much harder. The level of hacking, both in quantity and quality, at the turn of the millennium was insubstantial compared to today. Without processes like SDL in place for the last decade, computing would be in a sorry state under today's onslaught. Everyone deplores the weaknesses that remain in software today, but the truth is that if the guidelines had not been formulated and followed, the bar for a successful hacking exploit today would be much lower.

There is another aspect of security guidelines that is important to personal computer users: the guidelines work. Software that is produced under a strict security design and implementation regimen is safer than software that is not. Large companies like Microsoft, Google, Oracle, IBM, Apple, and so on follow SDL or similar processes. Good practices do not guarantee that software and hardware from these companies have no security defects; we all know that flaws occasionally appear in all vendors' products, but software that is not built following a security conscious process is much more likely to have hackable flaws. In addition, flaws in software developed under security guidelines are usually easier and quicker to diagnose and repair because the guidelines assume that flaws will be found and the software is designed to be patched. The guidelines include planning and budgeting for regular development and delivery of security patches.

Lone developers, or developers in a small shop or start-up, often do follow secure practices, but caution is needed. In a startup, a week of development time can mean life or death for the nascent business. This kind of pressure is not conducive to good security decisions. Organizations that are ignorant of or indifferent to good security practices do exist. Conventional

---

[3]For an overview of published process guidelines see Noopur Davis, "Secure Software Development Life Cycle Processes," Department of Homeland Security, Build Security In, Setting a Higher Standard For Software Assurance, July 13, 2013. `https://build securityin.us-cert.gov/articles/knowledge/sdlc-process/secure-software-development-life-cycle-processes#tsp`. Accessed September 2016.

products that are being connected to the Internet by designers and engineers who are not familiar with network security may inadvertently produce insecure designs. Apps from sources without known reputations for security must be treated with caution. The major vendors have public track records and reputations they are loath to lose. Does that mean you should never use an app from a small developer whom you have never heard of? No. There's great and safe software out there from small developers, often at higher quality and better price than the offerings of the big guys. But you should realize that there is some risk. Chapter 9 discusses some practices to follow when installing software from a less well-known source.

Patch and Update Processes

Perhaps the most important consequence of secure development processes is the development and proliferation of automated patch and update processes. One clue that the development team paid attention to security in a product is the presence of an automatic update process. We now have over 50 years of experience writing software and we should know by now that practically useful computer applications always are vulnerable to security breaches. No computer can ever be expected to be totally secure and error-free. Vendors can eliminate many issues by following development best practices, but these practices must include an active and on-going search for security flaws after the product is released. In addition, when defects are found, mechanisms must be in place to develop patches for the flaws rapidly and disseminate the patches expeditiously.

Why are automated patches and updates so important? When processes are automated, computer users no longer have to worry about applying the latest patches and updates. No one likes to find out that they have been stung by a virus that would have been stopped if they had remembered to apply the latest patch.

At many large corporations, patches must be tested with customized and bespoke applications[4] to make sure the patches won't cause problems with critical production processes. The IT departments in these organizations frequently have entire teams who do nothing but test and manage the application of patches and updates. Without automation, individuals would have to

---

[4]A bespoke application is written specifically for a given customer. Large enterprises often have bespoke applications that are written in house or by third parties to address the enterprise's unique requirement. Sometimes, a bespoke application is a commercial off-the-shelf (COTS) product that has been modified to meet special requirements. Bespoke applications often cause extra expense and security issues because the issues are unique and not identified or mitigated in the industry-wide environment.

do something similar, although individuals usually don't have customized and bespoke software to contend with, the amount of time and skill required for sound patch and update management is not trivial. For most of us, the time required would drive us to neglect this critical activity, and it would not be long before we landed in the soup. The security landscape moves so fast and our software is so complex that an individual user cannot keep up with everything even on the phones they hold in their hands. Automation takes the onus off the individual to choose when to apply patches.

Zero-Day Exploits

Zero-day exploits, attacks that exploit a flaw in a system that was previously unknown and therefore unstoppable, are rare. Government agencies such as the U.S. National Security Agency, law enforcement such as the Federal Bureau of Investigation, and military cyberwarfare groups are willing to pay millions of dollars for powerful zero-day exploits. Software and hardware vendors are also willing to pay for these. And it almost goes without saying that there is a ready black market on the criminal darkweb.

Zero-day exploits are scarce and becoming scarcer for two reasons. The first is that the industry, using better development methodologies and architectures, is producing more secure products with fewer exploits to be found. Second, the industry has built a robust system for discovering security flaws and patching them.

In a perverse way, the value of these zero-day exploits is increased by more secure architectures and powerful automated patching and updating services that are now available for all major operating systems and software. Today, zero-day exploits are hard to find and they don't stay zero-day for long. During their short life span, these exploits can be extremely valuable to an organization that knows how to use them to further their legitimate or illegitimate goals. High value, scarcity, and short life-span combine to induce competition that drives high prices.

A large network of researchers are continuously searching both for zero-day exploits and the effects of zero-day exploits. Many companies offer bounties to these researchers when they find a new flaw in the company's products. When the exploits are found, they are typically fixed and communicated to the security community.

Public and Private Vulnerability Management

Zero-day exploits are just one kind of vulnerability that must be managed to make computing safe. Vulnerabilities are flaws or weaknesses in software than can be used to violate the security policies of a system. For example, a flaw that causes a program to produce incorrect output is a flaw or defect, but it is not a vulnerability unless the bogus output could cause or permit a security violation. Frequently, a vulnerability will shift an application into a state in which it yields control to an unauthorized invader or hacker.

In the United States, a set of government and non-government institutions have grown up to coordinate responses to situations where computer security is compromised. These institutions work in concert with private enterprise, academics, and the public to discover and rectify vulnerabilities, flaws that may lead to security breaches. Unlike the FBI and other law enforcement agencies, these institutions do not exist to catch criminals and bring them to justice, although they frequently help law enforcement catch criminals. These groups main concern is making cybercrimes impossible.

Their approach is two pronged: when a security breach occurs that is not obviously due to a previously unknown vulnerability or technique, these groups examine the breach and determine if it is a new vulnerability. Then they work with the vendor of the system to develop a remedy. These groups also work to discover vulnerabilities that have not been used in an actual breach, or present theoretical flaws that could cause a vulnerability in some future situation. These too are documented and made available to systems vendors who may develop fixes or use theoretical deficiencies to strengthen future designs.

National Vulnerability Database (NVD)

The heart of the system is the National Vulnerabilities Database. The NVD is maintained by the Department of Homeland Security and the National Institute of Standards and Technology (NIST). In the NVD, a vulnerability is assigned an overall severity plus a ranking for exploitability, how technically difficult an exploit would be required to take advantage of the vulnerability, what kind of damage could be done, and so on. The entry also contains references to advisories, solutions, and tools that may be used to detect, research, or remediate the vulnerabilities. The NVD depends on Common Vulnerabilities and Exposures dictionary (CVE) to unambiguously identify vulnerabilities. Each vulnerability in the NVD has a corresponding entry in the CVE. See Figure 8-2. For more information on the CVE, see below.

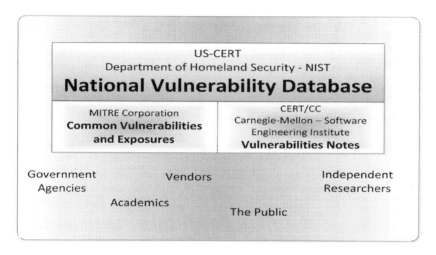

Figure 8-2. The National Vulnerability Database is a central repository for computer security vulnerability information that catalogs vulnerability issues and solutions

The NVD is a go-to public database open to anyone who wants to know about current software vulnerabilities. The team responsible for the NVD is the United States Computer Emergency Response Team (US-CERT). The US-CERT was formed to help protect U.S. government agencies from cyber-attacks, but it has grown beyond that limited role to act as a central clearing house for coordinating the engineering battle against all cybercrime.

Computer Emergency Response Team Coordination Center (CERT/CC)

CERT/CC is a division of the Software Engineering Institute (SEI). SEI is a private foundation that is funded by the US government and is based at Carnegie Mellon University. CERT/CC was formed in the late 1980s when cybersecurity began to emerge as an important topic. It is a research organization devoted to cybersecurity. CERT/CC predates the US-CERT. Although the two teams work together, they are distinct and have different functions.

CERT/CC brings together government, academic, and private engineers and researchers who focus on computer security-related issues and practices. They produce research papers and participate in security conferences. They collect and analyze data on security threats and solutions, develop security tools, and perform security analysis. They support the private sector as well as US government agencies such as the Department of Defense and Homeland Security.

CERT/CC collects, analyzes, and coordinates responses to vulnerabilities. The process begins with a report submitted to the CERT/CC site. Vendors, academics, independent researchers, the public, and CERT/CC staff all submit reports, which are examined, cross-referenced, and prioritized by severity. Usually, vendors are informed and given a chance to remediate the vulnerability before the reports are made public. When reports are made public, they are published in the CERT/CC Vulnerability Notes database.

Common Vulnerabilities and Exposures Dictionary (CVE)

MITRE Corporation is a non-profit research organization. MITRE maintains CVE, which is a list of publicly known computer security vulnerabilities. CVE assigns standard identifiers for vulnerabilities. Standard identifiers facilitate cooperation among investigators, researchers, engineers, and vendors in addressing vulnerabilities.[5]

The community working to reduce and eliminate vulnerabilities is large. MITRE Corporation is a US organization that works extensively with the US government. Major software and computing hardware vendors, such as Microsoft, Apple, Google, Intel, Cisco all participate in various capacities. However, the CVE community is international with contributors from many countries. The International Telecommunications Union (ITU) has adopted CVE as part of its standards.[6]

Without some form of unique identifiers, descriptions of vulnerabilities can easily be ambiguous. If vulnerabilities are not clearly and unambiguously identified, fixes can be misapplied, work duplicated, and issues overlooked. Obtaining a CVE identifier is the first step taken after a vulnerability is discovered. Often, the identifier will be assigned by the vendor of the vulnerable software. For example, Microsoft is the numbering authority for Microsoft issues and Hewlett Packard is the number authority for HP issues.

CVE-ID documents contain a brief description of the vulnerability and references to other documents that help identify the vulnerability. CVE entry also references the NVD. The CERT/CC Vulnerability Notes also relies on CVE identifiers.

---

[5]For more details about the CVE organization see Common Vulnerabilities and Exposures, "About CVE," http://cve.mitre.org/about/. Accessed September 2016.
[6]See "ITU-T Recommendations, ITU-T X.1520 (04/2011)," April 20, 2011. www.itu.int/ITU-T/recommendations/rec.aspx?rec=11061. Accessed September 2016.

US-CERT, CERT/CC, and Private Enterprise Working Together

The current mechanism for identifying and remediating computer vulnerabilities relies on a community of both private and public groups that work together with the goal of discovering and remediating vulnerabilities, both in the US and internationally. The cooperation works in a lot of different ways and is quite flexible. Rather than try to explain the relationships, here is an example that shows many parts working together.

The scenario begins with a small security consultancy, possibly only a principal or a few partners. In the last few years, many software companies have established bounty programs that pay researchers for discovering security flaws in their software. This practice has given rise to a swarm of bounty hunters who get some income from finding flaws and collecting the bounties.

Crosswalk is an Intel product for developing apps that will run on both Android and Apple iOS. A security researcher from a small consultancy discovered a flaw in Intel's implementation of Crosswalk that could be exploited by a hacker to launch a man-in-the-middle attack that would allow the hacker to listen in and interfere with supposedly secure communications.

The researcher, or perhaps bounty hunter, reported the vulnerability to Intel. Later, the researcher reported the vulnerability to CERT/CC. CERT/CC became involved and mediated communication between Intel and the researcher. CERT/CC obtained a CVE identifier for the vulnerability so it could be unambiguously cross-referenced in the community. Intel fixed the problem and sent the fix to the researcher. The researcher tested and confirmed the fix, and a public disclosure date was set. Until the disclosure date, the security researcher, CERT/CC, the CVE, and Intel kept the vulnerability confidential to discourage hackers from using the vulnerability before a fix was available. On the disclosure date, Intel published an account of the vulnerability and fix on their website and CERT/CC issued a public Vulnerability Note. Two days later, US-CERT published a Vulnerability Summary for the assigned CVE-ID on the Homeland Security-NIST National Vulnerability Database. The Vulnerability Notes, the NVD, and the CVE all cross-reference each other.[7] See Figure 8-3.

---

[7]The details are in the following: Vulnerability Notes Database, "Vulnerability Note VU#21781," July 29, 2016. www.kb.cert.org/vuls/id/217871. Accessed September 2016. Nightwatch Cybersecurity, "Advisory: Intel Crosswalk SSL Prompt Issue [CVE 2016-5672]," July 29, 2016. wwws.nightwatchcybersecurity.com/2016/07/29/advisory-intel-crosswalk-ssl-prompt-issue/. Accessed September 2016.
National Vulnerability Database. "Vulnerability Summary for CVE-2016-5672," July 31, 2016. https://web.nvd.nist.gov/view/vuln/detail?vulnId=CVE-2016-5672, and "Crosswalk security vulnerability,"
https://blogs.intel.com/evangelists/2016/07/28/crosswalk-security-vulnerability/. Accessed September 2016.

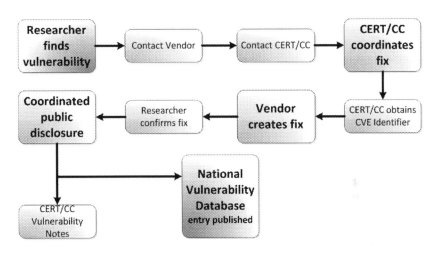

Figure 8-3. Example steps from discovery of a vulnerability to publication in the National Vulnerability Database

This vulnerability and resolution, which was chosen almost at random, is an example of cooperation between private enterprise, government agencies, and non-profits addressing significant security vulnerabilities before they become issues.

The vulnerability was rated as medium severity with a high exploitability score. In other words, worse vulnerabilities are possible, but this one would have been easy to exploit if a hacker discovered it. As far as anyone knows, the flaw discussed here was never exploited by a hacker, although it easily could have been.

In this case, the vulnerability was resolved by a patch from the vendor. If the vulnerability was a virus or other malware, the antimalware tool developers may respond by adding code to their tools to catch the malware in their scans. IT departments might have been alerted to watch for certain symptoms on their systems.

This example shows the importance of the automatic updating and patching mechanisms that are included now in most operating systems and software products. A vulnerability like the one described is important to users when a hacker takes advantage of it to steal information or wreak other havoc, but until that occurs, the vulnerability is benign. Uninformed users might even complain about the fix because they might see warning messages that they had not seen before. The symptoms of a man-in-the-middle attack are usually subtle and users may unknowingly prefer suffering the attack to the annoyance of repeating a transaction after an attack is stopped.

Under circumstances like these, without knowing about the vulnerability and its potential, end users have little incentive to apply this Crosswalk patch. Waiting for the next release is on the path of least resistance, but waiting also falls into the hands of hackers, giving them a long window in which to exploit the weakness. The CERT/CC Vulnerability Notes and the US-CERT National Vulnerability Database ordinarily do not release information on the issue until some fix is available but fixes do not always get applied promptly. Hackers are in the habit of scanning databases for new opportunities. Users who do not put fixes in place promptly are open to attack. Hackers do often find their own vulnerabilities to exploit, but they also take advantage of the vulnerability databases.

Automated patching and updating does a lot to shorten the susceptible period between publication of the vulnerability and fixes being applied to users systems. The user is usually the least informed player and the least capable of making informed decisions about what to patch or update and when to do it.

Security Theory

People have a natural tendency to think of security in a piecemeal fashion. When a criminal breaks through a fence, we rush to repair the hole in the fence, which is an obvious and expedient reaction, but it may be wiser or more cost efficient to examine the problem at a higher level as *perimeter enforcement* rather than fixing a hole in the fence. The more abstract view could lead to replacing the fence with a different kind of barrier, adding a motion detector to the alarm system, or moving valuables to a different location. The conclusion may be to fix the hole in the fence, but ignoring alternatives could also be a dangerous waste.

One way to look at computer security on a more general level is to examine the where computing is vulnerable on a general level. The goal is to realistically predict where computing is vulnerable and what is at risk before code is written and to take steps to preserve security in the face of unpredicted exploits. This is a complex subject that will only be touched on lightly here, but the subject is important because it helps sort out where to look for security issues and make sense of the effort (or lack of effort) by developers to improve cybersecurity.

The Security Triad

At the foundation of most security theory is a triad of goals: confidentiality, integrity, and availability. See Figure 8-4.

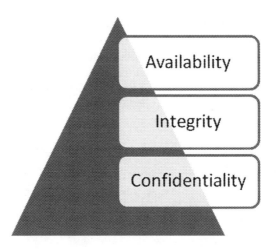

Figure 8-4. Security is a triad of goals

When a system is *confidential*, data and processes are only available to actors who have a legitimate right to access. Only the owner of a bank account and bank officials should have access to the amount in the account. Other account holders and bank employees not specifically assigned to managing the account should be barred from access.

When a system has *integrity*, data and processes will only be affected by authorized actors in a regulated fashion. A $100 deposit should never disappear or change to $75 dollars without a clearly defined and authorized audit trail and reason.

Finally, a system has *availability* when legitimate actors can get to data and processes in an orderly and predictable manner. If an authorized user is promised access to their account balance at 2 p.m. on Tuesdays, the user should, barring extraordinary events, always have access at the promised time.

As a computer user, the security triad can help you systematically review the security of features of a new laptop, tablet, or smartphone. They can help point out the weaknesses and strengths of applications you consider for installation. They can help you evaluate the safety of items from the Internet of Things you might place in your home or office and connect to your network.

When I consider installing a new application, I ask myself if the application exposes data in new ways, raising confidentiality issues. The sharing features of the newer versions of office tools like word processors are an example. I was prompted to look at the default access permissions and make sure information will not be exposed that I do not intend to expose. I then go on to ask questions about integrity and availability. This is an effective way to avoid security surprises with new functionality.

A key problem for computer security theorists is to discover ways in which confidentiality, integrity, and availability can be built into computer software and hardware in such a way that building applications that violate these principles is difficult or impossible. Computer operating systems such as Microsoft Windows, Apple iOS, OS X, Android, or Linux are the point where software and hardware come together, so operating systems are the focus of much of this effort.

Threat Modelling

One of the techniques developers use to design and construct more secure systems is called *threat modelling*. A developer, or group of developers, sit down to imagine all the threats that a system may be subject to and the consequences if the threats were carried out. The security triad provides a systematic pattern for thinking about threats.

Simply taking time to imagine the possible threats is a big step forward from the old days when security was an afterthought. Developers have taken threat modelling beyond a lightly structured "what if" exercise. The details of threat modeling techniques vary but they all identify the data processed by the system, the users of the system, and who the adversaries of the system might be and what they might be after. They also identify how data moves through the system and where it is stored. The next step is to spot the points where the system is vulnerable. That is easier than it may appear because almost all vulnerabilities occur when data moves from one module to another. One of the key tools in threat analysis is a data flow diagram that delineates the flow of data from one module to another.

With the system assets and points of vulnerability all listed out, the threat modelers evaluate each threat, rating them by the amount and seriousness of damage they could cause. The results of this evaluation are fed back into the project plans and developers are assigned to mitigate the threats.

Threat modeling is usually an iterative process. Modeling is repeated during development, continually modeling new threats as they may appear and testing the mitigation of old threats. This process replaces the old plan, where a developer would be assigned to code a solution to a security defect whenever defects happened to show up in testing or in the field, but no one systematically looked for vulnerabilities and developed plans for eliminating before they made it to testing.

Control Flow Integrity

One such effort is *control flow integrity*. Control flow integrity is important because it is an attempt to build resistance to one type of system attack into the operating system and application code, rather than address individual flaws.

Chapter 3 discussed how most computer hardware supports security by only allowing the most powerful and potentially destructive computer instructions to be executed when certain conditions are met.

Control flow integrity adds a layer of sophistication to the operating system software that determines the conditions when privileged instructions will be executed by looking at the flow of control from one software section to another. Researchers have identified patterns of shifts in control that indicate a program is doing something it was not intended to do.

For all the complexity of software and hardware, each core in a running computer is simply executing one instruction after another. The mechanisms that are used to determine which instruction will be executed next can be quite intricate, but they all answer a simple question: what next? If a hacker can insinuate a change into the control mechanism that will start the computer executing his sequence of instructions and abandon the legitimate sequence, the hacker has won and the computer is pwned.

There are many ways to trick your way into the control mechanism. One way is to throw a monkey wrench into the whole thing by stuffing more data into input than the program expects. Done with finesse, the excess data may be loaded into the control mechanism and will hand over control to the hacker.

If an application is programmed well, the excess data would be thrown out, either quietly or with an error message, but not all programs are written well. In fact, checking for *buffer overruns* (jargon for too much data) was not common until buffer overrun security breaches began occur regularly. Now, checking for buffer overruns is a routine part of most quality assurance testing, and software engineers are trained to prevent them in their code.

Buffer overrun vulnerabilities are becoming less common, but they have not been eliminated. Legacy code still exists with unpatched buffer overrun vulnerabilities, and buffer overruns can occur in subtle ways that good engineering and quality assurance practice can miss. Further, buffer overruns are by no means the only way control can be diverted to invaders.

Control flow integrity does not address how control is hijacked from its legitimate path. Instead, it detects when the control goes awry and raises a flag. No matter how the system was rigged by the hacker, if the program strays, control flow integrity detects the misadventure and guides it back to a safe path.

Enforcing control flow is a way of approaching the problem at a higher level. Rather than eliminate buffer overruns that cause control flow misadventures, control flow integrity measures detect deviations in flow control and stops the deviation. For example, Microsoft Windows 10 supports a feature called Control Flow Guard, which is an example of forcing control flow integrity. Developers use features built into the operating system to write applications that detect when the flow control of their code has been diverted from its intended direction.

Although Control Flow Guard does not protect flow control from every attack, it does make code more resistant. Developers must compile Control Flow Guard into their code. When used properly, Control Flow Guard provides an additional layer of protection for code in addition to the defensive and coding practices that security conscious developers have been following for a decade. Since it is a new feature, we do not know how effective it will be in preventing hackers from gaining control of applications, but if it is successful, there will be fewer exploits and security patches, which will mean that computing will be safer for everyone.

Control Flow Guard is an example of applying a high-level approach to attempt to eliminate entire classes of exploits. Most software and computer manufacturers are working hard to address security in this fashion. Microsoft is not unique in their diligence. Apple and Google are making similar efforts in iOS, OS X, and Android operating systems.[8]

An ideal computing system would be impossible to subvert. That would mean that the system would only ever be run by authorized users, the system would always do exactly what it was designed to, the system would only work with authorized input, and all output would always arrive at authorized targets and never be misdirected to unauthorized targets.

---

[8]Don't confuse Microsoft Control Flow Guard with network flow control, which addresses network congestion problems. The two are very different.

Personal Defense

Stay Safe

Personal cybersecurity is lopsided in favor of the criminals. Criminals may attack and be repulsed hundreds of times before they are successful, but the victim must deflect every single attack or they lose. Does that mean we all should give up and suffer? Or quit using our computers? No. There is no guarantee that anyone can stop every attack that the criminals throw at us, but the odds that the bad guys will be successful can be reduced. When they do succeed, the damage can be minimized.

Stopping the criminals does take some effort. You must gauge for yourself the effort you want to expend. Personally, I am a moderate. I am usually willing to accept some risk in exchange for convenience, and I always look for ways to reduce risk with minimal inconvenience. I am often willing to accept compromises.

When considering security, always question what is at risk. For instance, access to your brokerage account could place your life savings at risk, but a hacker turning your computer into a bot is an affront and annoyance, not necessarily a financial loss. Therefore, you may be willing to put more effort into maintaining a strong password on your brokerage account and avoiding compromising that password. You may be less willing to disable JavaScript on your web browser, which will prevent most drive-by malware infections, but make many popular websites unusable.

© Marvin Waschke 2017
M. Waschke, *Personal Cybersecurity*, DOI 10.1007/978-1-4842-2430-4_9

Most the subjects covered in this chapter have been mentioned previously. Here, you will learn how best to protect yourself from dangers using the technology that has been explained in earlier chapters.

Passwords

Passwords are the first line of defense against hackers breaking into your computer and data, but possibly not in the way you expect. Even a four-digit PIN is fairly effective against someone trying to break directly into your phone or your laptop because your device will begin throttling—forcing a pause between attempts—after a few wrong guesses and eventually stop accepting entries.

The real threat is from automated password cracking systems that can try millions of guesses in minutes. Password cracking was discussed in detail in Chapter 3.

It bears repeating that when choosing passwords, the challenge is stay off the "passwords for dummies" list and out of the dictionary. Easily remembered passwords, such as "1234", "password", "opensesame", and so on are on the dummies list. Assume that every name in the baby names books, every common pet name, and all cute phrases are there. For a while, you could strengthen passwords by substituting "@" for "a", "0" for "o", mixing in uppercase and lowercase letters, and so on, but processing speeds are much greater now and the hackers can try variations or the items in the dummies list. The common obfuscations, such "P@ssW0rd!" are on the list. And, yes, all the obscenities, vulgarities, and profanities are there too. One way to avoid the dummies list is to google your password choice. If there are a lot of hits, chances are good that your choice is on the list.

The strongest passwords are long, random sequences built from a large character set. A 64-character password, created from random choices from just a 90-character pool (all the usual characters and symbols) is uncrackable even by computers with many orders of magnitude more capacity than the best available today.

Password length is the cracker's enemy and your friend.[1] A long phrase is better than a short phrase. My trick is to open a book and choose a sequence of words at random that I can remember. I am not particularly concerned about adding symbols or mixing case, unless the symbols and case can help

---

[1] NIST is revising recommended password guidelines to reflect the need for length. For a good overview of the revision in process, see Jim Fenton, "Toward Better Password Requirements," www.slideshare.net/jim_fenton/toward-better-password-requirements. Accessed October 2016. Fenton is an independent researcher and consultant to NIST. This PowerPoint is not an official document, but it appears to reveal thinking on its way into the revised guidelines.

me remember how to type the phrase in correctly. As an example, "datapass-ingthroughyour" is one which I happened to pull out of a book on my shelf. I can probably remember that one. Another approach is to string together outlandish images like "purplegoatstretcher". I slightly prefer grabbing phrases at random from books because the mind plays tricks. Purple Goat Stretcher could be a submerged memory of a rock band I once heard and just might appear on some hacker's dummy list. The Google test is handy. Google returns "No results found for purplegoatstretcher," indicating that it is a good phrase.[2]

PASSWORD RULES

- Randomly generated passwords are strongest.
- Use long passwords. Over 12 characters. 20 is better.
- Long, memorable phrases are usually strong.
- Strong passwords get no Google hits.
- Never put a reused password on a critical account.
- Change the password on critical accounts immediately after a breach.

Choosing strong passwords is not the only thing to watch. Look carefully at your smartphone or tablet. Could an invader infer your PIN from the smudges and worn spots? Or do you always enter your laptop PIN at the same time and from the same seat in a coffee shop on your way to work? Could an attentive invader figure out your PIN or password by watching you? They don't have to look over your shoulder to pick up clues. When dealing with PINs, it isn't necessary for the invader to snatch the complete PIN. All they need are enough clues to reduce the number of tries it takes to guess correctly before the device locks up. And invaders can make very clever inferences.

There are solutions. Keep your devices smudge and wear free is for security as well as hygiene and appearances. If you see evidence that your PIN or password has been worn into any of your devices, it is time to change them. Don't give criminal invaders all the time in the world to mount an assault.

Reusing Passwords

Using the same password for more than one important account is extremely dangerous. Even carefully protected strong passwords can be skimmed by a keystroke recorder or weaseled out of you by a social engineer. Hackers know that people reuse passwords. If a hacker kips your work account password, he

---

[2]But don't rely on Google absolutely. No Google hits does not guarantee a good password. Your birthday in Roman numerals may not get hits, but it is still weak.

will try it on your bank account. And your medical accounts. And your Amazon account. And so on. Reusing passwords can cascade an annoyance into a major catastrophe.

Not reusing passwords is one of the most important cybersafety practices, but today, most people have many critical accounts and managing even a few unique strong passwords is a challenge. Practically, few people can do it without a system.

Changing Passwords

Conventional wisdom is that passwords should be changed monthly, and some systems force you to change your password on schedule. The new NIST guidelines relax the rules on changing passwords because people tend to use weaker passwords and reuse them more often if they are forced to change them frequently. You must always change a compromised password as quickly as possible, but changing passwords without reason is no longer advocated. Note that if you have broken the rules and you reused a compromised password, you must create a new unique password for every account where the compromised password was used. You should also periodically change any critical password that you enter frequently and regularly in public.

Password Management Systems

Passwords are difficult to manage well. If you have a steel trap memory, the best plan is to memorize them and never write them down, but with hundreds of online accounts, each with a different long password, few people are capable of that feat. Even if you are capable, you may want to be able to share your passwords in an emergency. For example, if an accident were to put you in a coma, you may want someone with power of attorney to be able to access your accounts. That requires something more than memory for tracking passwords.

Stratify Your Accounts

Not all accounts are equal and you don't have to manage them all the same. Your critical accounts, such as your bank account, PayPal account, accounts like Amazon that have your credit card number, and your email accounts are your first-tier accounts; they each must have a strong and unique password. You should also use multi-factor authentication if it is offered. More on email accounts later. You must be vigilant for any indication that the suppliers of those accounts have been hacked into and be prepared to change the password instantly. These accounts should be checked weekly or daily for odd activity. Be prepared to contact customer service immediately when something looks wrong.

The quicker you respond, the more contained the damage. The variability of time scales is a maddening aspect of cybersecurity. Sometimes the damage occurs in milliseconds as money is electronically transferred out of your account. But a hacker may wait for years to use a stolen password or personal data against you. No activity for days or weeks is no guarantee that a compromise will not be used for harm later.

Some accounts are not as important as the first tier. These are places where a hacker might steal information to use for stealing your identity, or information that you want to keep private for some reason. I place government accounts like Social Security, medical accounts, and online vendors that don't have my credit card on file but I do business with moderate frequency in this tier. Social media accounts will fit here for many people, although those, like Facebook, that can be used for authenticating other services should be tier one. Your online backup service may be in this tier, or, if you consider your data more valuable, you might place it in tier one.

Second tier accounts must also have strong and unique passwords, but they require less vigilance. You must be prepared to change passwords and take action, but not on a hair-trigger like the first tier.

And then there is the third tier. These include online subscriptions to magazines and newspapers. These are the accounts that don't know much about you and exist more to track your involvement on the site than any significant service. Convenience is more important than security in this tier. You probably would not care much if one of these accounts were hacked. Be a bit cautious, however. There may be more on these sites than you expect, and it may not be pleasant if someone were to log in to one of these sites and masquerade as you in a forum. Be suspicious and cautious. However, suspicions aside, reused passwords in this tier are probably are not so dangerous, as long as the reused password is not from the first or second tier, and shorter, weaker passwords are not so bad.

Paper Password Storage

The traditionally recommended best practice is to memorize your passwords. For most people, that is totally impractical. The practice has led to weak and reused passwords. The solution is a thoughtful management system.

You can record your passwords on paper. That practice has been discouraged by some, especially in offices. An intruder or a malicious insider can easily go through the office looking for passwords on notes stuck to computer displays, under keyboards, or in other obvious places, but keeping passwords on paper is not so much a problem for a personal user because you have more control over who is in your home. Nevertheless, a paper record gives a burglar or other invader an opportunity to steal both your computing gear and your passwords at the same time. You should treat your paper password record like cash or other highly portable valuables. Keep them under your control in your wallet or purse, or lock them up.

Web Browser Password Management

Another approach is to use the password management system that is built into most web browsers. This is not the best solution, but it is convenient. Google Chrome and Microsoft Internet Explorer and Edge use your Google and Microsoft accounts to control access to their stored passwords. You must be signed into the Google or Microsoft system to get access to the passwords stored in their respective browsers. Therefore, if a criminal can get into your Google or Microsoft account, they have access to all your passwords. Firefox requires you to set up a Firefox password and log in to access your passwords. Firefox will store passwords without a password, but that offers no security—anyone with access to your computer can access the passwords. Using browser password storage is convenient and it means you only need to know one password to access all your online passwords automatically.

Password Managers

Password managers encrypt and store passwords, often both locally and in a cloud repository. They resemble using a web browser with stored passwords. Users only need to know the password for the manager and it takes care of the rest. In addition to storing passwords, most of these tools will generate strong random passwords and help manage passwords by informing you of duplicate passwords and passwords that may need changing. You can also arrange to share access to passwords on several different devices and even among family members or other trusted partners.

For a long time, I opposed password management tools. I no longer do and I use one myself. My former objection was that these tools are single points of failure. If a hacker can hack into a password manager, they have unlimited access to all the accounts in the manager. The password management tool vendors must be special targets for hackers. You must trust that your password manager designers and developers will keep ahead of the hackers who are trying to beat them. One mistake and you lose everything.

For me, the strength of well-managed automatically generated random strong passwords is more important than single point of failure weaknesses. With my complex online life, I have found that I cannot maintain a long list of sufficiently strong passwords, even with a paper system, but a password manager meets the challenge. If a password manager uses strong local encryption, only you can access your passwords; not even a court order can compel your vendor to open them without your master password, which you have and your password manager vendor does not. An added convenience is that cloud-stored passwords are available to all your computers, tablets, and smartphones. For me, the security and convenience provided by a manager far exceeds the potential single point of failure weakness. However, you must be careful to choose reputable vendors who take proper care of the security of their product.

There are several password management tools available. Some have free versions. Their features change frequently and not all have the features I deem essential, so you must do some research when you make your choice. I look for automatically generated cryptographically random passwords, strong local encryption, and passwords accessible from more than one device. The last feature is important to me because I use Linux and Windows desktops, a Windows laptop, a Windows tablet, and an Android smartphone depending on what I am doing and where I am. Prior to using a password manager, I had nearly a two-inch stack of index cards to manage all my passwords. I no longer have duplicate passwords and they are all as strong as the account will allow.

If your passwords are now weak and duplicated, do the research and get a password manager.

Administrative Account Password

The default configuration for Windows assigns administrative privileges to the primary user account. As an administrator, you can add programs, change computer configurations, replace drivers, access files, and perform other actions forbidden to ordinary users.

This is convenient but it's not secure because administrative privileges are exactly what a hacker wants. Without administrative privileges, hackers can run programs, but they cannot turn your computer into a bot and their ransomware will likely fail. By changing the account you use every day to a regular user instead of administrator, you make the hacker's job much harder. For example, if a social engineering attack tricks you into opening a bad attachment, there is a good chance the attack will fail because it requires administrative privilege. When the attack runs, a pop-up asks for an administrative password and the attack stops there.

There is some inconvenience in not having administrative privilege because you are asked for an administrative password each time you want to add a new application or make other configuration changes, but most people don't make configuration changes often.

To configure a separate administrative account, first add a new administrative account. Then make your own account an ordinary user account. Removing administrative privileges from your account before you create another administrative account is like sawing off a tree limb while you are sitting on it. A computer must have at least one administrative account and an ordinary user can't create an administrative account, so creating an administrative account must come first. Make your administrative password long and strong. A password manager-generated random password is best.

On Apple OS X, ordinary users are not assigned administrative privileges. Instead, OS X follows the UNIX and Linux practice where administrative privilege is only assigned temporarily, which is more secure than Windows default practice. Android and iOS are similar. However, getting full administrative privilege on these UNIX-like systems is not impossible, and, in fact, is likely easier than getting administrative privilege on a Windows system with a single, strong, and seldom-used administrative account.

Consult your operating system manual for instructions on changing accounts. On Windows, it considerably increases the security of your system. It is easy, it generates only minor inconvenience, and it can stop many attacks.

Other Forms of Authentication

Passwords are difficult. Security experts (and hackers) agree that people reuse passwords and choose weak passwords frequently. Passwords don't mesh well with human capabilities—we have faulty memories and most of us have a lazy streak that dreams up a path-of-least-resistance solution when we know caution is required. Consequently, passwords have many failings when authenticating identity. These failings are compounded by increased use of computing, especially remote cloud computing, in our everyday lives. We must prove our identity for more accounts every month, and those accounts play an ever more crucial role in our lives. Whether passwords will be replaced by other forms of authentication is hard to predict, but there are alternatives available now and under development.

Password Hints and Questions

Don't use hints and secret questions if you can avoid it. Hackers can easily find your dog's name, your mother's maiden name, your spouse's birthday, etc. This method is still used, but they have proven to be a very weak form of authentication, especially with the advent of social media. NIST now recommends that US government systems not use them; I recommend that individuals not use them. The only time I would consider using these methods is in multi-factor authentication (see below).

Biometrics

Biometrics—finger print scans, face scans, retinal scans—have some important advantages: they can't be forgotten, they are complex and unique, and they are easily entered using the proper scanners. Biometric authentication is attractive and much effort is being put into improving the technologies.

Nevertheless, there are serious limitations to biometrics. If a biometric is compromised, it can't easily be replaced. When a password is compromised, a new password is easily substituted. Fingerprint scanners have been fooled with fake fingers made from fingerprints or molds taken from real fingers. If one fingerprint is compromised, you only have nine more to substitute. Retinal and face scans may be more difficult to fake, but when they are compromised, there are fewer alternates and crooks are working hard to devise ways to fake them.

These technologies are improving, but crooks are also working hard at compromising them. Ultra-high resolution photography and 3D printing can easily be sources of convincing fakes. In this race, my bet is on the crooks. However, as a factor in multi-factor authentication, biometrics could prove to be of great value.

Multi-Factor Authentication

Multi-factor authentication is a way of combining authentication methods so that the sum is stronger than the parts.

Authentication based only on a password is single-factor authentication, as is authentication based only on a fingerprint. Many laptops and phones can now authenticate using biometrics or a password or a PIN. This is not multi-factor authentication. Multi-factor authentication demands passing two or more authentication challenges, not one of several alternative challenges.

Many security systems are now based on two or more factors. The theory behind multi-factor authentication is simple probability. The probability of being dealt four aces in poker is low, but suppose you were dealt a poker hand and a blackjack hand at the same time. The probability of getting both four aces in the poker hand and a blackjack in the blackjack hand in the same deal is much lower than just getting four aces in a single poker hand. Multi-factor authentication takes advantage of this principle of probability.

Using multi-factor authentication, you might enter a password correctly only to get a pop-up instructing you to retrieve a code arriving by email and enter it within a limited time. Such a system is a two-factor system. A hacker who steals your password would also need access to your email to get into your account, which is unlikely. On the server side, a correct password not followed by a token from an email raises a flag that the password may be compromised. Using two-factor authentication, you may get emails or other messages saying one part of a two-part authentication failed. If you don't have a satisfactory explanation, it is time to change your password because a hacker has trifled with your system. Not only does multi-factor authentication make your account more secure, the system can generate useful warnings.

If authentication requires a fingerprint scan as well as a password and a token from email, it is a three-factor system. Adding a biometric factor further challenges an intruder.

Other factors that are used are special devices, often resembling credit cards, with a digital readout that generates numbers based on the time. Each card uses a different formula for generating the number. When you log in, you have to enter the number on the card. Variants plug into a USB slot. A smartphone app can also perform the same function. These methods have an advantage that there is no communication between the authenticator and your computer or phone to deliver the authenticating token. Hackers cannot divert messages to their devices, grab the token, and defeat the additional authentication factor.

Multi-factor authentication is much stronger than single factor authentication and an excellent choice when it is available. For critical accounts, opt for multi-factor authentication whenever you can, but try to avoid using texting as an authentication factor. It has proven too easy for hackers to divert messages sent to phones by tricking the cellular provider into reassigning your phone number to a hacker's phone. Email is often a more secure second factor than text messages or phone calls, although it means you must be careful that your email account is strongly secured.

Backup

I have seen more people lose their data because they did not back up, or had bad backups, than I have seen people rescue their data using a backup. The sad fact is that backing up properly is hard to set up and dreadfully easy to neglect.

You may go for years without needing to restore from a backup and easily drift into complacency, sure that your hard drives will last forever, ransomware will never strike you, some nasty malware will never require a full restore, and your house is immune from fire or flood. But those things happen to thousands of computers and their users each year.

Backups fail for many reasons. When you add storage devices or start to store things in new places on existing devices, your backup may have to be adjusted to grab data from new places. This can happen when you install a new application. If you neglect to make the changes, your backup will be incomplete. In extreme situations, it may not work at all.

Backups should be stored far enough from your computer that the backup won't be affected by whatever might destroy the data on your computer. In the past, that meant copying data to portable media like tapes, CDs, or portable hard drives and moving them to a distant place. For an individual, this effort that has no apparent benefit while things are going well. Consequently, many individuals neglect to keep their backup properly configured or entirely give up on the concept. Which is when disaster strikes.

BACKUP RULES

- Automate. Let the computer decide when to run the backups. Do not depend on a distractible human.
- Match the frequency of backups to the rate that you add data to your computer. If your files seldom change, your backups can be less frequent. After big changes, run an extra backup.
- Go wide. Back up more, rather than less. Storage is cheap; your data is priceless.
- Verify that you are backing up the files you think you are. Were the defaults right for you? If you chose manually, did you choose correctly?
- Rehearse. Periodically test-restore files. A full system restore is ideal, but seldom practical. Try a full system restore when you get a new computer.

I have a lot of experience with losing data and I fully understand the value of backups, yet there have been weeks when I have struggled to remember to rotate the portable drives I used for backups and stored in my detached garage. Storage in a garage close to my house was a compromise; storing them miles away would have been better, but even that compromise did not keep me on the straight and narrow.

Rather than use portable media, even with the simple and reliable backup utilities now built into operating systems, I prefer cloud backup services. I firmly believe in removing as much of the human element as possible from the backing up process. That means using a cloud backup service to back up everything; no saving storage space by selecting only important files; no storing portable media with relatives or at the office; no remembering to start backups. None of that. It can cost, but I regard it as money well-spent.

Placing backups in the hands of a cloud backup vendor may seem dangerous, but I think relying on fickle human habits is more dangerous. Cloud data storage centers are guarded and protected against disasters. The storage is often redundant; duplicate data is stored in physically remote locations so it not vulnerable to a single local disaster such as a flood. Encryption keeps your data private, probably more securely than portable media that can be lost or stolen. Like passwords, if your data is encrypted locally and the key is never transmitted to the service, not even a court order will get access to your files. Cloud backup depends on an Internet connection and a slow or unreliable connection is the only reason I would return to portable media backups.

CHOOSING A CLOUD BACKUP SERVICE

- If you back up extensive video and audio, an unlimited storage plan may be most practical.
- Plans that back up entire disks are simpler to configure.
- Some plans will back up more than one computer.
- Many plans have a free version.
- Local encryption and keys kept locally are most private.

Ransomware

The best defense against a ransomware invasion is the same as defending yourself against other cyberattacks. Keep your operating system and application up to date with the latest patches. Make sure your antimalware is up to date and run often. Avoid drive-bys by shunning questionable click-bait. Don't open attachments or click links in emails that are not from trusted sources.

Good backups will not prevent a ransomware attack, but if you are attacked, you must have a good current backup or you will be forced to pay the ransom and hope the criminals will keep their word about restoring your data. Restoring from a good current backup, you can be back to normal in a few hours without paying ransom.

There are some well-meaning products and services for dealing with ransomware that have not been as effective as one would hope. One version attempts to "vaccinate" computers against ransomware by making your computer appear to be already infected with ransomware. This works, in theory, because the ransomware hackers don't want to immediately reinfect computers that have paid the ransom. Unfortunately, this works for only a few ransomware variants and generates false confidence.

Other services propose to unlock the encrypted files. These services succeed in some, but not all cases. There is no substitute for good backups.

A note of caution: smart ransomware attempts to encrypt your backups as well as your regular data. For example, if your backup is a portable disk drive plugged into a USB port, assume that the ransomware will follow the connection and tamper with it also. If you use an external drive or a network drive for backup, disconnect the drives except when your backups are running. Cloud backup services are usually safe, but check on ransomware resistance before you sign up for the service.

Antimalware Tools

Antimalware and antivirus tools are the same thing. Viruses, self-reproducing bits of code that travel from computer to computer, are no longer as common as they were when the term "antivirus" was coined. Cybercrime has shifted its choice of weapons to "malware," which is a more generic term that includes anything that might land on your computer and do damage. If your device connects to the Internet, you must have antimalware tool installed and running that will identify and remove malware. Not to do so is inviting trouble. No antimalware tool is perfect, but they ward off many problems.

Choosing an antimalware tool can be confusing because the market is very competitive. The relative standings of the tools can change rapidly and new competitive features appear regularly. Many free versions are available. Automatic update is a required feature. You don't want to be caught unprepared for the latest nastiness.

When I shop for malware tools, I do not focus on which product will wipe out the most varieties of malware. The malware scene changes so rapidly that the leader one month may not be the leader next month. If the tool cleans up malware with respectable accuracy, I pay close attention to ease of installation, smooth auto-update, and unobtrusiveness, not the kill rate when the review was done. Poorly designed antimalware slows computers down and gets in the way even though they may wipe out every ugly thing in cyberspace. The biggest mistake you can make is to put off a scan or not to run any antimalware because your tool is clumsy, so easy and unobtrusive counts a lot for me.

On Windows, the easiest and least obtrusive antimalware tool is the built-in Windows Defender. There are other tools that have better kill rates, but Defender is respectable and it only takes a single click to activate it. Macs do not have an equivalent.

There are antimalware tools for tablets and smartphones also. Some experts do not recommend them because they are somewhat intrusive. These experts point out that antimalware does not prevent bad downloads from the app stores or lost or stolen devices, which are the most important attack vectors for phones. I recommend trying free versions. If you find one that doesn't get in the way, use it.

Firewalls

A firewall selectively stops messages from getting to your computer from the network and may prevent malware that has slipped into your computer from communicating back to its master.

The fundamental unit of information on computer networks is the packet. Packets contain the source and destination for the packet and some information on its status, along with the payload of information for transmission. A firewall examines each incoming and outgoing packet and decides whether to allow the packet to pass in or out based on rules. Some firewalls only examine the source and destination, others examine more, possibly going all the way to the contents of the payload.

One rule that is usually implemented blocks, with some exceptions, incoming packets that are not responses to previous outgoing packets. For example, your computer periodically requests email that may be waiting for you; the firewall will not allow it to accept email that it does not ask for. This policy protects your computer from malicious incoming messages and gives you control over what does arrive. Other firewall rules that may be implemented are blacklists or whitelists. A blacklist rule lists sources that the firewall will reject; all others will be accepted. A whitelist rule lists the sources that the firewall will let pass; all others will be rejected. Program or app installations may modify firewall rules to allow the installed software to operate.

A well-designed firewall is not inherently intrusive, but any firewall can be given a restrictive set of rules that slows network traffic to a trickle. Therefore, be careful if you decide to modify the configuration of your firewall. You may need to reverse the changes and try again before you get it right.

Is personal firewall protection necessary? Home network routers provide some similar protection. For typical home use, a personal firewall probably will not greatly increase protection. If a specific external site or program is a threat, then a firewall configured to stop the threat is useful, but such situations are more common for businesses, not home systems.

Nevertheless, I have the Windows firewall running on all my Windows computers. Why? Because it gives me one more layer of protection. If I found evidence that it was hindering performance or hassling me with error messages, I would reconsider, but, in recent years, it has been unobtrusive and has not raised issues, so it stays on. If it stops one threat, it has proved its worth. Apple also has a built-in firewall that I would treat in a similar fashion.

There are also many personal firewalls available beyond those supplied by the operating system manufacturers; some are free, some are part of antimalware packages. If you feel compelled to install one of these firewalls, you may prefer to use a firewall and antimalware tool from the same vendor.

Always set your firewall to the most restrictive level, and then relax the level if it interferes too much with your activities. Default restrictions are usually less the maximum. If you are comfortable with the more restrictive policy, you are safer.

Wi-Fi and Bluetooth

Wi-Fi and Bluetooth are two technologies that free us from cords. Wi-Fi connects computers to the network; Bluetooth connects peripherals, such as mice, keyboards, and headphones to computers, including smartphones and tablets. Both use radio signals to make computing more convenient. However, a radio signal is easier to intrude upon surreptitiously than a cord or cable. Both Wi-Fi and Bluetooth are great conveniences I would not be without, but some caution is necessary.

Wi-Fi

Public Wi-Fi sites have become more conscientious about warning users that public Wi-Fi is not secure, but you are still responsible for your safety. Anyone who is using a local area network can gain access to all the traffic in the local network. If the traffic is not protected in some way, other users can read and interfere with your traffic. When using public Wi-Fi, you are on a local network with all the other users of the Wi-Fi access point. You have no control over who might be interfering with your messages. To make matters worse, there are powerful and malicious tools for free download on the Internet that can turn any eighth-grader into a master invader of public Wi-Fi. You must protect yourself.

You can protect yourself by only interacting with sites that use secure communications for any high stakes transactions when on public Wi-Fi. Secure communication means using Transport Layer Security (TLS), formerly called Secure Socket Layer (SSL). You are using TLS when https (not http) shows up in the Internet address in your browser. Even better, avoid any financial or private information transactions over public Wi-Fi.

If you use public Wi-Fi frequently, you may want to consider subscribing to a Virtual Private Network (VPN). When using a VPN, all your Internet communications are almost as secure as on an actual private network. However, unsecured communication (non-https) can always be snooped. It's harder when you are on a private network, but still possible. When using a VPN, you must still be careful.

Another possibility is to use the Tor browser discussed in Chapter 5. Tor makes it difficult to trace connections and is therefore more private than ordinary browsing. However, Tor has a performance overhead and it is not a replacement for transport layer security. When using Tor on public Wi-Fi, you should still only connect to https sites or use a VPN. I would not bother with Tor on public Wi-Fi unless I felt compelled to use Tor for all my communications. I would subscribe to a VPN before I would set up Tor.

PUBLIC WI-FI RULES

- If the locked symbol or the s in https does not appear in your browser, assume that anyone in range of the Wi-Fi service can read anything you see in or enter into your browser. They can control what you see and do.
- An intruder may not be visible to you. Signals go through walls.
- If you do not trust every single user on a wireless network, treat the network as public. Networks that require a password given to customers, such as hotels and some businesses, are still public and NOT secure.
- Consider obtaining and using a VPN service if you use public Wi-Fi often.
- Secure communications (VPN or https) are relatively safe, but you should still avoid high-stakes transactions on public networks.
- Your phone may switch automatically from the cellular network to public Wi-Fi. Be aware!

Caution when using public Wi-Fi is not the end of the challenges. At home, your goal is to avoid turning your home Wi-Fi network into a public playground for neighborhood hackers or casual bandwidth thieves.[3] The Wi-Fi standards groups have made some security missteps in the past that have been corrected, but the weak security options live on. The Wi-Fi vendors, the hardware manufacturers, and the network providers who offer packages that include Wi-Fi gear are, as usual, more concerned with convenience than security. Default Wi-Fi configurations are often poorly secured. However, tightening up Wi-Fi security is not hard. If you happen to have an older Wi-Fi router that does not have the latest security, an upgrade is a good idea. It will probably improve performance also.

HOME WI-FI CONFIGURATION

- Consult your operating system documentation to find the IP address of your router.
- Enter the router IP address in the browser address field to bring up the router administrative interface. Consult your router manual for interface help.

---

[3] I expect bandwidth theft will increase as the Internet providers put more caps on data downloaded per month. The temptation to filch bandwidth from a neighbor's poorly secured Wi-Fi will be great.

- Use WPA2 security when possible. Avoid WEP. Avoid options that use short PINs.
- Do not use Wi-Fi Protected Setup (WPS).
- Put a long, strong password on your home Wi-Fi network.
- Put a long, strong password on your router—often neglected. If your computer is hacked, access to your router makes it much worse. Keep the criminals out with a strong password. A weak default password is an open door to your router becoming a bot for a hacker.
- Start with the maximum-security firewall setting. Relax the setting only if you have problems reaching sites or using network applications like some games.
- Do not enable advanced options unless you have a specific need. *Advanced* means *dangerous.*
- Periodically log in to the router and scan the connected list. If you see suspicious connections, change your network password and double-check that you are not using WPS. You can use MAC address filtering to whitelist the MACs you allow or blacklist those you don't. MACs are fakable, but filters up the game.

Bluetooth

Bluetooth is problematic because it can take many different forms. Some forms are secure, some not so secure. Common commercial Bluetooth headphones are so insecure that the NSA banned them in government agencies. The Bluetooth standard is written to accommodate many different applications using *profiles.* A profile narrows the scope of the standard to a specific purpose. Bluetooth has over 30 documented profiles. Some are secure, others not.

The profile that the NSA banned is terrible for top-secret communications, but it is fine if you don't care who might listen in on your tunes. Lax security makes the headphones easier to use and simplifies the electronics. It is up to you to sort out whether your Bluetooth devices are safe or not. One danger is an insecure Bluetooth keyboard that permits a hacker to log your keystrokes as you are typing in passwords. Since it is hard to determine what is secure, I assume all Bluetooth communications can be snooped upon, although I know some may be secure.

BLUETOOTH SAFETY

- Avoid high-stakes private activities, like banking transactions, when using Bluetooth peripherals in public.
- If you are not using Bluetooth, turn it off!
- Assume your Bluetooth connection is insecure unless you are positive it is encrypted and secured.

- Be aware of your surroundings, especially when pairing. Assume that low security Bluetooth transmissions can be snooped and intercepted from 30 feet in any direction, further with directional antennas. Beware of public areas and multi-dwelling buildings.
- Delete unused Bluetooth pairings. They are attack opportunities.
- Turn discoverability off when you are not pairing.
- If Internet traffic passes through a Bluetooth connection, your firewall may not monitor it. Check your firewall.

Email

Email is not private. Privacy was not a goal for early email designers; they aimed for convenience and simple implementation. Email today is more private than early implementations that forwarded messages from server to server, potentially leaving copies on unsecured servers all over, but email privacy today is still dependent on the security of both the sender and receiver's email service. Your email service may be secure, but that says nothing about the security of your recipient's service. Electronic discovery of email is a well-established practice under law. Email can be subpoenaed or subject to a search warrant and produced in court. Although you may not be involved in a lawsuit or criminal proceeding, your email may be caught up in discovery of your recipient and made public. If you or your recipient are using company email, the employers are in control, not you. Also, forwarding email takes only a few keystrokes and clicks; your mail may be accidentally, carelessly, or maliciously forwarded to the wrong place.

A practical personal policy for email is to assume that whatever goes into an email may become public. Make a habit of reminding yourself just before you click send that your message may go viral whether you want it to or not.

Email can be made more private by encrypting the email before it enters the email system. A strongly encrypted message with a key known only to you is nearly impossible for anyone to decrypt without your consent. The problem is that your recipient must have a key in order to read the message. Using asymmetric encryption, your correspondents can send you messages that only you can decrypt and vice versa. There are various commercial packages that support this.

Hackers use email to trick you into installing malware, revealing information, and clicking on poisonous websites. See the "Social Engineering" section below for more information.

Email Account Passwords

Email account passwords are important and deserve special attention. A hacker with access to your email account can read your email, send email in your name, and is already most of the way to having stolen your identity. Email is often a factor in multi-factor authentication and password resets. A hacker who controls your email account may be able to request a password reset on your bank account or other important accounts, locking you out and the hacker in. You may have many important accounts that the hacker can grab from your email. Therefore, be certain that your email account password is long, strong, and unique. It may be the most important password you own.

Social Engineering

Social engineering takes advantage of the ways humans think and act to execute computer-related crime. Most cybercrime begins by swiping access through social engineering. Social engineers have a relatively short list of goals. They want your accounts and passwords, opportunities to place malware on your computer, access to your computers, your identity, and your money. Social engineers use the same trickery and deception that con artists have used forever. Sometimes, a social engineer will appear on your doorstep in a uniform appearing to be from your ISP. They might call you, threatening your arrest by the IRS, Homeland Security, or your local law enforcement. Legitimate sources will oblige requests for further information and identification, and acknowledge your rights. Social engineers will evade, bully, and deceive.

Social engineers trick you with phony emails with attachments that install malware or lead you to dodgy websites that download malware onto your computer without your consent. They lure you into sending money that disappears, perhaps for a too-good to-be-true deal or free money from a distant country. A good social engineer knows how to sound legitimate. Always seek information from different sources before you respond to any email, phone call, or website, and then respond carefully.

AVOID SOCIAL ENGINEERING

- Never open an email attachment unless you know the source. Hackers often use names nabbed from your address list in emails for authenticity.
- Never click a link in a dodgy email.
- Avoid click-bait web sites. These sites lure you with the fantastic, too-good-to-be-true, or salacious come-ons.
- Do not yield personal information, access to your computer, or passwords in response to unsolicited calls. Government agencies are faked all the time. Hang up, look up the business, and call back if you feel compelled to respond.

- When calling back, be aware that fraudsters may be able to stay on the line and fake the sounds of a connection. Wait, or call someone whose voice you know to clear the line if you have doubts.
- Examine requests to wire money very carefully.
- Fraudulent car sales over the Internet are a lucrative form of crime. Be sure before you send money.
- Social engineers know how to tempt you. A deal that looks too good to be true probably is a scam.
- Scrutinize domain names in email and Internet addresses. "microsoft.computers.com" is not Microsoft.

Installing Software

Well designed and implemented software is a pleasure to use but, realistically, all software contains flaws that hackers exploit. Each app on your computer, tablet, or smartphone that you don't use adds hacking opportunities with no return benefits. Clogging up systems with software you don't use can impair performance. The simple solution is to uninstall anything you don't use. Create a system restore point before removing software that came with your computer, so you can restore easily if it is critical.

For a premium, you can buy laptops, tablets, and desktops that have no nonessential software installed. Impressively, a 10% to 20% performance improvement over comparable "loaded" devices has been reported. Software vendors pay hardware vendors and retailers to load free or ad-laden versions on new computing devices to market the for-a-fee versions of their software. The practice would be annoying but benign, except that each of these free programs is yet another opening for attack. Some hardware vendors have announced that they have reduced or eliminated non-essential software shipped on their products.

Be careful when you install new applications. A loosely written or hacker-written application can wreak havoc on your device and open it up to being taken over. Hackers also tamper with install scripts to install backdoors and other malware along with legitimate applications. When you download from a site other than the original developer, you run a risk of getting a doctored installation. This is especially easy with free open source products, even though many are high quality products. Make it a policy to download from the person or organization that developed the software, not sites with collections of free software.[4] Before installing any free or paid software, check it out. Bad reputations generally show up quickly on the Internet.

---

[4] If a free software program is good and useful to you, don't be a cheapskate. Pay the developers something for it. Support the good people.

The single greatest danger to tablets and smartphones is installing apps that contain threats. The vendors' app stores are supposed to prevent this by thoroughly examining apps before they are available in the stores. The app stores are safer than the free-for-all of downloads to desktops and laptops, but the vetting is not perfect. Malware does occasionally appear in all of the app stores. Apple, Google, and Microsoft may say that their stores are perfectly safe, and they may believe this, but hackers are smart and they find ways. The worst part is that an app that is intentionally installed by the user can often be hidden from antimalware scans. Whenever you install any software on any device from any source, be cautious. Use the search engines to scrutinize the reputation of any software before you install. It only takes a few minutes and it can prevent a world of grief.

SAFE SOFTWARE MANAGEMENT

- Uninstall software you do not use. Reinstall if you miss it.
- Never install software on a whim. Have a reason.
- Always download from sites you trust. Don't follow a dodgy link to an alternate download site. Identity certificates and cryptographic hashes prevent tampering.
- App stores vet for safety, but bad apples still get through.
- Beware of extras like custom browser toolbars or antimalware utilities that are tacked on to other installs. Opt out if you can; consider not installing if you can't. These add-ons are often trouble.
- Google applications you are not familiar with. Check reviews. If there are no reviews, wait a few days. Bad apps surface quickly on the Internet.
- Advanced tip: create a virtual machine to try questionable applications. If it acts out, delete the virtual machine.

Surfing the Web

The great dangers in surfing the Web are the result of social engineering trickery, man-in-the-middle attacks, and drive-bys.

Man-In-The-Middle

Your best protection against the man in the middle is communication secured with Transport Layer Security (TLS), the successor to Secure Sockets Layer (SSL). Any time you are doing anything that you don't want to be snooped on or tampered with, you should insist on TLS. Addresses of sites using TLS start with "https" and most browsers display a locked symbol when using TLS.[5]

Using TLS or SSL is the server's decision, not the client. When TLS was first used, performance was much lower for secure communication, so it was used sparingly. Computers and networks are more powerful today so the performance drop is negligible. Amazon, for example, formerly only used TLS when taking payments and executing orders, but today it uses TLS for all communication. If you can choose between sites, choose those that use TLS. Never do anything critical over simple and insecure HTTP. You can get extensions for most web browsers that will force use of HTTPS if the site supports it. HTTPS Everywhere is the most well-known.[6]

Certificates are an important part of TLS. A certificate is proof that you are communicating with the site you think you are communicating with and not hackers who have tricked their way in. If your browser comes up with a "faulty certificate" error when you try to connect with a site, the problem is often an expired certificate. The site has gotten behind on renewals. It happens. Or a hacker has gotten into the works and wants to tamper with your session. Many people are tempted to assume a clerical error and ignore the warning. I do not recommend succumbing to the temptation, but if you do, don't click the box that says to permanently ignore faulty certificates from the site. Don't ever exchange critical information over a connection that does not have a valid certificate. HTTPS Everywhere provides additional warnings on invalid certificates.

Drive-bys

Another danger while surfing the Web is a drive-by, a bit of malicious code that is downloaded with a web page and compromises your computer. There are two main culprits: Java and JavaScript. Both of these computer languages enhance web browsing. It would be hard to imagine the Web today without the contributions of code written in these languages. Although their names are similar, they are rather different.

---

[5]TLS replaced SSL in 1999, but the term SSL is still common. SSL has been declared insecure, but there are still old installations of SSL around, but there is not much an individual user can do about it.
[6]HTTPS Everywhere is available at www.eff.org/https-everywhere. Accessed October 2016.

The Java language was originally written for embedding into web pages, but it is not often used that way now because the original safety measures that were supposed to prevent local machines from being attacked via downloaded code have proven inadequate. However, Java has become the most popular language for large software projects and most business users need Java support.

For Java to work, you must have a Java Virtual Machine installed. Few popular websites now rely on Java. Therefore, unlike business users, most individual users don't need a Java Virtual Machine installed. You are safer without it. Don't install Java. If you have it installed, uninstall it. If you must have it for some reason, be diligent about keeping it updated because Java security flaws are patched frequently.

JavaScript bears a vague resemblance to Java, but most of the similarity is only in the name. You can't avoid JavaScript. Almost all websites use JavaScript and will not work properly without it. The best defenses are to avoid questionable sites, keep your antimalware tool up to date, and run scans frequently. You can turn off JavaScript in your web browser, but you will find that many websites no longer work properly. There are extensions to browsers that are designed to help. NoScript is an extension for Firefox, Chrome, and Opera web browsers that uses a whitelist.[7] Trusted sites on the whitelist can execute scripts. New sites are easily temporarily or permanently added to the whitelist. It also warns of especially risky scripts and blocks Java and Adobe Flash on non-whitelisted sites. This is an effective compromise, although by no means totally secure or convenient.

The Internet of Things—Dangerous Devices

Almost everyone has at least one dangerous online device in their home. These devices are things like home wired and wireless routers, webcams, DVRs, even printers that are connected to home networks and to the Internet. These present two dangers: hackers may gain control of these devices and turn them on you, and they may use them as bots in denial of service attacks. Some of the largest and most destructive denial of service attacks have come from massive networks of compromised IoT devices.

These devices are small computers, often running some variant of Linux. The usual line of attack is to gain access to the administrative account for the device, such as root or admin. These accounts often all have the same weak default password set at the factory. Criminals scan the Internet, searching for devices with this flimsy security. When they find them, they log on and begin to make trouble, like installing malware for launching denial of service attacks.

---

[7]NoScript can be downloaded from https://noscript.net/. Accessed October, 2016.

The solution is to place strong passwords on all your devices. You should begin by resetting the device to factory defaults, in case it has already been hacked. Consult your user manual. Resetting is usually a mechanical step: pushing a button or inserting a pin into a socket. Mechanical operations require physical access to the device, which is good in this case. Then follow user manual instructions for setting the device password. The process will be like setting the password on your router.

There is another step that may be necessary. The device may not block telnet or secure shell (ssh) access to the device. If you are familiar with and have access to a Linux installation, you can attempt to telnet or ssh into the device and change the root password. This step may not be necessary Your safest path is to choose IoT devices carefully, inquiring into their security and waiting for security issues to be resolved before risking and insecure installation. because the device password is often also the telnet or ssh root password, but there have been reports of devices that do not block telnet or ssh and still allow default access after the main account is changed. If telnet and ssh are beyond you, simply changing the device password still gives you much more protection than leaving the defaults. Manufactures already are said to be recalling and fixing these dangerous devices. Approach IoT devices cautiously. Inquire into their security and wait until security issues are resolved before installing them.

IoT-based denial of service attacks are particularly insidious because patching the problem is fraught with obstacles. Most of the vulnerable devices are manufactured as unlabeled generics, which become components in systems sold under many different labels. The manufacturers may have no record of where their products have been deployed and there is seldom any provision for updating the equipment after the end consumer has deployed it. Devices such as webcams are infrequently replaced or upgraded and by the time an issue appears, the manufacturer may no longer support the design or may even have gone out of business. The consumer whose IoT device is used in the attack probably does not know that their device is doing damage because a device participating in an attack may still work well. Therefore, the consumer has no direct incentive to fix or replace their devices and the victims have scant leverage.

Protecting Children

Children now appear on computers, use computers, and fall victim to cybercriminals.

Privacy

My childhood was in a rural community in the 1950s. My parents knew everyone residing within a mile of our farm. The entire county was knit together through ties of family, church, business, and acquaintance. Everyone seemed to know something about what everyone else was doing, and felt free to comment on it. These ties formed a granular news service that helped hold the society together.

People today reproduce that nostalgia-laden network of social ties using social media. But the new social media network is quite different. The old ties were symmetric. If I saw you, you saw me. If you knew what I was doing, I knew what you were up to. But Internet social media is not symmetric. I may have many friends on Facebook and receive many posts, but I reveal nothing about myself when I see a post, unless I choose comment or post myself. The relationship is symmetric only if I choose to make it so. In the social media world of asymmetric privacy, predators watch and prepare, leaving few clues to where they are or what they are thinking.

Parents must be aware of asymmetric privacy. In some cases, you can block it. Facebook postings are a good example. Posting photographs of children's birthday parties and Halloween costumes is a delight for everyone, including predators selecting their next victim. A predator who knows the names of relatives and details about a child's life, such a favorite meals and toys, has a powerful advantage when convincing a child to get into a vehicle or step into a secluded corner of the playground. You can reduce this risk by selecting your friends carefully and limiting visibility of posts to friends. But remember that your friends can repost and their friends might not be as careful as you about who sees the post.

Predators are not limited to pedophiles. They can be overly inquisitive potential boyfriends or girlfriends. Or a mildly aggressive neighbor kid, or a virulent bully who is spoiling to humiliate and push a child to suicide.

You must always consider the possibility of lurking predators when you post anything involving your child. Check privacy settings and set them properly, or don't post. These principles apply to all social media. As children mature, they may be prepared for greater exposure and they will almost certainly push for it. You may want to expose them to harsh reality gradually by loosening controls. That is a parent's decision, but think about it rather than let it happen.

Protection

At some point, your children will begin using computers on their own. We all know that there are many sites on the Internet that offer pornography and other material that most people consider inappropriate for children. There are tools you can install on your children's computer that offer varying degrees of protection. Both Apple and Microsoft have provisions for setting up children's accounts that restrict access to apps and websites.

These tools are useful, but they are fallible. They work through a combination of whitelisting, blacklisting, and pattern recognition. Blacklisting and whitelisting depends on you or the tool vendor having information about a site to make the decision to block it. Although the vendor may be diligent, there will be occasions when their information is absent or incorrect and an undesirable site gets through or a desirable site is blocked. Pattern recognition looks for certain words, or combinations of words, or visual patterns that identify a site as good or bad. The best of the pattern matching tools use the same kind of machine learning used in driverless cars. They do not rely on prior knowledge of sites, but be aware that these systems learn from mistakes and mistakes do happen.

Use these tools, but do not rely on them. They are not a replacement for supervision and preparation for lapses in protection.

You may want to take steps to preserve your child's identity. If an identity thief has your child's social security number, they may start applying for loans and credit cards in the child's name. You can prevent this by opening credit records with the credit bureaus (Equifax, Experian, Trans Union, and Innovis) and then freezing the records. When a financial institution does a credit check, a flag will raise, blocking the exploitation. Exactly how this can be done depends on the credit bureau and state regulations. Some people argue against establishing a child's credit record because the record becomes a public record of the child's existence.[8]

Attack

The simple fact is that children lack experience and judgment. Younger children have less experience and weaker judgment. Adults are social engineered and hacked often enough. Children are even more likely to be hacked.

Reducing cybermishaps for children is difficult, but possible. One of the first steps is to limit the sites and applications that the child may access using access control tools and built-in operating system tools. This includes limiting access to email and messaging. Children are easily tricked into opening malware attachments, falling for clickbait links, offering up information to miscreants, and responding to dangerous messages. Until they are old enough to make good decisions, they must be shielded.

---

[8]See Brian Krebs "The Lowdown on Freezing Your Kid's Credit," KrebsonSecurity, January 20, 2016. https://krebsonsecurity.com/2016/01/the-lowdown-on-freezing-your-kids-credit/. Accessed October 2016. Krebs provides detail on current regulations. The comments offer some insight into the controversy over the prudence of establishing a child's credit file.

The other important step is to prevent a hack on the child from affecting the rest of the family's resources, especially financial resources and opportunities for identity theft. Unless children are strictly supervised, they should never sign on to any kind of computer using their parents' accounts. They should not know their parents' passwords. They must have their own accounts, not necessarily in their name, but with limited privilege.

It may be counterintuitive, but you are often safer if your children are on their own computer; if a hacker gets into a child's computer, it is more difficult for the hacker to get to the parents' resources from a separate child's computer than from an account on the parents' computer. The child's account on the child's computer should still be a child account, never an account with administrative privilege. If the child is hacked often, or you are very cautious, completely restore the system periodically, in the same way that public computers in libraries are restored daily to purge them of data and malware left by public users.

Disaster Recovery

When, Not If, You Become a Victim

Your antimalware (antivirus) appliance is up and running. It's updated with the latest information and automated updates keep it that way. Your operating system is fully patched and set for automatic update, as is your web browser, and all your applications. You've eliminated programs and apps that you don't use and you are cautious when installing new ones. All the miscellaneous devices connected to your network have strong, non-default passwords. Your passwords are long, strong, and well-managed with no duplicates. You run backups regularly, store them remotely, and check them periodically. You have separate administrative accounts on all your computers that you only use when necessary. Your firewalls are all set for maximum security. Your Wi-Fi network has a long, strong password as does your network router. You are careful with public Wi-Fi and Bluetooth. You are on the alert for malicious social engineers.

Congratulations! You are among the elite who use computer systems with intelligent regard for cybercrime.

Now let's talk about what happens when all these precautions are of no avail and the worst happens. The worst is not likely to happen, much less likely for you because you are careful, but it can happen.

© Marvin Waschke 2017
M. Waschke, *Personal Cybersecurity*, DOI 10.1007/978-1-4842-2430-4_10

Cybercriminals are smart and diligent, and there is always a chance that they will get to your equipment before it has been patched against the latest exploit or artful social engineers will weasel their way into your confidence despite your caution. But when an attack occurs, all is not lost. With prompt and reasonable action, most attacks can be reduced to annoyances, not grow into catastrophes.

Third-Party Data Theft

Sometimes it is not your fault. Things just happen. For instance, a department store is hacked and your credit or debit card data falls into criminal hands, or a government agency is attacked and other records are exposed.

Detection

Detecting third-party data theft is not easy. The hacked systems are not under your control. Those in charge of the compromised system may not inform you because they want to avoid adverse publicity. Sometimes legal departments recommend keeping security breaches private to avoid publicizing evidence of negligence.

There are things you can do. Review your financial accounts and check your credit reports regularly. Identity theft often appears as credit checks that you did not initiate or new lines of credit you did not open in your credit report.

Beware of passwords that change without warning. An unexpected password change may mean that a hacker has your password and has changed it. Contact the site immediately and have them help you secure your account again. If you made the mistake of using the compromised password on more than one account, you must also resecure those accounts. You don't remember all the accounts that have the same password? Then resecure all your accounts. If possible, when resecuring, choose multi-factor authentication, especially if you do not know how the hacker got your password and you don't know how to prevent it from happening again. Multi-factor authentication will stop the hacker if your password is stolen again. Assume that any of your computing devices could have been hacked.

The sooner you spot a problem, the sooner it will be resolved and the more likely the resolution will be in your favor. The optimum frequency depends on the activity on the account or report. A good goal is to spot anything out of order within a week of its occurrence. A charge to a store that you do not patronize, an unexpectedly large charge, a charge from a remote location are all candidates, any charge you do not recognize. Report any anomaly to the card issuer or institution involved immediately. Your financial institution may allow you more time, but don't delay. The longer you wait, the less likely it becomes that the criminal will be caught and the more likely that you will be forced to jump through hoops to be made whole.

Payment Card Information Theft

Before a hack occurs, there is little you can do to force a department store to be diligent about security, and most people do not have the information or expertise to evaluate corporate security controls. Payment card theft is usually handled by your bank or credit card company. Your old card will be terminated and you will be issued a new card. In the meantime, you are not liable for illegitimate charges against your card, but you are obliged to point out to your bank or payment card company the charges to your account that are not yours. If you see a problem, you should report it immediately.

CREDIT VS. DEBIT CARDS

There is little difference between credit and debit cards in terms of liability. In either case, if you report a loss promptly, the issuer is responsible for all but a nominal amount, and issuers frequently ignore the nominal amount as a goodwill gesture.

But there is an important difference in the way you, the victim, are reimbursed. When a criminal uses your debit card illegally, the amount of the charge immediately leaves your account, as it does when you make a legitimate debit. When a criminal uses your credit card, the amount is charged to your credit account, but money does not leave your possession until you pay your credit card bill.

This difference is not trivial. When a credit card is compromised, charges are made that you don't have to pay, although you will still be liable for making the minimum payment. Using a debit card, the issuer replaces money that has already left your account. If the criminal makes a substantial charge with your debit card, you could be out thousands of dollars until your debit card issuer reimburses you. In the meantime, you may have insufficient funds for legitimate bills, resulting in penalties and overdraft charges for rejected transactions. Depending on your debit card issuer's policies, the situation could continue for months and do serious damage to your credit rating.

When there is a payment card theft, credit cards are easier to deal with.

Identity Theft

Identity theft can begin with a direct invasion into your computer, tablet, or smartphone, but more often, identity thieves purchase information on the darknet and use it to grab assets. The information on the darknet comes from big raids on all sorts of institutions. You can purchase services that monitor your credit and accounts to spot spurious activity, but many experts suggest that if you have the discipline to monitor yourself, you are likely to be more accurate than a service that uses general rules about consumer behavior rather than the intimate knowledge you have of yourself and your family's habits.

When you detect questionable activity, the first step is to notify any payment card companies that may be affected. The next step is to freeze credit reporting at all the major credit reporting services (currently TransUnion, Experian, Equifax, and Innovis.) Whenever someone requests a new line of credit, the bank or other institution requests a report from the credit reporting service. If there is a freeze on the account, the credit reporting service will refuse to send a report. This stops most requests for a new line of credit. Very few, if any, organizations will extend credit to an individual with a freeze on their account, and criminals are usually unwilling to identify themselves further by arguing.[1]

The freeze is the most effective tool you have for curtailing identity theft. Some people choose to freeze their credit as a defensive measure before their information is compromised. You play the odds. If you freeze your credit reports, you must unfreeze them whenever you want a new line of credit, and the credit bureaus sometimes charge for putting on a freeze. That's a hassle. Is it worth the peace of mind that comes from knowing that your identity is difficult to steal? You must answer for yourself. My credit reports are not frozen, but I reconsider the decision regularly. I would freeze them immediately if I suspected someone was trifling with my identity.

You may be offered a free subscription to an identity theft monitoring service by an organization that lost your data. Take their offer. Another layer of protection is always useful. In theory, these services take over the job of monitoring your accounts, although, as I mentioned above, I don't think they are a good replacement of your own scrutiny.

Should you subscribe to one of those services on your own? If you are diligent about monitoring your accounts, you probably are more capable of spotting anomalies than the algorithms of the monitoring service, but that assumes you have the time and discipline to monitor your accounts carefully.

I do not subscribe to a monitoring service because, between my wife and I, we watch our accounts and credit reports closely, but if I felt we were slacking, I would subscribe.

---

[1] See Brian Krebs, "How I Learned to Stop Worrying and Embrace the Security Freeze," KrebsonSecurity, June 15, 2015. http://krebsonsecurity.com/2015/06/how-i-learned-to-stop-worrying-and-embrace-the-security-freeze/. Accessed October 2016. Brian Krebs is a cybersecurity journalist whom hackers attack regularly in retaliation for exposing their nefarious schemes. He has experience with resisting and recovering from attack.

Hacking

When your computer, tablet, or smartphone is invaded by a malicious intruder, you have been hacked. The hacker is usually trying to gain access to your critical accounts, gather information that can be used for identity theft type operations, requisition your device for a botnet, or extort some form of ransom.

Detection

There are no strict rules for knowing when you have been hacked. Sometimes it is obvious, such as when a ransomware message pops up with instructions for paying ransom to release your files. Or it might be an unbidden pop-up from some service that offers to "fix" your computer. Other times, an indication is subtler but still obvious, such as a command line screen popping up and responding to an unseen typist or a screen cursor that suddenly takes on a mind of its own. Other signs are inexplicable password changes, or your friends receiving a flood of phishing or spam emails that are from you or traceable to you. If your computer has been pressed into a botnet, the only sign may be periodic sluggishness that can't be attributed to anything you do. Your ISP may inform you that your home network is emitting suspicious traffic. In that case, the culprit may be an appliance such as a thermostat that can be controlled from a smartphone app or even a hacked Internet router.

Unfortunately, the signs are often ambiguous. An overly sensitive touchpad and a wandering thumb can make it seem that a phantom has taken over the cursor on your laptop. Poorly written, but benign, software can also cause weird pop-ups and messages. A hacked system is only one among many causes of a sluggish system. You must think before you act, but acting fast when you think you have been hacked is important.

Immediate Action

First, stop the damage. Power down your computer, tablet, or smartphone immediately. You may want to save any unsaved work. This is your decision and you will probably want to consider how much work could be lost, but if I were certain I had been hacked, I would cut power without hesitation. On battery-powered devices, I would remove the battery as fast as I could. On smartphones and tablets, follow whatever procedure your device has for a full power off. Why? Because the damage that could be done by a hacker is worse in my estimation than losing a few minutes work. If you must keep running, at least disconnect from the Internet.

After your computing device is shut down, take a minute to think and plot a strategy. Most of the time, the next step is to start your device in safe mode. That means not connected to the network. Unplugging your Ethernet cable or turning off your Wi-Fi radio is also a good idea, just in case you don't start in safe mode through some mishap.

Recovery

When you are up and running and off the network, run a thorough antimalware scan. Hopefully antimalware will find the culprit and remove it. You may need to update your antimalware tool to catch the latest infections. If your antimalware tool did find a problem and removed it, you can cautiously restart and connect to the network. Make a note of the name of the malware that was removed. You can look it up and learn more about the invasion, which may be helpful.

At this point, your ordeal may be over, but do not assume that you are safe yet. Antimalware threat removal is not always perfect and there is always a possibility that the infection involved additional threats that were not detected or removed.

If you have a backup, restoring from backup is an excellent idea, even if your antimalware scan assures you that the threat has been removed. You may want to try an alternative antimalware tool just in case your tool missed something. If your antimalware did not detect any threats to remove, it is certain you should restore from a backup. After the restoration, run another scan to check if the restored system is clean. You may have to go through a regression, restoring successively older backups until you find an uninfected version.

When you think your system is clean, you are not finished. You don't know what the hackers hauled into their clutches during the time your system was infected. They may have passwords and identity data that they can use for future attacks. You must be vigilant. Take the same precautions that you would after a site that has your information has been hacked. Change all your critical passwords and look out for anomalies on your system. There are a few kinds of attacks, such as BIOS attacks, that are lodged so deep in your system that they are not wiped out by a full restore.

Ransomware

Ransomware is a special variety of malicious software that threatens to damage your computing device or expose you in some way, if you do not pay the ransom. The most common form encrypts your files, but other varieties threaten legal action, fines, or exposure to social sanctions such accusations of viewing objectionable material. Most of these threats are idle and can safely be ignored.

Legitimate orders to pay from agencies like the Internal Revenue Service can always be confirmed by calling the agency at their public phone number.

Immediate Action

Ransomware that encrypts your files requires immediate intervention. Some ransomware is reported to bring up the ransom demand when they start encrypting. Encryption is slow and you may be able to minimize damage by switching off your computer as quickly as possible. Follow the procedure you would follow for any hack. I would not try for an orderly shutdown; just go for the power switch or the wall socket as quickly as you can. Remove the battery from battery powered devices. Block the criminal from communicating with your system. Disconnect from the Internet by unplugging Ethernet cable and turning off your wireless radio. If you are quick enough, you may spare yourself a lot of effort.

Recovery

Good and frequent backups are the key to recovery. There are some services that offer to unlock your files based on keys discovered from previous attacks. If the hacker is clever, those methods are not likely to work, because most hackers understand strong unique passwords.

After you have shut the system down, let it rest for a while. If the attackers are waiting for your system to come back up, give them a little time to lose interest. Get a cup of coffee, take a walk in the fresh air. The break will do you good.

If you have a good backup, you are set to restore your system and return to normal operation. However, your immediate goal is to remove the ransomware from your system. Restart and run an antimalware scan, if you can. You may not be able to if the hacker has disabled your antimalware software.

If antimalware removes the source of infection, you only need to restore the encrypted files. If nothing is detected, you should do a full restore, including reinstalling the operating system. This can be several hours wait, but not difficult if your backup system is good. At this point, you are restored to your state at the time of the backup. If your system is still infected, you may have to restore again from an earlier backup.

You should always try to analyze the source of the infection and use your knowledge to avoid future infections. Frequently, the infection stems from opening a malicious attachment to an email, but think about any recent downloads or software installations. Did you surf your way onto a click-bait site? Office documents with embedded macros are often used by hackers for delivering malware. Microsoft often puts up a warning when a document contains embedded macros. When you see the warning, think carefully about the possibility that a criminal inserted something undesirable. Above all, be aware!

Reporting Cybercrime

Cybercrime tends to be under-reported. When you are hacked, when your payment card information is taken, when you are subjected to ransomware, you are the victim of a crime. The unfortunate truth is that law enforcement is not likely to offer much help to the victim of small cybercrimes. However, we cannot expect cybercrime to decrease and cybersecurity to increase if the authorities do not have reliable information on the extent of the problem.

All cybercrimes can be reported to the FBI's Internet Crime Complaint Center (IC3).[2] The IC3 will analyze the complaint and forward it to the appropriate international, federal, state, or local agency. For most cybercrime, this is your most effective step. The IC3 may be able to bundle your issue with other issues and inspire action that an isolated issue could not create.

Complaints that are clearly local, such as a neighbor stealing bandwidth or local email fraud, are most effective when reported to local authorities. Many states' attorneys general have cybercrime offices. How much activity your complaint will generate is hard to predict, but consider that your goal of recording the crime is so that authorities can plan for appropriate future enforcement.

A Final Note

Cybercrime may seem to be a miasma that is dragging us all down. For every advance in computing, there seems to be a corresponding surge in cybercrime and new ways that our devices can be used against us.[3] As a computer veteran, I sometimes feel that hackers are about to invalidate over half a century of progress in computing, progress that has made the work force more efficient, ushered tremendous scientific and medical progress, and brought us Flappy Bird and Pokémon GO.

---

[2]File complaints at www.ic3.gov/complaint/default.aspx. Accessed October 2016.
[3]Artificial intelligence and machine learning are examples of progress on both sides of the law. Artificial intelligence can be used to both prevent cybercrimes and perform crimes. See John Markoff, "As Artificial Intelligence Evolves, So Does Its Criminal Potential," New York Times, October 23, 2016. www.nytimes.com/2016/10/24/technology/artificial-intelligence-evolves-with-its-criminal-potential.html. Accessed October 2016.

Nevertheless, I am optimistic. Developers have been serious about security only since the turn of the century. Computing gallops ahead at breakneck speed, but its foundations change slowly; resistance to cybercrime must be built into those slowly changing foundations as well as into the superstructure. The insecure foundational code that was written in the 80s and 90s is going away gradually. If you listen carefully to the dialog on exploits and patches, you will find that many exploits today are based on mistakes made 10 or 20 years ago. Although new security issues always come up, the code written today to replace the old foundation is more secure and each year hackers are forced to work harder for their exploits. The unpleasant counterbalance to improved code is increasing reliance on computing for financial transactions and business, which make cybercrime more lucrative and worth extra effort.

At present, most law enforcement is still poorly prepared to deal with cybercrime and the system of laws and international agreements are still heavily grounded in the concepts of physical, not electronic, crime. Cybercrime is difficult to address because it involves complex engineering problems as well as moral and ethical issues. Few legislators are prepared to evaluate the engineering sides of the issues and may tend to dismiss them or enact suboptimal laws. Legislators must be informed that cybercrime is a real danger that damages their constituents, not just a theoretical annoyance. It is important to let them know of your concerns and to lodge complaints with law enforcement. They must not look away and say that cybercrime is a problem for engineers and technology vendors.

The battle against cybercrime occurs on several fronts. One is engineering, building systems that are more resistant to crime. The second is regulation to restrain insecure practices such as the hackable Internet of Things. A third is laws that make it easier to prosecute cybercrime, such as streamlined extradition laws and agreements. Yet another is adequate funding of law enforcement for execution of cybercrime laws.

The final front in the battle is fought by individual computer users. The sorry fact is that the victims of cybercrime become victims when they leave themselves open to attack. Reasonably securing your computer, laptop, tablet, and smartphone takes some effort, but not more effort than securing the doors and windows of your house and locking your car. If you follow the practices in Chapter 9, even only a few of them, you will be much safer and the probability that your devices will be hacked will go down. If you pay attention to what happens in your payment card accounts, the probability that you will lose money to payment card theft is low. Watch your credit reports and the chance you will be stung with identity theft is also low.

You can be safe!

I

Index

M. Waschke, *Personal Cybersecurity*, DOI 10.1007/978-1-4842-2430-4

Get the eBook for only $4.99!

Why limit yourself?

Now you can take the weightless companion with you wherever you go and access your content on your PC, phone, tablet, or reader.

Since you've purchased this print book, we are happy to offer you the eBook for just $4.99.

Convenient and fully searchable, the PDF version enables you to easily find and copy code—or perform examples by quickly toggling between instructions and applications.

To learn more, go to http://www.apress.com/us/shop/companion or contact support@apress.com.

he United States
ters